MznLnx

Missing Links Exam Preps

Exam Prep for

Corporate Finance

Ross, Westerfield, & Jaffe, 8th Edition

The MznLnx Exam Prep is your link from the texbook and lecture to your exams.
The MznLnx Exam Preps are unauthorized and comprehensive reviews of your textbooks.

All material provided by MznLnx and Rico Publications (c) 2010
Textbook publishers and textbook authors do not particpate in or contribute to these reviews.

MznLnx

Rico Publications

Exam Prep for Corporate Finance
8th Edition
Ross, Westerfield, & Jaffe

Publisher: Raymond Houge
Assistant Editor: Michael Rouger
Text and Cover Designer: Lisa Buckner
Marketing Manager: Sara Swagger
Project Manager, Editorial Production: Jerry Emerson
Art Director: Vernon Lowerui

Product Manager: Dave Mason
Editorial Assitant: Rachel Guzmanji
Pedagogy: Debra Long
Cover Image: Jim Reed/Getty Images
Text and Cover Printer: City Printing, Inc.
Compositor: Media Mix, Inc.

(c) 2010 Rico Publications
ALL RIGHTS RESERVED. No part of this work covered by the copyright may be reproduced or used in any form or by an means--graphic, electronic, or mechanical, including photocopying, recording, taping, Web distribution, information storage, and retrieval systems, or in any other manner--without the written permission of the publisher.

Printed in the United States
ISBN:

For more information about our products, contact us at:
Dave.Mason@RicoPublications.com

For permission to use material from this text or product, submit a request online to:
Dave.Mason@RicoPublications.com

Contents

CHAPTER 1
Introduction to Corporate Finance — 1

CHAPTER 2
Financial Statements and Cash Flow — 12

CHAPTER 3
Financial Statements Analysis and Long-Term Planning — 19

CHAPTER 4
Discounted Cash Flow Valuation — 29

CHAPTER 5
How to Value Bonds and Stocks — 34

CHAPTER 6
Net Present Value and Other Investment Rules — 45

CHAPTER 7
Making Capital Investment Decisions — 50

CHAPTER 8
Risk Analysis, Real Options, and Capital Budgeting — 57

CHAPTER 9
Risk and Return: Lessons from Market History — 61

CHAPTER 10
Return and Risk: The Capital Asset Pricing Model (CAPM) — 66

CHAPTER 11
An Alternative View of Risk and Return: The Arbitrage Pricing Theory — 71

CHAPTER 12
Risk, Cost of Capital, and Capital Budgeting — 74

CHAPTER 13
Corporate Financing Decisions and Efficient Capital Markets — 81

CHAPTER 14
Long-Term Financing: An Introduction — 88

CHAPTER 15
Capital Structure: Basic Concepts — 98

CHAPTER 16
Capital Structure: Limits to the Use of Debt — 102

CHAPTER 17
Valuation and Capital Budgeting for the Levered Firm — 108

CHAPTER 18
Dividends and Other Payouts — 112

CHAPTER 19
Issuing Securities to the Public — 119

CHAPTER 20
Long-Term Debt — 128

Contents (Cont.)

CHAPTER 21
Leasing — 138

CHAPTER 22
Options and Corporate Finance — 145

CHAPTER 23
Options and Corporate Finance: Extensions and Applications — 152

CHAPTER 24
Warrants and Convertibles — 155

CHAPTER 25
Derivatives and Hedging Risk — 159

CHAPTER 26
Short-Term Finance and Planning — 165

CHAPTER 27
Cash Management — 170

CHAPTER 28
Credit Management — 176

CHAPTER 29
Mergers and Acquisitions — 179

CHAPTER 30
Financial Distress — 187

CHAPTER 31
International Corporate Finance — 189

ANSWER KEY — 199

TO THE STUDENT

COMPREHENSIVE

The *MznLnx* Exam Prep series is designed to help you pass your exams. Editors at MznLnx review your textbooks and then prepare these practice exams to help you master the textbook material. Unlike study guides, workbooks, and practice tests provided by the texbook publisher and textbook authors, *MznLnx* gives you **all** of the material in each chapter in exam form, not just samples, so you can be sure to nail your exam.

MECHANICAL

The MznLnx Exam Prep series creates exams that will help you learn the subject matter as well as test you on your understanding. Each question is designed to help you master the concept. Just working through the exams, you gain an understanding of the subject--its a simple mechanical process that produces success.

INTEGRATED STUDY GUIDE AND REVIEW

MznLnx is not just a set of exams designed to test you, its also a comprehensive review of the subject content. Each exam question is also a review of the concept, making sure that you will get the answer correct without having to go to other sources of material. You learn as you go! Its the easiest way to pass an exam.

HUMOR

Studying can be tedious and dry. MznLnx's instructional design includes moderate humor within the exam questions on occassion, to break the tedium and revitalize the brain

Chapter 1. Introduction to Corporate Finance

1. In financial accounting, a _____ or statement of financial position is a summary of a person's or organization's balances. Assets, liabilities and ownership equity are listed as of a specific date, such as the end of its financial year. A _____ is often described as a snapshot of a company's financial condition.
   - a. Balance sheet
   - b. Financial statements
   - c. Statement on Auditing Standards No. 70: Service Organizations
   - d. Statement of retained earnings

2. _____ is a measure of the ability of a debtor to pay their debts as and when they fall due. It is usually expressed as a ratio or a percentage of current liabilities.

   For a corporation with a published balance sheet there are various ratios used to calculate a measure of liquidity.
   - a. Invested capital
   - b. Operating leverage
   - c. Operating profit margin
   - d. Accounting liquidity

3. In business and accounting, _____s are everything of value that is owned by a person or company. The balance sheet of a firm records the monetary value of the _____s owned by the firm. The two major _____ classes are tangible _____s and intangible _____s.
   - a. Income
   - b. Asset
   - c. Accounts payable
   - d. EBITDA

4. _____ is the planning process used to determine whether a firm's long term investments such as new machinery, replacement machinery, new plants, new products, and research development projects are worth pursuing. It is budget for major capital, or investment, expenditures.

   Many formal methods are used in _____, including the techniques such as

   - Net present value
   - Profitability index
   - Internal rate of return
   - Modified Internal Rate of Return
   - Equivalent annuity

   These methods use the incremental cash flows from each potential investment, or project. Techniques based on accounting earnings and accounting rules are sometimes used - though economists consider this to be improper - such as the accounting rate of return, and 'return on investment.' Simplified and hybrid methods are used as well, such as payback period and discounted payback period.
   - a. Financial distress
   - b. Shareholder value
   - c. Preferred stock
   - d. Capital budgeting

5. In finance, _____ refers to the way a corporation finances its assets through some combination of equity, debt, or hybrid securities. A firm's _____ is then the composition or 'structure' of its liabilities. For example, a firm that sells $20 billion in equity and $80 billion in debt is said to be 20% equity-financed and 80% debt-financed.
   - a. Market for corporate control
   - b. Book building
   - c. Rights issue
   - d. Capital structure

Chapter 1. Introduction to Corporate Finance

6. In accounting, a _____ is an asset on the balance sheet which is expected to be sold or otherwise used up in the near future, usually within one year, or one business cycle - whichever is longer. Typical _____s include cash, cash equivalents, accounts receivable, inventory, the portion of prepaid accounts which will be used within a year, and short-term investments.

On the balance sheet, assets will typically be classified into _____s and long-term assets.

   a. Historical cost
   b. Long-term liabilities
   c. Write-off
   d. Current asset

7. In accounting, _____ are considered liabilities of the business that are to be settled in cash within the fiscal year or the operating cycle, whichever period is longer.

For example accounts payable for goods, services or supplies that were purchased for use in the operation of the business and payable within a normal period of time would be _____.

Bonds, mortgages and loans that are payable over a term exceeding one year would be fixed liabilities.

   a. Gross sales
   b. Net income
   c. Closing entries
   d. Current liabilities

8. _____ is that which is owed; usually referencing assets owed, but the term can cover other obligations. In the case of assets, _____ is a means of using future purchasing power in the present before a summation has been earned. Some companies and corporations use _____ as a part of their overall corporate finance strategy.
   a. Cross-collateralization
   b. Credit cycle
   c. Partial Payment
   d. Debt

9. In business and finance, a _____ (also referred to as equity _____) of stock means a _____ of ownership in a corporation (company.) In the plural, stocks is often used as a synonym for _____s especially in the United States, but it is less commonly used that way outside of North America.

In the United Kingdom, South Africa, and Australia, stock can also refer to completely different financial instruments such as government bonds or, less commonly, to all kinds of marketable securities.

   a. Margin
   b. Procter ' Gamble
   c. Bucket shop
   d. Share

10. _____ is a term in Corporate Finance used to indicate a condition when promises to creditors of a company are broken or honored with difficulty. Sometimes _____ can lead to bankruptcy. _____ is usually associated with some costs to the company and these are known as Costs of _____.
   a. Commercial paper
   b. Cashflow matching
   c. Capital structure
   d. Financial distress

11. _____ plant, and equipment, is a term used in accountancy for assets and property which cannot easily be converted into cash. This can be compared with current assets such as cash or bank accounts, which are described as liquid assets. In most cases, only tangible assets are referred to as fixed.

Chapter 1. Introduction to Corporate Finance

a. Percentage of Completion
b. Remittance advice
c. Petty cash
d. Fixed asset

12. _____ are defined as identifiable non-monetary assets that cannot be seen, touched or physically measured, which are created through time and/or effort and that are identifiable as a separate asset. There are two primary forms of intangibles - legal intangibles (such as trade secrets (e.g., customer lists), copyrights, patents, trademarks, and goodwill) and competitive intangibles (such as knowledge activities (know-how, knowledge), collaboration activities, leverage activities, and structural activities.) Legal intangibles generate legal property rights defensible in a court of law.
   a. ABN Amro
   b. AAB
   c. A Random Walk Down Wall Street
   d. Intangible assets

13. _____ is a financial metric which represents operating liquidity available to a business. Along with fixed assets such as plant and equipment, _____ is considered a part of operating capital. It is calculated as current assets minus current liabilities.
   a. 529 plan
   b. Working capital management
   c. 4-4-5 Calendar
   d. Working capital

14. The phrase _____ refers to the aspect of corporate strategy, corporate finance and management dealing with the buying, selling and combining of different companies that can aid, finance, or help a growing company in a given industry grow rapidly without having to create another business entity.

An acquisition, also known as a takeover, is the buying of one company (the 'target') by another. An acquisition may be friendly or hostile.

   a. Mergers and acquisitions
   b. 7-Eleven
   c. 4-4-5 Calendar
   d. 529 plan

15. A _____ is a contract entered into between which regulates the terms of a loan. they usually relate to loans of cash, but market specific contracts are also used to regulate securities lending.

They are usually in written form, but there is no legal reason why a _____ cannot be a purely oral contract (although in some countries this may be limited by the Statute of frauds or equivalent legislation).

   a. Loan agreement
   b. Lien
   c. Foreclosure
   d. Royalties

16. A _____ is a fungible, negotiable instrument representing financial value. They are broadly categorized into debt securities (such as banknotes, bonds and debentures), and equity securities; e.g., common stocks. The company or other entity issuing the _____ is called the issuer.
   a. Securities lending
   b. Book entry
   c. Tracking stock
   d. Security

17. A _____ is a party (e.g. person, organization, company, or government) that has a claim to the services of a second party. The first party, in general, has provided some property or service to the second party under the assumption (usually enforced by contract) that the second party will return an equivalent property or service. The second party is frequently called a debtor or borrower.

a. NOPLAT
b. Redemption value
c. False billing
d. Creditor

18. In economic models, the _____ time frame assumes no fixed factors of production. Firms can enter or leave the marketplace, and the cost (and availability) of land, labor, raw materials, and capital goods can be assumed to vary. In contrast, in the short-run time frame, certain factors are assumed to be fixed, because there is not sufficient time for them to change.
   a. Long-run
   b. 4-4-5 Calendar
   c. 529 plan
   d. Short-run

19. Decisions relating to working capital and short term financing are referred to as _____. These involve managing the relationship between a firm's short-term assets and its short-term liabilities. The goal of _____ is to ensure that the firm is able to continue its operations and that it has sufficient cash flow to satisfy both maturing short-term debt and upcoming operational expenses.
   a. 529 plan
   b. Working capital management
   c. Working capital
   d. 4-4-5 Calendar

20. In finance, _____ (or gearing) is borrowing money to supplement existing funds for investment in such a way that the potential positive or negative outcome is magnified and/or enhanced. It generally refers to using borrowed funds, or debt, so as to attempt to increase the returns to equity. Deleveraging is the action of reducing borrowings.
   a. Leverage
   b. Pension fund
   c. Limited partnership
   d. Financial endowment

21. In finance, _____ is the ability of an entity to pay its debts with available cash. _____ can also be described as the ability of a corporation to meet its long-term fixed expenses and to accomplish long-term expansion and growth. The better a company's _____, the better it is financially.
   a. Solvency
   b. Political risk
   c. Capital asset
   d. Mid price

22. _____ is the standard framework of guidelines for financial accounting used in the United States of America. It includes the standards, conventions, and rules accountants follow in recording and summarizing transactions, and in the preparation of financial statements. _____ are now issued by the Financial Accounting Standards Board (FASB).
   a. Net income
   b. Depreciation
   c. Revenue
   d. Generally accepted accounting principles

23. The institution most often referenced by the word '_____' is a public or publicly traded _____, the shares of which are traded on a public stock exchange (e.g., the New York Stock Exchange or Nasdaq in the United States) where shares of stock of _____s are bought and sold by and to the general public. Most of the largest businesses in the world are publicly traded _____s. However, the majority of _____s are said to be closely held, privately held or close _____s, meaning that no ready market exists for the trading of shares.
   a. Protect
   b. Depository Trust Company
   c. Federal Home Loan Mortgage Corporation
   d. Corporation

24. A sole _____, or simply _____ is a type of business entity which legally has no separate existence from its owner. Hence, the limitations of liability enjoyed by a corporation and limited liability partnerships do not apply to sole proprietors. All debts of the business are debts of the owner.

Chapter 1. Introduction to Corporate Finance

a. Proprietorship
c. Product life cycle
b. Just-in-time
d. Free cash flow

25. A _____ is a type of business entity in which partners (owners) share with each other the profits or losses of the business undertaking in which all have invested. _____s are often favored over corporations for taxation purposes, as the _____ structure does not generally incur a tax on profits before it is distributed to the partners (i.e. there is no dividend tax levied.) However, depending on the _____ structure and the jurisdiction in which it operates, owners of a _____ may be exposed to greater personal liability than they would as shareholders of a corporation.
   a. Clayton Antitrust Act
   c. National Securities Markets Improvement Act of 1996
   b. Fiduciary
   d. Partnership

26. A _____ is a form of partnership similar to a general partnership, except that in addition to one or more general partners (GPs), there are one or more limited partners (_____s). It is a partnership in which only one partner is required to be a general partner.

The GPs are, in all major respects, in the same legal position as partners in a conventional firm, i.e. they have management control, share the right to use partnership property, share the profits of the firm in predefined proportions, and have joint and several liability for the debts of the partnership.

   a. Limited liability company
   c. Leverage
   b. Fund of funds
   d. Limited partnership

27. The _____ are the primary rules governing the management of a corporation in the United States and Canada, and are filed with a state or other regulatory agency. The equivalent in the United Kingdom and various other countries is Articles of Association.

A corporation's _____ generally provide information such as:

- The corporation's name, which has to be unique from any other corporation in that jurisdiction. As part of the corporation's name, certain words such as 'incorporated', 'limited', 'corporation', (or their abbreviations) or some equivalent term in countries whose language is not English, are usually required as part of the name as a 'flag' to indicate to persons doing business with the organization that it is a corporation as opposed to an individual or partnership (with unlimited liability.) In some cases, certain types of names are prohibited except by special permission, such as words implying the corporation is a government agency or has powers to act in ways it is not otherwise allowed.
- The name of the person(s) organizing the corporation (usually members of the board of directors.)
- Whether the corporation is a stock corporation or a non-stock corporation.
- Whether the corporation's existence is permanent or limited for a specific period of time. Generally the rule is that a corporation existence is forever, or until (1) it stops paying the yearly corporate renewal fees or otherwise fails to do something required to continue its existence such as file certain paperwork each year; or (2) it files a request to 'wind up and dissolve.'
- In some cases, a corporation must state the purposes for which it is formed. Some jurisdictions permit a general statement such as 'any lawful purpose' but some require explicit specifications.
- If a non-stock corporation, whether it is for profit or non-profit. However, some jurisdictions differentiate by 'for profit' or 'non profit' and some by 'stock or non-stock'.
- In the United States, if a corporation is to be organized as a non-profit, to be recognized as such by the Internal Revenue Service, such as for eligibility for tax exemption, certain specific wording must be included stating no part of the assets of the corporation are to benefit the members.
- If a stock corporation, the number of shares the corporation is authorized to issue, or the maximum amount in a specific currency of stock that may be issued, e.g. a maximum of $25,000.
- The number and names of the corporation's initial Board of Directors (though this is optional in most cases.)
- The initial director(s) of the corporation (in some cases the incorporator or the registered agent must be a director, if not an attorney or another corporation.)
- The location of the corporation's 'registered office' - the location at which legal papers can be served to the corporation if necessary. Some states further require the designation of a Registered Agent: a person to whom such papers could be delivered.

Most states permit a corporation to be formed by one person; in some cases (such as non-profit corporations) it may require three or five or more. This change has come about as a result of Delaware liberalizing its corporation rules to allow corporations to be formed by one person, and states not wanting to lose corporate charters to Delaware had to revise their rules as a result.

a. Expedited Funds Availability Act
b. External risks
c. Articles of Partnership
d. Articles of incorporation

28. A _____ is a type of business entity: it is a type of corporation or partnership between two companies. Certificates of ownership (or stocks) are issued by the company in return for each contribution, and the shareholders are free to transfer their ownership interest at any time by selling their stockholding to others.

Chapter 1. Introduction to Corporate Finance 7

There are two kinds of _____. The private company kind and the open market. The shares are usually only held by the directors and Company Secretary. Debt for which they agree to be liable.

a. 529 plan
b. 4-4-5 Calendar
c. Subsidiary
d. Joint stock company

29. _____ is a concept whereby a person's financial liability is limited to a fixed sum, most commonly the value of a person's investment in a company or partnership with _____. A shareholder in a limited company is not personally liable for any of the debts of the company, other than for the value of his investment in that company. The same is true for the members of a _____ partnership and the limited partners in a limited partnership.

a. Personal property
b. Beneficial owner
c. Sarbanes-Oxley Act
d. Limited liability

30. A _____ in the law of the vast majority of United States jurisdictions is a legal form of business company that provides limited liability to its owners. It is a hybrid business entity having certain characteristics of both a corporation and a partnership or sole proprietorship (depending on how many owners there are.) The primary characteristic an _____ shares with a corporation is limited liability, and the primary characteristic it shares with a partnership is the availability of pass-through income taxation.

a. Pension fund
b. Fund of funds
c. Financial endowment
d. Limited liability company

31. A _____ is a type of limited company in the United Kingdom and the Republic of Ireland which is permitted to offer its shares to the public.

a. 4-4-5 Calendar
b. 7-Eleven
c. 529 plan
d. Public limited company

32. In business, _____ is income that a company receives from its normal business activities, usually from the sale of goods and services to customers. Some companies also receive _____ from interest, dividends or royalties paid to them by other companies. _____ may refer to business income in general, or it may refer to the amount, in a monetary unit, received during a period of time, as in 'Last year, Company X had _____ of $32 million.'

In many countries, including the UK, _____ is referred to as turnover.

a. Revenue
b. Bottom line
c. Matching principle
d. Furniture, Fixtures and Equipment

33. _____ is the imposition of two or more taxes on the same income (in the case of income taxes), asset (in the case of capital taxes), or financial transaction (in the case of sales taxes.) It refers to two distinct situations:

- taxation of dividend income without relief or credit for taxes paid by the company paying the dividend on the income from which the dividend is paid. This arises in the so-called 'classical' system of corporate taxation, used in the United States.
- taxation by two or more countries of the same income, asset or transaction, for example income paid by an entity of one country to a resident of a different country. The double liability is often mitigated by tax treaties between countries.

It is not unusual for a business or individual who is resident in one country to make a taxable gain (earnings, profits) in another. This person may find that he is obliged by domestic laws to pay tax on that gain locally and pay again in the country in which the gain was made. Since this is inequitable, many nations make bilateral _____ agreements with each other.

a. 4-4-5 Calendar
b. 529 plan
c. 7-Eleven
d. Double taxation

34. In the most general sense, a _____ is anything that is a hindrance, or puts individuals at a disadvantage.

Before we discuss the financial terms, we should note that a _____ can also have a much more important slang meaning.

This is best described in an example.

a. McFadden Act
b. Covenant
c. Limited liability
d. Liability

35. _____ is a form of corporation equity ownership represented in the securities. It is dangerous in comparison to preferred shares and some other investment options, in that in the event of bankruptcy, _____ investors receive their funds after preferred stockholders, bondholders, creditors, etc. On the other hand, common shares on average perform better than preferred shares or bonds over time.

a. Stop-limit order
b. Stock market bubble
c. Stock split
d. Common stock

36. In economics, a _____ is a mechanism that allows people to easily buy and sell (trade) financial securities (such as stocks and bonds), commodities (such as precious metals or agricultural goods), and other fungible items of value at low transaction costs and at prices that reflect the efficient-market hypothesis.

_____s have evolved significantly over several hundred years and are undergoing constant innovation to improve liquidity.

Both general markets (where many commodities are traded) and specialized markets (where only one commodity is traded) exist.

a. Delta hedging
b. Financial market
c. Cost of carry
d. Secondary market

Chapter 1. Introduction to Corporate Finance

37. An _____ is an economic concept that relates to the cost incurred by an entity (such as organizations) associated with problems such as divergent management-shareholder objectives and information asymmetry. The costs consist of two main sources:

1. The costs inherently associated with using an agent (e.g., the risk that agents will use organizational resource for their own benefit) and
2. The costs of techniques used to mitigate the problems associated with using an agent (e.g., the costs of producing financial statements or the use of stock options to align executive interests to shareholder interests.)

Though effects of _____ are present in any agency relationship, the term is most used in business contexts.

The information asymmetry that exists between shareholders and the Chief Executive Officer is generally considered to be a classic example of a principal-agent problem. The agent (the manager) is working on behalf of the principal (the shareholders), who does not observe the actions of the agent.

a. AAB
b. ABN Amro
c. Agency cost
d. A Random Walk Down Wall Street

38. In political science and economics, the _____ or agency dilemma treats the difficulties that arise under conditions of incomplete and asymmetric information when a principal hires an agent. Various mechanisms may be used to try to align the interests of the agent with those of the principal, such as piece rates/commissions, profit sharing, efficiency wages, performance measurement (including financial statements), the agent posting a bond, or fear of firing. The _____ is found in most employer/employee relationships, for example, when stockholders hire top executives of corporations.

a. 7-Eleven
b. Principal-agent problem
c. 4-4-5 Calendar
d. 529 plan

39. _____ is the field of accountancy concerned with the preparation of financial statements for decision makers, such as stockholders, suppliers, banks, employees, government agencies, owners, and other stakeholders. The fundamental need for _____ is to reduce principal-agent problem by measuring and monitoring agents' performance and reporting the results to interested users.

_____ is used to prepare accounting information for people outside the organization or not involved in the day to day running of the company.

a. Financial Accounting
b. 529 plan
c. 4-4-5 Calendar
d. 7-Eleven

40. In economics, business, and accounting, a _____ is the value of money that has been used up to produce something, and hence is not available for use anymore. In business, the _____ may be one of acquisition, in which case the amount of money expended to acquire it is counted as _____. In this case, money is the input that is gone in order to acquire the thing.

a. Cost
b. Fixed costs
c. Marginal cost
d. Sliding scale fees

Chapter 1. Introduction to Corporate Finance

41. _____ is a fee paid on borrowed assets. It is the price paid for the use of borrowed money, or, money earned by deposited funds. Assets that are sometimes lent with _____ include money, shares, consumer goods through hire purchase, major assets such as aircraft, and even entire factories in finance lease arrangements.
   a. AAB
   b. Interest
   c. Insolvency
   d. A Random Walk Down Wall Street

42. The _____ is the market for securities, where companies and governments can raise longterm funds. The _____ includes the stock market and the bond market. Financial regulators, such as the U.S. Securities and Exchange Commission, oversee the _____s in their designated countries to ensure that investors are protected against fraud.
   a. Capital market
   b. Delta neutral
   c. Forward market
   d. Spot rate

43. In finance, the _____ is the global financial market for short-term borrowing and lending. It provides short-term liquidity funding for the global financial system. The _____ is where short-term obligations such as Treasury bills, commercial paper and bankers' acceptances are bought and sold.
   a. Money market
   b. Debt-for-equity swap
   c. Cramdown
   d. Consumer debt

44. The _____ is a stock exchange based in New York City, New York. It is the largest stock exchange in the world by dollar value of its listed companies securities. As of October 2008, the combined capitalization of all domestic _____ listed companies was $10.1 trillion.
   a. 529 plan
   b. 7-Eleven
   c. 4-4-5 Calendar
   d. New York Stock Exchange

45. The _____ is that part of the capital markets that deals with the issuance of new securities. Companies, governments or public sector institutions can obtain funding through the sale of a new stock or bond issue. This is typically done through a syndicate of securities dealers.
   a. Sector rotation
   b. Volatility clustering
   c. Peer group analysis
   d. Primary market

46. The _____ is the financial market where previously issued securities and financial instruments such as stock, bonds, options, and futures are bought and sold. The term '_____' is also used refer to the market for any used goods or assets, or an alternative use for an existing product or asset where the customer base is the second market

With primary issuances of securities or financial instruments, or the primary market, investors purchase these securities directly from issuers such as corporations issuing shares in an IPO or private placement, or directly from the federal government in the case of treasuries.

   a. Delta neutral
   b. Financial market
   c. Secondary market
   d. Performance attribution

47. The U.S. _____ is an independent agency of the United States government which holds primary responsibility for enforcing the federal securities laws and regulating the securities industry, the nation's stock and options exchanges, and other electronic securities markets. The SEC was created by section 4 of the SEC of 1934 (now codified as 15 U.S.C. Â§ 78d and commonly referred to as the 1934 Act.)

a. 529 plan
b. 7-Eleven
c. 4-4-5 Calendar
d. Securities and Exchange Commission

48. A _____, securities exchange or (in Europe) bourse is a corporation or mutual organization which provides 'trading' facilities for stock brokers and traders, to trade stocks and other securities. _____s also provide facilities for the issue and redemption of securities as well as other financial instruments and capital events including the payment of income and dividends. The securities traded on a _____ include: shares issued by companies, unit trusts and other pooled investment products and bonds.
   a. Stock Exchange
   b. 529 plan
   c. 4-4-5 Calendar
   d. 7-Eleven

49. The _____ is an American stock exchange. It is the largest electronic screen-based equity securities trading market in the United States. With approximately 3,200 companies, it has more trading volume per day than any other stock exchange in the world.
   a. 529 plan
   b. 4-4-5 Calendar
   c. 7-Eleven
   d. NASDAQ

50. The _____ of 2002 (Pub.L. 107-204, 116 Stat. 745, enacted July 30, 2002), also known as the Public Company Accounting Reform and Investor Protection Act of 2002 and commonly called Sarbanes-Oxley, Sarbox or SOX, is a United States federal law enacted on July 30, 2002 in response to a number of major corporate and accounting scandals including those affecting Enron, Tyco International, Adelphia, Peregrine Systems and WorldCom.
   a. Sarbanes-Oxley Act
   b. Blue sky law
   c. Duty of loyalty
   d. Foreign Corrupt Practices Act

Chapter 2. Financial Statements and Cash Flow

1. In business and accounting, _____s are everything of value that is owned by a person or company. The balance sheet of a firm records the monetary value of the _____s owned by the firm. The two major _____ classes are tangible _____s and intangible _____s.

   a. Income
   b. Accounts payable
   c. EBITDA
   d. Asset

2. In financial accounting, a _____ or statement of financial position is a summary of a person's or organization's balances. Assets, liabilities and ownership equity are listed as of a specific date, such as the end of its financial year. A _____ is often described as a snapshot of a company's financial condition.

   a. Financial statements
   b. Statement on Auditing Standards No. 70: Service Organizations
   c. Statement of retained earnings
   d. Balance sheet

3. _____ are formal records of a business' financial activities.

   _____ provide an overview of a business' financial condition in both short and long term. There are four basic _____:

   1. **Balance sheet**: also referred to as statement of financial position or condition, reports on a company's assets, liabilities, and net equity as of a given point in time.
   2. **Income statement**: also referred to as Profit and Loss statement (or a 'P'L'), reports on a company's income, expenses, and profits over a period of time.
   3. **Statement of retained earnings**: explains the changes in a company's retained earnings over the reporting period.
   4. **Statement of cash flows**: reports on a company's cash flow activities, particularly its operating, investing and financing activities.

   a. Statement of retained earnings
   b. Financial statements
   c. Notes to the Financial Statements
   d. Statement on Auditing Standards No. 70: Service Organizations

4. The phrase _____ refers to the aspect of corporate strategy, corporate finance and management dealing with the buying, selling and combining of different companies that can aid, finance, or help a growing company in a given industry grow rapidly without having to create another business entity.

   An acquisition, also known as a takeover, is the buying of one company (the 'target') by another. An acquisition may be friendly or hostile.

   a. 529 plan
   b. 7-Eleven
   c. Mergers and acquisitions
   d. 4-4-5 Calendar

5. _____, in bookkeeping, refers to assets, liabilities, income, and expenses recorded on individual pages of the so called book of final entry or ledger. Changes in _____ value are made by chronologically posting debit (DR) and credit (CR) entries to its page. Examples of _____s are cash, _____s receivable, mortgages, loans, land and buildings, common stock, sales, services provided, wages, and payroll overhead.

a. Alpha
b. Account
c. Accretion
d. Option

6. _____ is one of a series of accounting transactions dealing with the billing of customers who owe money to a person, company or organization for goods and services that have been provided to the customer. In most business entities this is typically done by generating an invoice and mailing or electronically delivering it to the customer, who in turn must pay it within an established timeframe called credit or payment terms.

An example of a common payment term is Net 30, meaning payment is due in the amount of the invoice 30 days from the date of invoice.

a. Accounts receivable
b. Income
c. Impaired asset
d. Accounting methods

7. In accounting, a _____ is an asset on the balance sheet which is expected to be sold or otherwise used up in the near future, usually within one year, or one business cycle - whichever is longer. Typical _____s include cash, cash equivalents, accounts receivable, inventory, the portion of prepaid accounts which will be used within a year, and short-term investments.

On the balance sheet, assets will typically be classified into _____s and long-term assets.

a. Long-term liabilities
b. Historical cost
c. Write-off
d. Current asset

8. _____ plant, and equipment, is a term used in accountancy for assets and property which cannot easily be converted into cash. This can be compared with current assets such as cash or bank accounts, which are described as liquid assets. In most cases, only tangible assets are referred to as fixed.

a. Remittance advice
b. Petty cash
c. Percentage of Completion
d. Fixed asset

9. _____ is a list for goods and materials held available in stock by a business. It is also used for a list of the contents of a household and for a list for testamentary purposes of the possessions of someone who has died. In accounting _____ is considered an asset.

a. Inventory
b. ABN Amro
c. A Random Walk Down Wall Street
d. AAB

10. _____ is a measure of the ability of a debtor to pay their debts as and when they fall due. It is usually expressed as a ratio or a percentage of current liabilities.

For a corporation with a published balance sheet there are various ratios used to calculate a measure of liquidity.

a. Invested capital
b. Accounting liquidity
c. Operating leverage
d. Operating profit margin

11. The term _____ is often used to refer to the investment management of collective investments, (not necessarily) whilst the more generic fund management may refer to all forms of institutional investment as well as investment management for private investors. Investment managers who specialize in advisory or discretionary management on behalf of (normally wealthy) private investors may often refer to their services as wealth management or portfolio management often within the context of so-called 'private banking'.

The provision of 'investment management services' includes elements of financial analysis, asset selection, stock selection, plan implementation and ongoing monitoring of investments.

    a. ABN Amro
    b. A Random Walk Down Wall Street
    c. AAB
    d. Asset management

12. In accounting, _____ or *Carrying value* is the value of an asset according to its balance sheet account balance. For assets, the value is based on the original cost of the asset less any depreciation, amortization or impairment costs made against the asset. A company's _____ is its total assets minus intangible assets and liabilities.

    a. Current liabilities
    b. Retained earnings
    c. Pro forma
    d. Book value

13. In economics, business, and accounting, a _____ is the value of money that has been used up to produce something, and hence is not available for use anymore. In business, the _____ may be one of acquisition, in which case the amount of money expended to acquire it is counted as _____. In this case, money is the input that is gone in order to acquire the thing.

    a. Cost
    b. Fixed costs
    c. Marginal cost
    d. Sliding scale fees

14. _____ is that which is owed; usually referencing assets owed, but the term can cover other obligations. In the case of assets, _____ is a means of using future purchasing power in the present before a summation has been earned. Some companies and corporations use _____ as a part of their overall corporate finance strategy.

    a. Cross-collateralization
    b. Partial Payment
    c. Credit cycle
    d. Debt

15. _____ is a term in Corporate Finance used to indicate a condition when promises to creditors of a company are broken or honored with difficulty. Sometimes _____ can lead to bankruptcy. _____ is usually associated with some costs to the company and these are known as Costs of _____.

    a. Commercial paper
    b. Capital structure
    c. Financial distress
    d. Cashflow matching

16. The free _____ of a public company is an estimate of the proportion of shares that are not held by large owners and that are not stock with sales restrictions (restricted stock that cannot be sold until they become unrestricted stock.)

Chapter 2. Financial Statements and Cash Flow 15

The free _____ or a public _____ is usually defined as being all shares held by investors other than:

- shares held by owners owning more than 5% of all shares (those could be institutional investors, 'strategic shareholders,' founders, executives, and other insiders' holdings)
- restricted stocks (granted to executives that can be, but don't have to be, registered insiders)
- insider holdings (it is assumed that insiders hold stock for the very long term)

The free _____ is an important criterion in quoting a share on the stock market.

To _____ a company means to list its shares on a public stock exchange through an initial public offering (or 'flotation'.)

- Open market
- Outstanding shares
- Market capitalization
- Public _____ *loat*
- Reverse takeover

a. Float
c. Golden parachute
b. Trade finance
d. Synthetic CDO

17. _____ is the standard framework of guidelines for financial accounting used in the United States of America. It includes the standards, conventions, and rules accountants follow in recording and summarizing transactions, and in the preparation of financial statements. _____ are now issued by the Financial Accounting Standards Board (FASB).
    a. Revenue
    b. Depreciation
    c. Net income
    d. Generally accepted accounting principles

18. _____ are defined as identifiable non-monetary assets that cannot be seen, touched or physically measured, which are created through time and/or effort and that are identifiable as a separate asset. There are two primary forms of intangibles - legal intangibles (such as trade secrets (e.g., customer lists), copyrights, patents, trademarks, and goodwill) and competitive intangibles (such as knowledge activities (know-how, knowledge), collaboration activities, leverage activities, and structural activities.) Legal intangibles generate legal property rights defensible in a court of law.
    a. A Random Walk Down Wall Street
    b. AAB
    c. ABN Amro
    d. Intangible assets

19. _____ is the price at which an asset would trade in a competitive Walrasian auction setting. _____ is often used interchangeably with open _____, fair value or fair _____, although these terms have distinct definitions in different standards, and may differ in some circumstances.

International Valuation Standards defines _____ as 'the estimated amount for which a property should exchange on the date of valuation between a willing buyer and a willing seller in an arm'e;s-length transaction after proper marketing wherein the parties had each acted knowledgeably, prudently, and without compulsion.'

16   *Chapter 2. Financial Statements and Cash Flow*

_____ is a concept distinct from market price, which is 'e;the price at which one can transact'e;, while _____ is 'e;the true underlying value'e; according to theoretical standards.

a. Wrap account
b. T-Model
c. Debt restructuring
d. Market value

20. _____ is the balance of the amounts of cash being received and paid by a business during a defined period of time, sometimes tied to a specific project. Measurement of _____ can be used

- to evaluate the state or performance of a business or project.
- to determine problems with liquidity. Being profitable does not necessarily mean being liquid. A company can fail because of a shortage of cash, even while profitable.
- to generate project rate of returns. The time of _____s into and out of projects are used as inputs to financial models such as internal rate of return, and net present value.
- to examine income or growth of a business when it is believed that accrual accounting concepts do not represent economic realities. Alternately, _____ can be used to 'validate' the net income generated by accrual accounting.

_____ as a generic term may be used differently depending on context, and certain _____ definitions may be adapted by analysts and users for their own uses. Common terms include operating _____ and free _____.

_____s can be classified into:

1. Operational _____s: Cash received or expended as a result of the company's core business activities.
2. Investment _____s: Cash received or expended through capital expenditure, investments or acquisitions.
3. Financing _____s: Cash received or expended as a result of financial activities, such as interests and dividends.

All three together - the net _____ - are necessary to reconcile the beginning cash balance to the ending cash balance. Loan draw downs or equity injections, that is just shifting of capital but no expenditure as such, are not considered in the net _____.

a. Corporate finance
b. Cash flow
c. Shareholder value
d. Real option

21. _____, refers to consumption opportunity gained by an entity within a specified time frame, which is generally expressed in monetary terms. However, for households and individuals, '_____ is the sum of all the wages, salaries, profits, interests payments, rents and other forms of earnings received... in a given period of time.' For firms, _____ generally refers to net-profit: what remains of revenue after expenses have been subtracted.

a. OIBDA
b. Accrual
c. Annual report
d. Income

22. An _____ is a financial statement for companies that indicates how Revenue is transformed into net income The purpose of the _____ is to show managers and investors whether the company made or lost money during the period being reported.

The important thing to remember about an _____ is that it represents a period of time.

a. AAB
c. A Random Walk Down Wall Street
b. ABN Amro
d. Income statement

23. _____ refers to a tax levied by various jurisdictions on the profits made by companies or associations. It is a tax on the value of the corporation's profits.

The measure of taxable profits varies from country to country.

a. Corporate tax
c. Proxy fight
b. Trade finance
d. First-mover advantage

24. _____, in accrual accounting, is any account where the asset or liability is not realized until a future date, e.g. annuities, charges, taxes, income, etc. The _____ item may be carried, dependent on type of deferral, as either an asset or liability.See also: accrual

_____ is also used in the university admissions process. It is the action by which a school rejects a student for early admission but still opts to review that student in the general admissions pool.

a. Net profit
c. Deferred
b. Current asset
d. Revenue

25. _____ is an accounting concept, meaning a future tax liability or asset, resulting from temporary differences between book (accounting) value of assets and liabilities and their tax value, or timing differences between the recognition of gains and losses in financial statements and their recognition in a tax computation.

Temporary differences are differences between the carrying amount of an asset or liability recognised in the balance sheet and the amount attributed to that asset or liability for tax purposes (the tax base.)

Temporary differences may be either:

- taxable temporary differences, which are temporary differences that will result in taxable amounts in determining taxable profit (tax loss) of future periods when the carrying amount of the asset or liability is recovered or settled; or
- deductible temporary differences, which are temporary differences that will result in deductible amounts in determining taxable profit (tax loss) of future periods when the carrying amount of the asset or liability is recovered or settled.

Chapter 2. Financial Statements and Cash Flow

The tax base of an asset or liability is the amount attributed to that asset or liability for tax purposes:

- the tax base of an asset is the amount that will be deductible for tax purposes against any taxable economic benefits that will flow to an entity when it recovers the carrying amount of the asset.

- the tax base of a liability is its carrying amount, less any amount that will be deductible for tax purposes in respect of that liability in future periods.

The basic principle of accounting for _____ under a temporary difference approach can be illustrated using a common example in which a company has fixed assets which qualify for tax depreciation.

a. Qualified residence interest
b. Monetary policy
c. Tax exemption
d. Deferred tax

26. _____ is a financial metric which represents operating liquidity available to a business. Along with fixed assets such as plant and equipment, _____ is considered a part of operating capital. It is calculated as current assets minus current liabilities.
a. 529 plan
b. Working capital management
c. 4-4-5 Calendar
d. Working capital

27. A _____ is a party (e.g. person, organization, company, or government) that has a claim to the services of a second party. The first party, in general, has provided some property or service to the second party under the assumption (usually enforced by contract) that the second party will return an equivalent property or service. The second party is frequently called a debtor or borrower.
a. False billing
b. NOPLAT
c. Creditor
d. Redemption value

Chapter 3. Financial Statements Analysis and Long-Term Planning   19

1. In financial accounting, a _____ or statement of financial position is a summary of a person's or organization's balances. Assets, liabilities and ownership equity are listed as of a specific date, such as the end of its financial year. A _____ is often described as a snapshot of a company's financial condition.

   a. Statement on Auditing Standards No. 70: Service Organizations
   b. Financial statements
   c. Balance sheet
   d. Statement of retained earnings

2. _____, refers to consumption opportunity gained by an entity within a specified time frame, which is generally expressed in monetary terms. However, for households and individuals, '_____ is the sum of all the wages, salaries, profits, interests payments, rents and other forms of earnings received... in a given period of time.' For firms, _____ generally refers to net-profit: what remains of revenue after expenses have been subtracted.

   a. Annual report
   b. Accrual
   c. OIBDA
   d. Income

3. An _____ is a financial statement for companies that indicates how Revenue is transformed into net income The purpose of the _____ is to show managers and investors whether the company made or lost money during the period being reported.

   The important thing to remember about an _____ is that it represents a period of time.

   a. ABN Amro
   b. Income statement
   c. A Random Walk Down Wall Street
   d. AAB

4. The _____ is a financial ratio that measures whether or not a firm has enough resources to pay its debts over the next 12 months. It compares a firm's current assets to its current liabilities. It is expressed as follows:

$$\text{Current ratio} = \frac{\text{Current Assets}}{\text{Current Liabilities}}$$

   For example, if WXY Company's current assets are $50,000,000 and its current liabilities are $40,000,000, then its _____ would be $50,000,000 divided by $40,000,000, which equals 1.25.

   a. PEG ratio
   b. Current ratio
   c. Sustainable growth rate
   d. Debt service coverage ratio

5. In economics, the concept of the _____ refers to the decision-making time frame of a firm in which at least one factor of production is fixed. Costs which are fixed in the _____ have no impact on a firms decisions. For example a firm can raise output by increasing the amount of labour through overtime.

   a. Long-run
   b. 529 plan
   c. 4-4-5 Calendar
   d. Short-run

6. In finance, _____ is the ability of an entity to pay its debts with available cash. _____ can also be described as the ability of a corporation to meet its long-term fixed expenses and to accomplish long-term expansion and growth. The better a company's _____, the better it is financially.

   a. Capital asset
   b. Mid price
   c. Political risk
   d. Solvency

Chapter 3. Financial Statements Analysis and Long-Term Planning

7. In finance, the Acid-test or _____ or liquid ratio measures the ability of a company to use its near cash or quick assets to immediately extinguish or retire its current liabilities. Quick assets include those current assets that presumably can be quickly converted to cash at close to their book values.

>

Generally, the acid test ratio should be 1:1 or better, however this varies widely by industry.

a. Net assets
b. P/E ratio
c. Quick ratio
d. Financial ratio

8. The _____ is a bank regulation that sets the minimum reserves each bank must hold to customer deposits and notes. These reserves are designed to satisfy withdrawal demands, and would normally be in the form of fiat currency stored in a bank vault (vault cash), or with a central bank.

The reserve ratio is sometimes used as a tool in the monetary policy, influencing the country's economy, borrowing, and interest rates.

a. Reserve requirement
b. Wall Street Journal prime rate
c. Variable rate mortgage
d. Prime rate

9. _____ is a fee paid on borrowed assets. It is the price paid for the use of borrowed money, or, money earned by deposited funds. Assets that are sometimes lent with _____ include money, shares, consumer goods through hire purchase, major assets such as aircraft, and even entire factories in finance lease arrangements.

a. AAB
b. A Random Walk Down Wall Street
c. Interest
d. Insolvency

10. Times interest earned (TIE) or _____ is a measure of a company's ability to honor its debt payments. It may be calculated as either EBIT or EBITDA divided by the total interest payable.

$$\text{Times-Interest-Earned} = \frac{\text{EBIT or EBITDA}}{\text{Interest Charges}}$$

- Financial ratio
- Financial leverage
- EBIT
- EBITDA
- Debt service coverage ratio

Interest Charges = Traditionally 'charges' refers to interest expense found on the income statement.

Times Interest Earned or Interest Coverage is a great tool when measuring a company's ability to meet its debt obligations.

Chapter 3. Financial Statements Analysis and Long-Term Planning

a. Earnings per share
b. Interest coverage ratio
c. Information ratio
d. Assets turnover

11. In economic models, the _____ time frame assumes no fixed factors of production. Firms can enter or leave the marketplace, and the cost (and availability) of land, labor, raw materials, and capital goods can be assumed to vary. In contrast, in the short-run time frame, certain factors are assumed to be fixed, because there is not sufficient time for them to change.
   a. Short-run
   b. 4-4-5 Calendar
   c. Long-run
   d. 529 plan

12. In finance, the value of an option consists of two components, its intrinsic value and its _____. Time value is simply the difference between option value and intrinsic value. _____ is also known as theta, extrinsic value, or instrumental value.
   a. Debt buyer
   b. Time value
   c. Conservatism
   d. Global Squeeze

13. Simply put, _____ is the value of money figuring in a given amount of interest for a given amount of time. For example 100 dollars of todays money held for a year at 5 percent interest is worth 105 dollars, therefore 100 dollars paid now or 105 dollars paid exactly one year from now is the same amount of payment of money with that given intersest at that given amount of time. This notion dates at least to Martín de Azpilcueta of the School of Salamanca.

All of the standard calculations for _____ derive from the most basic algebraic expression for the present value of a future sum, 'discounted' to the present by an amount equal to the _____. For example, a sum of FV to be received in one year is discounted (at the rate of interest r) to give a sum of PV at present: PV = FV -- rÂ·PV = FV/(1+r).

   a. Current account
   b. Coefficient of variation
   c. Zero-coupon bond
   d. Time value of money

14. _____ is that which is owed; usually referencing assets owed, but the term can cover other obligations. In the case of assets, _____ is a means of using future purchasing power in the present before a summation has been earned. Some companies and corporations use _____ as a part of their overall corporate finance strategy.
   a. Debt
   b. Partial Payment
   c. Credit cycle
   d. Cross-collateralization

15. _____ is a financial ratio that indicates the percentage of a company's assets are provided via debt. It is the ratio of total debt (the sum of current liabilities and long-term liabilities) and total assets (the sum of current assets, fixed assets, and other assets such as 'goodwill'.)

>

or alternatively:

>

Chapter 3. Financial Statements Analysis and Long-Term Planning

For example, a company with $2 million in total assets and $500,000 in total liabilities would have a _____ of 25%

Like all financial ratios, a company's _____ should be compared with their industry average or other competing firms.

a. Debt ratio
b. Capitalization rate
c. Cash management
d. Cash concentration

16. _____ is typically a higher ranking stock than voting shares, and its terms are negotiated between the corporation and the investor.

_____ usually carry no voting rights, but may carry superior priority over common stock in the payment of dividends and upon liquidation. _____ may carry a dividend that is paid out prior to any dividends to common stock holders.

a. Preferred stock
b. Trade-off theory
c. Follow-on offering
d. Second lien loan

17. _____ or interest coverage ratio is a measure of a company's ability to honor its debt payments. It may be calculated as either EBIT or EBITDA divided by the total interest payable.

$$\text{Times-Interest-Earned} = \frac{\text{EBIT or EBITDA}}{\text{Interest Charges}}$$

- Financial ratio
- Financial leverage
- EBIT
- EBITDA
- Debt service coverage ratio

Interest Charges = Traditionally 'charges' refers to interest expense found on the income statement.

_____ or Interest Coverage is a great tool when measuring a company's ability to meet its debt obligations.

a. Net assets
b. Return of capital
c. Cash conversion cycle
d. Times interest earned

18. In business and accounting, _____s are everything of value that is owned by a person or company. The balance sheet of a firm records the monetary value of the _____s owned by the firm. The two major _____ classes are tangible _____s and intangible _____s.

a. EBITDA
b. Asset
c. Income
d. Accounts payable

Chapter 3. Financial Statements Analysis and Long-Term Planning

19. The term _____ is often used to refer to the investment management of collective investments, (not necessarily) whilst the more generic fund management may refer to all forms of institutional investment as well as investment management for private investors. Investment managers who specialize in advisory or discretionary management on behalf of (normally wealthy) private investors may often refer to their services as wealth management or portfolio management often within the context of so-called 'private banking'.

The provision of 'investment management services' includes elements of financial analysis, asset selection, stock selection, plan implementation and ongoing monitoring of investments.

a. ABN Amro
b. Asset management
c. A Random Walk Down Wall Street
d. AAB

20. _____ is a list for goods and materials held available in stock by a business. It is also used for a list of the contents of a household and for a list for testamentary purposes of the possessions of someone who has died. In accounting _____ is considered an asset.

a. A Random Walk Down Wall Street
b. ABN Amro
c. AAB
d. Inventory

21. The _____ is an equation that equals the cost of goods sold divided by the average inventory. Average inventory equals beginning inventory plus ending inventory divided by 2.

The formula for _____:

$$\text{Inventory Turnover} = \frac{\text{Cost of Goods Sold}}{\text{Average Inventory}}$$

The formula for average inventory:

$$\text{Average Inventory} = \frac{\text{Beginning inventory} + \text{Ending inventory}}{2}$$

A low turnover rate may point to overstocking, obsolescence, or deficiencies in the product line or marketing effort.

a. Earnings yield
b. Operating leverage
c. Inventory turnover
d. Information ratio

22. _____ is one of the Accounting Liquidity ratios, a financial ratio. This ratio measures the number of times, on average, the inventory is sold during the period. Its purpose is to measure the liquidity of the inventory.

a. AAB
b. ABN Amro
c. A Random Walk Down Wall Street
d. Inventory turnover Ratio

23. _____ is one of the accounting liquidity ratios, a financial ratio. This ratio measures the number of times, on average, receivables (e.g. Accounts Receivable) are collected during the period. A popular variant of the _____ is to convert it into an Average Collection Period in terms of days.

a. Sharpe ratio
b. Return on equity
c. Receivables turnover Ratio
d. PEG ratio

24. _____ is a financial ratio that measures the efficiency of a company's use of its assets in generating sales revenue or sales income to the company.

$$Asset\ Turnover = \frac{Sales}{Average Total Assets}$$

- 'Sales' is the value of 'Net Sales' or 'Sales' from the company's income statement
- 'Average Total Assets' is the value of 'Total assets' from the company's balance sheet in the beginning and the end of the fiscal period divided by 2.
- Assets turnover

a. Earnings yield
b. Average accounting return
c. Asset turnover
d. Inventory turnover

25. In finance, a _____ is collateral that the holder of a position in securities, options, or futures contracts has to deposit to cover the credit risk of his counterparty (most often his broker.) This risk can arise if the holder has done any of the following:

- borrowed cash from the counterparty to buy securities or options,
- sold securities or options short, or
- entered into a futures contract.

The collateral can be in the form of cash or securities, and it is deposited in a _____ account. On U.S. futures exchanges, '_____' was formally called performance bond.

_____ buying is buying securities with cash borrowed from a broker, using other securities as collateral.

a. Procter ' Gamble
b. Share
c. Credit
d. Margin

26. _____ are the earnings returned on the initial investment amount.

In the US, the Financial Accounting Standards Board (FASB) requires companies' income statements to report _____ for each of the major categories of the income statement: continuing operations, discontinued operations, extraordinary items, and net income.

The _____ formula does not include preferred dividends for categories outside of continued operations and net income.

a. Inventory turnover
c. Average accounting return
b. Assets turnover
d. Earnings per share

27. _____ is the price at which an asset would trade in a competitive Walrasian auction setting. _____ is often used interchangeably with open _____, fair value or fair _____, although these terms have distinct definitions in different standards, and may differ in some circumstances.

International Valuation Standards defines _____ as 'the estimated amount for which a property should exchange on the date of valuation between a willing buyer and a willing seller in an arm'e;s-length transaction after proper marketing wherein the parties had each acted knowledgeably, prudently, and without compulsion.'

_____ is a concept distinct from market price, which is 'e;the price at which one can transact'e;, while _____ is 'e;the true underlying value'e; according to theoretical standards.

a. Market value
c. Debt restructuring
b. Wrap account
d. T-Model

28. The _____ percentage shows how profitable a company's assets are in generating revenue.

_____ can be computed as:

$$ROA = \frac{\text{Net Income}}{\text{Total Assets}}$$

This number tells you 'what the company can do with what it's got', i.e. how many dollars of earnings they derive from each dollar of assets they control. It's a useful number for comparing competing companies in the same industry.

a. Receivables turnover ratio
c. P/E ratio
b. Return on assets
d. Return on sales

29. _____ measures the rate of return on the ownership interest (shareholders' equity) of the common stock owners. _____ is viewed as one of the most important financial ratios. It measures a firm's efficiency at generating profits from every dollar of shareholders' equity (also known as net assets or assets minus liabilities.)

a. Return on sales
c. Return of capital
b. Diluted Earnings Per Share
d. Return on equity

30. In business, _____ is the total assets minus total outside liabilities of an individual or a company. For a company, this is called shareholders' equity and may be referred to as book value. _____ is stated as at a particular point in time.

a. Moneylender
c. Restructuring
b. Certified International Investment Analyst
d. Net worth

31. In business and finance, a _____ (also referred to as equity _____) of stock means a _____ of ownership in a corporation (company.) In the plural, stocks is often used as a synonym for _____ s especially in the United States, but it is less commonly used that way outside of North America.

In the United Kingdom, South Africa, and Australia, stock can also refer to completely different financial instruments such as government bonds or, less commonly, to all kinds of marketable securities.

a. Procter ' Gamble
b. Margin
c. Bucket shop
d. Share

32. The _____ is a financial ratio used to compare a company's book value to its current market price. Book value is an accounting term denoting the portion of the company held by the shareholders; in other words, the company's total tangible assets less its total liabilities. The calculation can be performed in two ways, but the result should be the same each way. In the first way, the company's market capitalization can be divided by the company's total book value from its balance sheet. The second way, using per-share values, is to divide the company's current share price by the book value per share (i.e. its book value divided by the number of outstanding shares).

a. Stock repurchase
b. Stop order
c. Price-to-book ratio
d. Whisper numbers

33. _____ is the practice of comparing a firm's results to those of similar companies or competitors.

a. False billing
b. Trade date
c. Capital guarantee
d. Peer group analysis

34. The term _____ is a term applied to practices that are perfunctory, or seek to satisfy the minimum requirements or to conform to a convention or doctrine. It has different meanings in different fields.

In accounting, _____ earnings are those earnings of companies in addition to actual earnings calculated under the Generally Accepted Accounting Principles (GAAP) in their quarterly and yearly financial reports.

a. Pro forma
b. Deferred income
c. Deferred financing costs
d. Long-term liabilities

35. _____ is the standard framework of guidelines for financial accounting used in the United States of America. It includes the standards, conventions, and rules accountants follow in recording and summarizing transactions, and in the preparation of financial statements. _____ are now issued by the Financial Accounting Standards Board (FASB).

a. Depreciation
b. Generally Accepted Accounting Principles
c. Revenue
d. Net income

36. A _____ is a payment made by a corporation to its shareholder members. When a corporation earns a profit or surplus, that money can be put to two uses: it can either be re-invested in the business (called retained earnings), or it can be paid to the shareholders as a _____. Many corporations retain a portion of their earnings and pay the remainder as a _____.

a. Dividend puzzle
b. Dividend yield
c. Dividend
d. Special dividend

37. _____ is the fraction of net income a firm pays to its stockholders in dividends:

Chapter 3. Financial Statements Analysis and Long-Term Planning   27

The part of the earnings not paid to investors is left for investment to provide for future earnings growth. Investors seeking high current income and limited capital growth prefer companies with high _____. However investors seeking capital growth may prefer lower payout ratio because capital gains are taxed at a lower rate.

a. Dividend payout ratio
b. Dividend puzzle
c. Dividend imputation
d. Dividend yield

38. _____ indicates the percentage of a company's earnings that are not paid out in dividends but credited to retained earnings. It is the opposite of the dividend payout ratio, so that also called the retention rate.

_____ = 1 - Dividend Payout Ratio

a. Bankassurer
b. Fair market value
c. Retention ratio
d. Dow Jones Indexes

39. _____ is a measure of the ability of a debtor to pay their debts as and when they fall due. It is usually expressed as a ratio or a percentage of current liabilities.

For a corporation with a published balance sheet there are various ratios used to calculate a measure of liquidity.

a. Accounting liquidity
b. Invested capital
c. Operating leverage
d. Operating profit margin

40. _____ is the term in economics for the amount of fixed or real capital present in relation to other factors of production, especially labor. At the level of either a production process or the aggregate economy, it may be estimated by the capital/labor ratio, such as from the points along a capital/labor isoquant.

Since the use of tools and machinery makes labor more effective, rising _____ pushes up the productivity of labor, so a society that is more capital intensive tends to have a higher standard of living over the long run than one with low _____.

a. Cost of capital
b. Weighted average cost of capital
c. 4-4-5 Calendar
d. Capital intensity

41. _____ is the maximum rate at which a company can grow revenue without having to invest new equity capital. If a company earns a 15% return on equity (ROE), it can grow 15% simply by reinvesting all the earnings in new opportunities and maintaining a stable debt to equity ratio. In order to grow faster, the company would have to invest more equity capital or increase its financial leverage.

a. Current ratio
b. Price/cash flow ratio
c. Return on capital employed
d. Sustainable growth rate

42. _____, in bookkeeping, refers to assets, liabilities, income, and expenses recorded on individual pages of the so called book of final entry or ledger. Changes in _____ value are made by chronologically posting debit (DR) and credit (CR) entries to its page. Examples of _____s are cash, _____s receivable, mortgages, loans, land and buildings, common stock, sales, services provided, wages, and payroll overhead.

a. Option
b. Accretion
c. Account
d. Alpha

43. _____ is a type of risk faced by investors, corporations, and governments. It is a risk that can be understood and managed with proper aforethought and investment.

Broadly, _____ refers to the complications businesses and governments may face as a result of what are commonly referred to as political decisions--or 'any political change that alters the expected outcome and value of a given economic action by changing the probability of achieving business objectives.' .

a. Mid price
b. Capital asset
c. Single-index model
d. Political risk

Chapter 4. Discounted Cash Flow Valuation

1. In finance, _____ is the process of estimating the potential market value of a financial asset or liability. they can be done on assets (for example, investments in marketable securities such as stocks, options, business enterprises, or intangible assets such as patents and trademarks) or on liabilities (e.g., Bonds issued by a company.) _____ s are required in many contexts including investment analysis, capital budgeting, merger and acquisition transactions, financial reporting, taxable events to determine the proper tax liability, and in litigation.

   a. Valuation
   b. Margin
   c. Share
   d. Procter ' Gamble

2. A '_____' is a 'Charge' that is paid to obtain the right to delay a payment. Essentially, the payer purchases the right to make a given payment in the future instead of in the Present. The '_____', or 'Charge' that must be paid to delay the payment, is simply the difference between what the payment amount would be if it were paid in the present and what the payment amount would be paid if it were paid in the future.

   a. Risk modeling
   b. Risk aversion
   c. Discount
   d. Value at risk

3. The _____ is an interest rate a central bank charges depository institutions that borrow reserves from it.

   The term _____ has two meanings:

   - the same as interest rate; the term 'discount' does not refer to the meaning of the word, but to the purpose of using the quantity, such as computations of present value, e.g. net present value / discounted cash flow

   - the annual effective _____, which is the annual interest divided by the capital including that interest; this rate is lower than the interest rate; it corresponds to using the value after a year as the nominal value, and seeing the initial value as the nominal value minus a discount; it is used for Treasury Bills and similar financial instruments

   The annual effective _____ is the annual interest divided by the capital including that interest, which is the interest rate divided by 100% plus the interest rate. It is the annual discount factor to be applied to the future cash flow, to find the discount, subtracted from a future value to find the value one year earlier.

   For example, suppose there is a government bond that sells for $95 and pays $100 in a year's time.

   a. Black-Scholes
   b. Fisher equation
   c. Discount rate
   d. Stochastic volatility

4. _____ measures the nominal future sum of money that a given sum of money is 'worth' at a specified time in the future assuming a certain interest rate rate of return; it is the present value multiplied by the accumulation function.

   The value does not include corrections for inflation or other factors that affect the true value of money in the future. This is used in time value of money calculations.

   a. Discounted cash flow
   b. Future-oriented
   c. Future value
   d. Present value of costs

5. _____ or net present worth (NPW) is defined as the total present value (PV) of a time series of cash flows. It is a standard method for using the time value of money to appraise long-term projects. Used for capital budgeting, and widely throughout economics, it measures the excess or shortfall of cash flows, in present value terms, once financing charges are met.

a. Present value of costs
b. Negative gearing
c. Tax shield
d. Net present value

6. _____ is the value on a given date of a future payment or series of future payments, discounted to reflect the time value of money and other factors such as investment risk. _____ calculations are widely used in business and economics to provide a means to compare cash flows at different times on a meaningful 'like to like' basis.

The most commonly applied model of the time value of money is compound interest.

a. Present value of benefits
b. Net present value
c. Negative gearing
d. Present value

7. _____ is the concept of adding accumulated interest back to the principal, so that interest is earned on interest from that moment on. The act of declaring interest to be principal is called compounding (i.e., interest is compounded.) A loan, for example, may have its interest compounded every month: in this case, a loan with $100 principal and 1% interest per month would have a balance of $101 at the end of the first month.

a. Risk management
b. Penny stock
c. 4-4-5 Calendar
d. Compound interest

8. A _____ is a financial contract whose value is derived from the value of something else (known as the underlying.) The underlying on which a _____ is based can be an asset, weather conditions bonds or other forms of credit.

a. Derivative
b. 4-4-5 Calendar
c. 529 plan
d. 7-Eleven

9. The _____ is a capital budgeting metric used by firms to decide whether they should make investments. It is an indicator of the efficiency or quality of an investment, as opposed to net present value (NPV), which indicates value or magnitude.

The IRR is the annualized effective compounded return rate which can be earned on the invested capital, i.e., the yield on the investment.

a. A Random Walk Down Wall Street
b. AAB
c. Internal rate of return
d. ABN Amro

10. _____ is a fee paid on borrowed assets. It is the price paid for the use of borrowed money , or, money earned by deposited funds . Assets that are sometimes lent with _____ include money, shares, consumer goods through hire purchase, major assets such as aircraft, and even entire factories in finance lease arrangements.

a. A Random Walk Down Wall Street
b. Interest
c. AAB
d. Insolvency

11. An _____ is the price a borrower pays for the use of money they do not own, and the return a lender receives for deferring the use of funds, by lending it to the borrower. _____s are normally expressed as a percentage rate over the period of one year.

_____s targets are also a vital tool of monetary policy and are used to control variables like investment, inflation, and unemployment.

 a. Interest rate
 b. ABN Amro
 c. A Random Walk Down Wall Street
 d. AAB

12. The terms _____ , nominal _____, and effective _____ describe the interest rate for a whole year (annualized), rather than just a monthly fee/rate, as applied on a loan, mortgage, credit card, etc. Those terms have formal, legal definitions in some countries or legal jurisdictions, but in general:

- The nominal _____ is the simple-interest rate (for a year.)
- The effective _____ is the fee+compound interest rate (calculated across a year.)

The nominal _____ is calculated as: the rate, for a payment period, multiplied by the number of payment periods in a year. However, the exact legal definition of 'effective _____' can vary greatly in each jurisdiction, depending on the type of fees included, such as participation fees, loan origination fees, monthly service charges, or late fees. The effective _____ has been called the 'mathematically-true' interest rate for each year. The computation for the effective _____, as the fee+compound interest rate, can also vary depending on whether the up-front fees, such as origination or participation fees, are added to the entire amount, or treated as a short-term loan due in the first payment.

 a. ABN Amro
 b. AAB
 c. A Random Walk Down Wall Street
 d. Annual percentage rate

13. The _____, effective annual interest rate, Annual Equivalent Rate (AER) or simply effective rate is the interest rate on a loan or financial product restated from the nominal interest rate as an interest rate with annual compound interest. It is used to compare the annual interest between loans with different compounding terms (daily, monthly, annually, or other.)

The _____ differs in two important respects from the annual percentage rate (APR):

1. the _____ generally does not incorporate one-time charges such as front-end fees;
2. the _____ is (generally) not defined by legal or regulatory authorities (as APR is in many jurisdictions.)

By contrast, the 'effective APR' is used as a legal term, where front-fees and other costs can be included, as defined by local law.

Annual Percentage Yield or effective annual yield is the analogous concept used for savings or investment products, such as a certificate of deposit.

a. ABN Amro
c. A Random Walk Down Wall Street
b. Effective interest rate
d. AAB

14. In finance, the term _____ describes the amount in cash that returns to the owners of a security. Normally it does not include the price variations, at the difference of the total return. _____ applies to various stated rates of return on stocks (common and preferred, and convertible), fixed income instruments (bonds, notes, bills, strips, zero coupon), and some other investment type insurance products (e.g. annuities.)

a. Yield to maturity
c. Macaulay duration
b. 4-4-5 Calendar
d. Yield

15. _____ are a form of British government bond (gilt), dating originally from the 18th century. _____ are one of the rare examples of an actual perpetuity: although they may be redeemed by the British government, they are unlikely to do so in the foreseeable future.

In 1752, the Chancellor of the Exchequer and Prime Minister Sir Henry Pelham converted all outstanding issues of redeemable government stock into one bond, Consolidated 3.5% Annuities, in order to reduce the coupon rate paid on the government debt.

a. Revenue bonds
c. Serial bond
b. Brady bonds
d. Consols

16. The phrase _____ refers to the aspect of corporate strategy, corporate finance and management dealing with the buying, selling and combining of different companies that can aid, finance, or help a growing company in a given industry grow rapidly without having to create another business entity.

An acquisition, also known as a takeover, is the buying of one company (the 'target') by another. An acquisition may be friendly or hostile.

a. 4-4-5 Calendar
c. Mergers and acquisitions
b. 7-Eleven
d. 529 plan

17. A _____ is an annuity in which the periodic payments begin on a fixed date and continue indefinitely. It is sometimes referred to as a perpetual annuity. Fixed coupon payments on permanently invested (irredeemable) sums of money are prime examples of these. Scholarships paid perpetually from an endowment fit the definition of _____.

a. Stochastic volatility
c. LIBOR market model
b. Current yield
d. Perpetuity

18. An _____ can be defined as a contract which provides an income stream in return for an initial payment.

An immediate _____ is an _____ for which the time between the contract date and the date of the first payment is not longer than the time interval between payments. A common use for an immediate _____ is to provide a pension to a retired person or persons.

a. AT'T Inc.
c. Amortization
b. Annuity
d. Intrinsic value

19. _____ is a legal term for a type of debt which is overdue after missing an expected payment. It is also used (in the form in _____) for payments that occur at the end of a period.

_____ accrue from the date on the first missed payment was due.

a. A Random Walk Down Wall Street
b. AAB
c. Arrears
d. Interest

Chapter 5. How to Value Bonds and Stocks

1. In business and accounting, _____s are everything of value that is owned by a person or company. The balance sheet of a firm records the monetary value of the _____s owned by the firm. The two major _____ classes are tangible _____s and intangible _____s.
   a. EBITDA
   b. Accounts payable
   c. Income
   d. Asset

2. The term _____ is often used to refer to the investment management of collective investments, (not necessarily) whilst the more generic fund management may refer to all forms of institutional investment as well as investment management for private investors. Investment managers who specialize in advisory or discretionary management on behalf of (normally wealthy) private investors may often refer to their services as wealth management or portfolio management often within the context of so-called 'private banking'.

   The provision of 'investment management services' includes elements of financial analysis, asset selection, stock selection, plan implementation and ongoing monitoring of investments.

   a. ABN Amro
   b. A Random Walk Down Wall Street
   c. AAB
   d. Asset management

3. In finance, a _____ is a debt security, in which the authorized issuer owes the holders a debt and, depending on the terms of the _____, is obliged to pay interest (the coupon) and/or to repay the principal at a later date, termed maturity.

   Thus a _____ is a loan: the issuer is the borrower, the _____ holder is the lender, and the coupon is the interest. _____s provide the borrower with external funds to finance long-term investments, or, in the case of government _____s, to finance current expenditure.

   a. Catastrophe bonds
   b. Convertible bond
   c. Puttable bond
   d. Bond

4. In economic models, the _____ time frame assumes no fixed factors of production. Firms can enter or leave the marketplace, and the cost (and availability) of land, labor, raw materials, and capital goods can be assumed to vary. In contrast, in the short-run time frame, certain factors are assumed to be fixed, because there is not sufficient time for them to change.
   a. Short-run
   b. 529 plan
   c. Long-run
   d. 4-4-5 Calendar

5. A _____ is a document that indicates that the bearer of the document has title to property, such as shares or bonds. They differ from normal registered instruments, in that no records are kept of who owns the underlying property, or of the transactions involving transfer of ownership. Whoever physically holds the bearer bond papers owns the property.
   a. Bearer instrument
   b. Book entry
   c. Securities lending
   d. Marketable

6. In finance, the binomial options pricing model (BOPM) provides a generalisable numerical method for the valuation of options. The _____ was first proposed by Cox, Ross and Rubinstein (1979.) Essentially, the model uses a 'discrete-time' model of the varying price over time of the underlying financial instrument.

Chapter 5. How to Value Bonds and Stocks

a. Binomial model
b. Discount rate
c. Modified Internal Rate of Return
d. Perpetuity

7. _____ is that which is owed; usually referencing assets owed, but the term can cover other obligations. In the case of assets, _____ is a means of using future purchasing power in the present before a summation has been earned. Some companies and corporations use _____ as a part of their overall corporate finance strategy.
 a. Partial Payment
 b. Debt
 c. Cross-collateralization
 d. Credit cycle

8. A '_____' is a 'Charge' that is paid to obtain the right to delay a payment. Essentially, the payer purchases the right to make a given payment in the future instead of in the Present. The '_____', or 'Charge' that must be paid to delay the payment, is simply the difference between what the payment amount would be if it were paid in the present and what the payment amount would be paid if it were paid in the future.
 a. Risk aversion
 b. Risk modeling
 c. Value at risk
 d. Discount

9. A _____ is a bond bought at a price lower than its face value, with the face value repaid at the time of maturity. It does not make periodic interest payments, or so-called 'coupons,' hence the term zero-coupon bond. Investors earn return from the compounded interest all paid at maturity plus the difference between the discounted price of the bond and its par value.
 a. Zero coupon bond
 b. Callable bond
 c. Municipal bond
 d. Bowie bonds

10. The phrase _____ refers to the aspect of corporate strategy, corporate finance and management dealing with the buying, selling and combining of different companies that can aid, finance, or help a growing company in a given industry grow rapidly without having to create another business entity.

An acquisition, also known as a takeover, is the buying of one company (the 'target') by another. An acquisition may be friendly or hostile.

 a. 529 plan
 b. 7-Eleven
 c. 4-4-5 Calendar
 d. Mergers and acquisitions

11. In finance, _____ is the process of estimating the potential market value of a financial asset or liability. they can be done on assets (for example, investments in marketable securities such as stocks, options, business enterprises, or intangible assets such as patents and trademarks) or on liabilities (e.g., Bonds issued by a company.) _____s are required in many contexts including investment analysis, capital budgeting, merger and acquisition transactions, financial reporting, taxable events to determine the proper tax liability, and in litigation.
 a. Valuation
 b. Margin
 c. Procter ' Gamble
 d. Share

12. The coupon or _____ of a bond is the amount of interest paid per year expressed as a percentage of the face value of the bond.

For example if you hold $10,000 nominal of a bond described as a 4.5% loan stock, you will receive $450 in interest each year (probably in two installments of $225 each.)

Chapter 5. How to Value Bonds and Stocks

Not all bonds have coupons.

a. Revenue bonds
c. Coupon rate
b. Puttable bond
d. Zero-coupon bond

13. _____ is a fee paid on borrowed assets. It is the price paid for the use of borrowed money , or, money earned by deposited funds . Assets that are sometimes lent with _____ include money, shares, consumer goods through hire purchase, major assets such as aircraft, and even entire factories in finance lease arrangements.

a. Insolvency
c. AAB
b. A Random Walk Down Wall Street
d. Interest

14. An _____ is the price a borrower pays for the use of money they do not own, and the return a lender receives for deferring the use of funds, by lending it to the borrower. _____s are normally expressed as a percentage rate over the period of one year.

_____s targets are also a vital tool of monetary policy and are used to control variables like investment, inflation, and unemployment.

a. A Random Walk Down Wall Street
c. AAB
b. Interest rate
d. ABN Amro

15. _____ is a life of security. It may also refer to the final payment date of a loan or other financial instrument, at which point all remaining interest and principal is due to be paid.

1, 3, 6 months _____ band can be calculated by using 30-day per month periods.

a. Maturity
c. Primary market
b. False billing
d. Replacement cost

16. _____, in finance and accounting, means stated value or face value. From this comes the expressions at par (at the _____), over par (over _____) and under par (under _____.)

The term '_____' has several meanings depending on context and geography.

a. Par value
c. Sinking fund
b. FIDC
d. Global Squeeze

17. The terms _____ , nominal _____, and effective _____ describe the interest rate for a whole year (annualized), rather than just a monthly fee/rate, as applied on a loan, mortgage, credit card, etc. Those terms have formal, legal definitions in some countries or legal jurisdictions, but in general:

- The nominal _____ is the simple-interest rate (for a year.)
- The effective _____ is the fee+compound interest rate (calculated across a year.)

Chapter 5. How to Value Bonds and Stocks 37

The nominal _____ is calculated as: the rate, for a payment period, multiplied by the number of payment periods in a year. However, the exact legal definition of 'effective _____' can vary greatly in each jurisdiction, depending on the type of fees included, such as participation fees, loan origination fees, monthly service charges, or late fees. The effective _____ has been called the 'mathematically-true' interest rate for each year. The computation for the effective _____, as the fee+compound interest rate, can also vary depending on whether the up-front fees, such as origination or participation fees, are added to the entire amount, or treated as a short-term loan due in the first payment.

a. ABN Amro
b. AAB
c. A Random Walk Down Wall Street
d. Annual percentage rate

18. _____ are a form of British government bond (gilt), dating originally from the 18th century. _____ are one of the rare examples of an actual perpetuity: although they may be redeemed by the British government, they are unlikely to do so in the foreseeable future.

In 1752, the Chancellor of the Exchequer and Prime Minister Sir Henry Pelham converted all outstanding issues of redeemable government stock into one bond, Consolidated 3.5% Annuities, in order to reduce the coupon rate paid on the government debt.

a. Serial bond
b. Consols
c. Revenue bonds
d. Brady bonds

19. _____ is a type of bond that allows the issuer of the bond to retain the privilege of redeeming the bond at some point before the bond reaches the date of maturity. In other words, on the call dates, the issuer has the right, but not the obligation, to buy back the bonds from the bond holders at the call price. Technically speaking, the bonds are not really bought and held by the issuer but cancelled immediately.

a. Coupon rate
b. Gilts
c. Bond fund
d. Callable bond

20. _____ is typically a higher ranking stock than voting shares, and its terms are negotiated between the corporation and the investor.

_____ usually carry no voting rights, but may carry superior priority over common stock in the payment of dividends and upon liquidation. _____ may carry a dividend that is paid out prior to any dividends to common stock holders.

a. Follow-on offering
b. Preferred stock
c. Trade-off theory
d. Second lien loan

21. In financial accounting, _____s are precautions for which the amount or probability of occurrence are not known. Typical examples are _____s for warranty costs and _____ for taxes the term reserve is used instead of term _____; such a use, however, is inconsistent with the terminology suggested by International Accounting Standards Board.

a. Money measurement concept
c. Petty cash
b. Provision
d. Momentum Accounting and Triple-Entry Bookkeeping

22. _____ is the value on a given date of a future payment or series of future payments, discounted to reflect the time value of money and other factors such as investment risk. _____ calculations are widely used in business and economics to provide a means to compare cash flows at different times on a meaningful 'like to like' basis.

The most commonly applied model of the time value of money is compound interest.

a. Negative gearing
c. Present value of benefits
b. Net present value
d. Present value

23. In finance, the term _____ describes the amount in cash that returns to the owners of a security. Normally it does not include the price variations, at the difference of the total return. _____ applies to various stated rates of return on stocks (common and preferred, and convertible), fixed income instruments (bonds, notes, bills, strips, zero coupon), and some other investment type insurance products (e.g. annuities.)

a. Yield
c. Macaulay duration
b. 4-4-5 Calendar
d. Yield to maturity

24. The _____ or redemption yield is the yield promised to the bondholder on the assumption that the bond or other fixed-interest security such as gilts will be held to maturity, that all coupon and principal payments will be made and coupon payments are reinvested at the bond's promised yield at the same rate as invested. It is a measure of the return of the bond. This technique in theory allows investors to calculate the fair value of different financial instruments.

a. Macaulay duration
c. 4-4-5 Calendar
b. Yield to maturity
d. Yield

25. An _____ can be defined as a contract which provides an income stream in return for an initial payment.

An immediate _____ is an _____ for which the time between the contract date and the date of the first payment is not longer than the time interval between payments. A common use for an immediate _____ is to provide a pension to a retired person or persons.

a. Annuity
c. Amortization
b. Intrinsic value
d. AT'T Inc.

26. A _____ is different from normal stock in that it is unregistered - no records are kept of the owner, or the transactions involving ownership. Whoever physically holds the _____ papers owns the stock or corporation. This is useful for investors and corporate officers who wish to retain anonymity.

a. Gilts
c. Clean price
b. Revenue bonds
d. Bearer bond

27. The _____ is a financial market where participants buy and sell debt securities, usually in the form of bonds. As of 2006, the size of the international _____ is an estimated $45 trillion, of which the size of the outstanding U.S. _____ debt was $25.2 trillion.

Chapter 5. How to Value Bonds and Stocks

Nearly all of the $923 billion average daily trading volume in the U.S. _____ takes place between broker-dealers and large institutions in a decentralized, over-the-counter market.

- a. Fixed income
- b. 529 plan
- c. Bond market
- d. 4-4-5 Calendar

28. In finance, a _____ is a security that entitles the holder to buy stock of the company that issued it at a specified price, which is usually higher than the stock price at time of issue.

_____s are frequently attached to bonds or preferred stock as a sweetener, allowing the issuer to pay lower interest rates or dividends. They can be used to enhance the yield of the bond, and make them more attractive to potential buyers.

- a. Warrant
- b. Clearing house
- c. Credit
- d. Clearing

29. A _____ is a profit that results from investments into a capital asset, such as stocks, bonds or real estate, which exceeds the purchase price. It is the difference between a higher selling price and a lower purchase price, resulting in a financial gain for the seller. Conversely, a capital loss arises if the proceeds from the sale of a capital asset are less than the purchase price.

- a. Tax brackets
- b. Capital gain
- c. Capital gains tax
- d. Payroll tax

30. _____ is a form of corporation equity ownership represented in the securities. It is dangerous in comparison to preferred shares and some other investment options, in that in the event of bankruptcy, _____ investors receive their funds after preferred stockholders, bondholders, creditors, etc. On the other hand, common shares on average perform better than preferred shares or bonds over time.

- a. Stock market bubble
- b. Stop-limit order
- c. Stock split
- d. Common stock

31. A _____ is a payment made by a corporation to its shareholder members. When a corporation earns a profit or surplus, that money can be put to two uses: it can either be re-invested in the business (called retained earnings), or it can be paid to the shareholders as a _____. Many corporations retain a portion of their earnings and pay the remainder as a _____.

- a. Dividend puzzle
- b. Special dividend
- c. Dividend yield
- d. Dividend

32. In business and finance, a _____ (also referred to as equity _____) of stock means a _____ of ownership in a corporation (company.) In the plural, stocks is often used as a synonym for _____s especially in the United States, but it is less commonly used that way outside of North America.

In the United Kingdom, South Africa, and Australia, stock can also refer to completely different financial instruments such as government bonds or, less commonly, to all kinds of marketable securities.

a. Share
b. Procter ' Gamble
c. Bucket shop
d. Margin

33. In finance, _____ are stocks that appreciate in value and yield a high return on equity (ROE.) Analysts compute ROE by taking the company's net income and dividing it by the company's equity. To be classified as a growth stock, analysts expect to see at least 15 percent return on equity.
   a. Stock valuation
   b. Growth stocks
   c. 4-4-5 Calendar
   d. Security Analysis

34. _____ is an estimate of the fair value of corporations and their stocks, by using fundamental economic criteria. This theoretical valuation has to be perfected with market criteria, as the final purpose is to determine potential market prices.
   a. Stock valuation
   b. Security Analysis
   c. 4-4-5 Calendar
   d. Growth stocks

35. _____ is a theory that all economic activities and policies should be oriented towards achieving a state of equilibrium, a steady state.

The theory asserts that the continuous growth model is inherently unstable resulting in a 'boom/bust' cycle, and that continuous growth in the context of finite resources is unlikely to support current levels of prosperity indefinitely.

Proponents of this theory also explicitly challenge the popular equation of economic growth with progress - an equation they have labelled Growth Fetish - and posit that sustainability has inherent value.

   a. 4-4-5 Calendar
   b. 529 plan
   c. 7-Eleven
   d. Zero growth

36. In accounting, _____ refers to the portion of net income which is retained by the corporation rather than distributed to its owners as dividends. Similarly, if the corporation makes a loss, then that loss is retained and called variously retained losses, accumulated losses or accumulated deficit. _____ and losses are cumulative from year to year with losses offsetting earnings.
   a. Historical cost
   b. Generally Accepted Accounting Principles
   c. Matching principle
   d. Retained earnings

37. _____ is the maximum rate at which a company can grow revenue without having to invest new equity capital. If a company earns a 15% return on equity (ROE), it can grow 15% simply by reinvesting all the earnings in new opportunities and maintaining a stable debt to equity ratio. In order to grow faster, the company would have to invest more equity capital or increase its financial leverage.
   a. Current ratio
   b. Sustainable growth rate
   c. Return on capital employed
   d. Price/cash flow ratio

38. The _____ on a company stock is the company's annual dividend payments divided by its market cap, or the dividend per share divided by the price per share. It is often expressed as a percentage.

Dividend payments on preferred shares are stipulated by the prospectus.

a. Dividend reinvestment plan
b. Dividend yield
c. Dividend imputation
d. Special dividend

39. _____ is the fraction of net income a firm pays to its stockholders in dividends:

The part of the earnings not paid to investors is left for investment to provide for future earnings growth. Investors seeking high current income and limited capital growth prefer companies with high _____. However investors seeking capital growth may prefer lower payout ratio because capital gains are taxed at a lower rate.

a. Dividend payout ratio
b. Dividend yield
c. Dividend puzzle
d. Dividend imputation

40. In business, a _____ is a product or a business unit that generates unusually high profit margins: so high that it is responsible for a large amount of a company's operating profit. This profit far exceeds the amount necessary to maintain the _____ business, and the excess is used by the business for other purposes.

A firm is said to be acting as a _____ when its earnings per share (EPS) is equal to its dividends per share (DPS), or in other words, when a firm pays out 100% of its free cash flow (FCF) to its shareholders as dividends at the end of each accounting term.

a. Cash cow
b. Corporate Transparency
c. Performance measurement
d. Management by exception

41. _____ are the earnings returned on the initial investment amount.

In the US, the Financial Accounting Standards Board (FASB) requires companies' income statements to report _____ for each of the major categories of the income statement: continuing operations, discontinued operations, extraordinary items, and net income.

The _____ formula does not include preferred dividends for categories outside of continued operations and net income.

a. Inventory turnover
b. Earnings per share
c. Average accounting return
d. Assets turnover

42. _____ or net present worth (NPW) is defined as the total present value (PV) of a time series of cash flows. It is a standard method for using the time value of money to appraise long-term projects. Used for capital budgeting, and widely throughout economics, it measures the excess or shortfall of cash flows, in present value terms, once financing charges are met.

a. Tax shield
b. Negative gearing
c. Present value of costs
d. Net present value

43. The _____ is an interest rate a central bank charges depository institutions that borrow reserves from it.

Chapter 5. How to Value Bonds and Stocks

The term _____ has two meanings:

- the same as interest rate; the term 'discount' does not refer to the meaning of the word, but to the purpose of using the quantity, such as computations of present value, e.g. net present value / discounted cash flow

- the annual effective _____, which is the annual interest divided by the capital including that interest; this rate is lower than the interest rate; it corresponds to using the value after a year as the nominal value, and seeing the initial value as the nominal value minus a discount; it is used for Treasury Bills and similar financial instruments

The annual effective _____ is the annual interest divided by the capital including that interest, which is the interest rate divided by 100% plus the interest rate. It is the annual discount factor to be applied to the future cash flow, to find the discount, subtracted from a future value to find the value one year earlier.

For example, suppose there is a government bond that sells for $95 and pays $100 in a year's time.

a. Fisher equation
b. Stochastic volatility
c. Black-Scholes
d. Discount rate

44. _____ refers to any one of several methods by which a company, for 'financial accounting' and/or tax purposes, depreciates a fixed asset in such a way that the amount of depreciation taken each year is higher during the earlier years of an asset's life. For financial accounting purposes, _____ is generally used when an asset is expected to be much more productive during its early years, so that depreciation expense will more accurately represent how much of an asset's usefulness is being used up each year. For tax purposes, _____ provides a way of deferring corporate income taxes by reducing taxable income in current years, in exchange for increased taxable income in future years.

a. Accelerated depreciation
b. ABN Amro
c. A Random Walk Down Wall Street
d. AAB

45. Two primary _____, cash and accrual basis, and their combination, called modified cash basis, are used in recognizing income (revenues) and expenses in bookkeeping in order to measure net income for a specified time interval (accounting period.) Both methods differ on such recognition leading to varying income recordings, which may be subject to error or - manipulation. Many financial scandals involved accounting manipulations.

a. Outstanding balance
b. Accounting equation
c. Asset
d. Accounting methods

46. _____ is a term used in accounting, economics and finance to spread the cost of an asset over the span of several years.

In simple words we can say that _____ is the reduction in the value of an asset due to usage, passage of time, wear and tear, technological outdating or obsolescence, depletion or other such factors.

In accounting, _____ is a term used to describe any method of attributing the historical or purchase cost of an asset across its useful life, roughly corresponding to normal wear and tear.

Chapter 5. How to Value Bonds and Stocks

a. Matching principle
b. Bottom line
c. Deferred financing costs
d. Depreciation

47. _____ or First In, First Out, is an abstraction in ways of organizing and manipulation of data relative to time and prioritization. This expression describes the principle of a queue processing technique or servicing conflicting demands by ordering process by first-come, first-served (FCFS) behaviour: what comes in first is handled first, what comes in next waits until the first is finished, etc.

Thus it is analogous to the behaviour of persons queueing (or 'standing in line', in common American parlance), where the persons leave the queue in the order they arrive, or waiting one's turn at a traffic control signal.

a. Penny stock
b. 4-4-5 Calendar
c. FIFO
d. Risk management

48. _____ is a list for goods and materials held available in stock by a business. It is also used for a list of the contents of a household and for a list for testamentary purposes of the possessions of someone who has died. In accounting _____ is considered an asset.

a. AAB
b. ABN Amro
c. A Random Walk Down Wall Street
d. Inventory

49. _____ is an acronym which stands for last in, first out. In computer science and queueing theory this refers to the way items stored in some types of data structures are processed. By definition, in a _____ structured linear list, elements can be added or taken off from only one end, called the 'top'.

a. 529 plan
b. 4-4-5 Calendar
c. 7-Eleven
d. LIFO

50. _____ (PoC) is an accounting method of work-in-progress evaluation, for recording long-term contracts. For such tasks, this is the only method authorised by the International Financial Reporting Standards (IFRS.)

Revenues and gross profit are recognized each period based on the construction progress-in other words, the _____.

a. Remittance advice
b. Percentage of Completion
c. Fixed asset
d. Suspense account

51. A _____, securities exchange or (in Europe) bourse is a corporation or mutual organization which provides 'trading' facilities for stock brokers and traders, to trade stocks and other securities. _____s also provide facilities for the issue and redemption of securities as well as other financial instruments and capital events including the payment of income and dividends. The securities traded on a _____ include: shares issued by companies, unit trusts and other pooled investment products and bonds.

a. 4-4-5 Calendar
b. 529 plan
c. 7-Eleven
d. Stock exchange

Chapter 5. How to Value Bonds and Stocks

52. Depreciation methods that provide for a higher depreciation charge in the first year of an asset's life and gradually decreasing charges in subsequent years are called accelerated depreciation methods. This may be a more realistic reflection of an asset's actual expected benefit from the use of the asset: many assets are most useful when they are new. One popular accelerated method is the declining-balance method. Under this method the Book Value is multiplied by a fixed rate.

The most common rate used is double the straight-line rate. For this reason, this technique is referred to as the _____. To illustrate, suppose a business has an asset with $1,000 Original Cost, $100 Salvage Value, and 5 years useful life. First, calculate straight-line depreciation rate. Since the asset has 5 years useful life, the straight-line depreciation rate equals (100% / 5) 20% per year. With _____, as the name suggests, double that rate, or 40% depreciation rate is used.

a. Doctrine of the Proper Law
b. The Goodyear Tire ' Rubber Company
c. Double-declining-balance method
d. Database auditing

53. The _____ is the market for securities, where companies and governments can raise longterm funds. The _____ includes the stock market and the bond market. Financial regulators, such as the U.S. Securities and Exchange Commission, oversee the _____s in their designated countries to ensure that investors are protected against fraud.

a. Capital market
b. Spot rate
c. Delta neutral
d. Forward market

54. A _____ is an exchange of promises between two or more parties to do an act which is enforceable in a court of law. It is where an unqualified offer meets a qualified acceptance and the parties reach Consensus ad Idem. The parties must have the necessary capacity to _____ and the _____ must not be either trifling, indeterminate, impossible or illegal.

a. 529 plan
b. 7-Eleven
c. 4-4-5 Calendar
d. Contract

55. In economics, business, and accounting, a _____ is the value of money that has been used up to produce something, and hence is not available for use anymore. In business, the _____ may be one of acquisition, in which case the amount of money expended to acquire it is counted as _____. In this case, money is the input that is gone in order to acquire the thing.

a. Sliding scale fees
b. Fixed costs
c. Cost
d. Marginal cost

56. In finance, the yield curve is the relation between the interest rate (or cost of borrowing) and the time to maturity of the debt for a given borrower in a given currency. For example, the current U.S. dollar interest rates paid on U.S. Treasury securities for various maturities are closely watched by many traders, and are commonly plotted on a graph such as the one on the right which is informally called 'the yield curve.' More formal mathematical descriptions of this relation are often called the _____.

The yield of a debt instrument is the annualized percentage increase in the value of the investment.

a. 529 plan
b. Term structure of Interest rates
c. 7-Eleven
d. 4-4-5 Calendar

Chapter 6. Net Present Value and Other Investment Rules

1. _____ is the planning process used to determine whether a firm's long term investments such as new machinery, replacement machinery, new plants, new products, and research development projects are worth pursuing. It is budget for major capital, or investment, expenditures.

Many formal methods are used in _____, including the techniques such as

- Net present value
- Profitability index
- Internal rate of return
- Modified Internal Rate of Return
- Equivalent annuity

These methods use the incremental cash flows from each potential investment, or project. Techniques based on accounting earnings and accounting rules are sometimes used - though economists consider this to be improper - such as the accounting rate of return, and 'return on investment.' Simplified and hybrid methods are used as well, such as payback period and discounted payback period.

    a. Preferred stock   b. Capital budgeting
    c. Shareholder value   d. Financial distress

2. _____ or net present worth (NPW) is defined as the total present value (PV) of a time series of cash flows. It is a standard method for using the time value of money to appraise long-term projects. Used for capital budgeting, and widely throughout economics, it measures the excess or shortfall of cash flows, in present value terms, once financing charges are met.

    a. Present value of costs   b. Negative gearing
    c. Net present value   d. Tax shield

3. _____ is the value on a given date of a future payment or series of future payments, discounted to reflect the time value of money and other factors such as investment risk. _____ calculations are widely used in business and economics to provide a means to compare cash flows at different times on a meaningful 'like to like' basis.

The most commonly applied model of the time value of money is compound interest.

    a. Net present value   b. Present value of benefits
    c. Negative gearing   d. Present value

4. _____ are a class of computational algorithms that rely on repeated random sampling to compute their results. _____ are often used when simulating physical and mathematical systems. Because of their reliance on repeated computation and random or pseudo-random numbers, _____ are most suited to calculation by a computer.

_____ in finance are often used to calculate the value of companies, to evaluate investments in projects at corporate level or to evaluate financial derivatives. The method is intended for financial analysts who want to construct stochastic or probabilistic financial models as opposed to the traditional static and deterministic models.

Chapter 6. Net Present Value and Other Investment Rules

    a. Semivariance
    c. Sample size
    b. Correlation
    d. Monte Carlo methods

5. _____ or economic opportunity loss is the value of the next best alternative foregone as the result of making a decision. _____ analysis is an important part of a company's decision-making processes but is not treated as an actual cost in any financial statement. The next best thing that a person can engage in is referred to as the _____ of doing the best thing and ignoring the next best thing to be done.
    a. Opportunity cost
    c. ABN Amro
    b. AAB
    d. A Random Walk Down Wall Street

6. _____ in business and economics refers to the period of time required for the return on an investment to 'repay' the sum of the original investment. For example, a $1000 investment which returned $500 per year would have a two year _____. It intuitively measures how long something takes to 'pay for itself.' _____ is widely used due to its ease of use despite recognized limitations.
    a. Financial Gerontology
    c. Consignment stock
    b. Seasoned equity offering
    d. Payback period

7. In economics, business, and accounting, a _____ is the value of money that has been used up to produce something, and hence is not available for use anymore. In business, the _____ may be one of acquisition, in which case the amount of money expended to acquire it is counted as _____. In this case, money is the input that is gone in order to acquire the thing.
    a. Fixed costs
    c. Cost
    b. Marginal cost
    d. Sliding scale fees

8. _____ is the balance of the amounts of cash being received and paid by a business during a defined period of time, sometimes tied to a specific project. Measurement of _____ can be used

- to evaluate the state or performance of a business or project.
- to determine problems with liquidity. Being profitable does not necessarily mean being liquid. A company can fail because of a shortage of cash, even while profitable.
- to generate project rate of returns. The time of _____s into and out of projects are used as inputs to financial models such as internal rate of return, and net present value.
- to examine income or growth of a business when it is believed that accrual accounting concepts do not represent economic realities. Alternately, _____ can be used to 'validate' the net income generated by accrual accounting.

_____ as a generic term may be used differently depending on context, and certain _____ definitions may be adapted by analysts and users for their own uses. Common terms include operating _____ and free _____.

Chapter 6. Net Present Value and Other Investment Rules

_____s can be classified into:

1. Operational _____s: Cash received or expended as a result of the company's core business activities.
2. Investment _____s: Cash received or expended through capital expenditure, investments or acquisitions.
3. Financing _____s: Cash received or expended as a result of financial activities, such as interests and dividends.

All three together - the net _____ - are necessary to reconcile the beginning cash balance to the ending cash balance. Loan draw downs or equity injections, that is just shifting of capital but no expenditure as such, are not considered in the net _____.

a. Shareholder value
b. Real option
c. Corporate finance
d. Cash flow

9. The _____ is the average project earnings after taxes and depreciation, divided by the average book value of the investment during its life.

There are three steps to calculating the _____.

First, determine the average net income of each year of the project's life. Second, determine the average investment, taking depreciation into account. Third, determine the _____ by dividing the average net income by the average investment.

a. Assets turnover
b. Operating leverage
c. Average accounting return
d. Information ratio

10. Depreciation methods that provide for a higher depreciation charge in the first year of an asset's life and gradually decreasing charges in subsequent years are called accelerated depreciation methods. This may be a more realistic reflection of an asset's actual expected benefit from the use of the asset: many assets are most useful when they are new. One popular accelerated method is the declining-balance method. Under this method the Book Value is multiplied by a fixed rate.

The most common rate used is double the straight-line rate. For this reason, this technique is referred to as the _____. To illustrate, suppose a business has an asset with $1,000 Original Cost, $100 Salvage Value, and 5 years useful life. First, calculate straight-line depreciation rate. Since the asset has 5 years useful life, the straight-line depreciation rate equals (100% / 5) 20% per year. With _____, as the name suggests, double that rate, or 40% depreciation rate is used.

a. Database auditing
b. Double-declining-balance method
c. Doctrine of the Proper Law
d. The Goodyear Tire ' Rubber Company

11. _____ is a term used in accounting, economics and finance to spread the cost of an asset over the span of several years.

Chapter 6. Net Present Value and Other Investment Rules

In simple words we can say that _____ is the reduction in the value of an asset due to usage, passage of time, wear and tear, technological outdating or obsolescence, depletion or other such factors.

In accounting, _____ is a term used to describe any method of attributing the historical or purchase cost of an asset across its useful life, roughly corresponding to normal wear and tear.

a. Matching principle
b. Bottom line
c. Deferred financing costs
d. Depreciation

12. _____, refers to consumption opportunity gained by an entity within a specified time frame, which is generally expressed in monetary terms. However, for households and individuals, '_____ is the sum of all the wages, salaries, profits, interests payments, rents and other forms of earnings received... in a given period of time.' For firms, _____ generally refers to net-profit: what remains of revenue after expenses have been subtracted.

a. Annual report
b. Accrual
c. OIBDA
d. Income

13. _____ is equal to the income that a firm has after subtracting costs and expenses from the total revenue. _____ can be distributed among holders of common stock as a dividend or held by the firm as retained earnings. _____ is an accounting term; in some countries (such as the UK) profit is the usual term.

a. Historical cost
b. Furniture, Fixtures and Equipment
c. Write-off
d. Net income

14. The _____ is a capital budgeting metric used by firms to decide whether they should make investments. It is an indicator of the efficiency or quality of an investment, as opposed to net present value (NPV), which indicates value or magnitude.

The IRR is the annualized effective compounded return rate which can be earned on the invested capital, i.e., the yield on the investment.

a. ABN Amro
b. A Random Walk Down Wall Street
c. Internal rate of return
d. AAB

15. A '_____' is a 'Charge' that is paid to obtain the right to delay a payment. Essentially, the payer purchases the right to make a given payment in the future instead of in the Present. The '_____', or 'Charge' that must be paid to delay the payment, is simply the difference between what the payment amount would be if it were paid in the present and what the payment amount would be paid if it were paid in the future.

a. Risk modeling
b. Value at risk
c. Risk aversion
d. Discount

16. The _____ is an interest rate a central bank charges depository institutions that borrow reserves from it.

Chapter 6. Net Present Value and Other Investment Rules

The term _____ has two meanings:

- the same as interest rate; the term 'discount' does not refer to the meaning of the word, but to the purpose of using the quantity, such as computations of present value, e.g. net present value / discounted cash flow

- the annual effective _____, which is the annual interest divided by the capital including that interest; this rate is lower than the interest rate; it corresponds to using the value after a year as the nominal value, and seeing the initial value as the nominal value minus a discount; it is used for Treasury Bills and similar financial instruments

The annual effective _____ is the annual interest divided by the capital including that interest, which is the interest rate divided by 100% plus the interest rate. It is the annual discount factor to be applied to the future cash flow, to find the discount, subtracted from a future value to find the value one year earlier.

For example, suppose there is a government bond that sells for $95 and pays $100 in a year's time.

a. Black-Scholes
c. Stochastic volatility
b. Discount rate
d. Fisher equation

17. In finance, _____, also known as return on investment is the ratio of money gained or lost on an investment relative to the amount of money invested. The amount of money gained or lost may be referred to as interest, profit/loss, gain/loss, or net income/loss. The money invested may be referred to as the asset, capital, principal, or the cost basis of the investment.
a. Stock or scrip dividends
c. Doctrine of the Proper Law
b. Composiition of Creditors
d. Rate of return

18. _____ or financing is to provide capital (funds), which means money for a project, a person, a business or any other private or public institutions.

Those funds can be allocated for either short term or long term purposes. The health fund is a new way of _____ private healthcare centers.

a. Product life cycle
c. Funding
b. Synthetic CDO
d. Proxy fight

Chapter 7. Making Capital Investment Decisions

1. _____ is the field of accountancy concerned with the preparation of financial statements for decision makers, such as stockholders, suppliers, banks, employees, government agencies, owners, and other stakeholders. The fundamental need for _____ is to reduce principal-agent problem by measuring and monitoring agents' performance and reporting the results to interested users.

_____ is used to prepare accounting information for people outside the organization or not involved in the day to day running of the company.

   a. 7-Eleven
   b. 4-4-5 Calendar
   c. 529 plan
   d. Financial accounting

2. _____, refers to consumption opportunity gained by an entity within a specified time frame, which is generally expressed in monetary terms. However, for households and individuals, '_____ is the sum of all the wages, salaries, profits, interests payments, rents and other forms of earnings received... in a given period of time.' For firms, _____ generally refers to net-profit: what remains of revenue after expenses have been subtracted.
   a. OIBDA
   b. Annual report
   c. Accrual
   d. Income

3. In economics and business decision-making, _____ are costs that cannot be recovered once they have been incurred. _____ are sometimes contrasted with variable costs, which are the costs that will change due to the proposed course of action, and prospective costs which are costs that will be incurred if an action is taken. In microeconomic theory, only variable costs are relevant to a decision.
   a. Hindsight bias
   b. Hyperbolic discounting
   c. 4-4-5 Calendar
   d. Sunk costs

4. The phrase _____ refers to the aspect of corporate strategy, corporate finance and management dealing with the buying, selling and combining of different companies that can aid, finance, or help a growing company in a given industry grow rapidly without having to create another business entity.

An acquisition, also known as a takeover, is the buying of one company (the 'target') by another. An acquisition may be friendly or hostile.

   a. 7-Eleven
   b. 529 plan
   c. Mergers and acquisitions
   d. 4-4-5 Calendar

5. _____ is the balance of the amounts of cash being received and paid by a business during a defined period of time, sometimes tied to a specific project. Measurement of _____ can be used

   - to evaluate the state or performance of a business or project.
   - to determine problems with liquidity. Being profitable does not necessarily mean being liquid. A company can fail because of a shortage of cash, even while profitable.
   - to generate project rate of returns. The time of _____s into and out of projects are used as inputs to financial models such as internal rate of return, and net present value.
   - to examine income or growth of a business when it is believed that accrual accounting concepts do not represent economic realities. Alternately, _____ can be used to 'validate' the net income generated by accrual accounting.

Chapter 7. Making Capital Investment Decisions 51

_____ as a generic term may be used differently depending on context, and certain _____ definitions may be adapted by analysts and users for their own uses. Common terms include operating _____ and free _____.

_____s can be classified into:

1. Operational _____s: Cash received or expended as a result of the company's core business activities.
2. Investment _____s: Cash received or expended through capital expenditure, investments or acquisitions.
3. Financing _____s: Cash received or expended as a result of financial activities, such as interests and dividends.

All three together - the net _____ - are necessary to reconcile the beginning cash balance to the ending cash balance. Loan draw downs or equity injections, that is just shifting of capital but no expenditure as such, are not considered in the net _____.

a. Shareholder value
c. Real option
b. Cash flow
d. Corporate finance

6. In economics, business, and accounting, a _____ is the value of money that has been used up to produce something, and hence is not available for use anymore. In business, the _____ may be one of acquisition, in which case the amount of money expended to acquire it is counted as _____. In this case, money is the input that is gone in order to acquire the thing.
   a. Fixed costs
   c. Marginal cost
   b. Sliding scale fees
   d. Cost

7. _____ or economic opportunity loss is the value of the next best alternative foregone as the result of making a decision. _____ analysis is an important part of a company's decision-making processes but is not treated as an actual cost in any financial statement. The next best thing that a person can engage in is referred to as the _____ of doing the best thing and ignoring the next best thing to be done.
   a. ABN Amro
   c. A Random Walk Down Wall Street
   b. Opportunity cost
   d. AAB

8. _____ is a financial metric which represents operating liquidity available to a business. Along with fixed assets such as plant and equipment, _____ is considered a part of operating capital. It is calculated as current assets minus current liabilities.
   a. 529 plan
   c. 4-4-5 Calendar
   b. Working capital management
   d. Working capital

9. The _____ is the current method of accelerated asset depreciation required by the United States income tax code. Under _____, all assets are divided into classes which dictate the number of years over which an asset's cost will be recovered.

Chapter 7. Making Capital Investment Decisions

Prior to the Accelerated Cost Recovery System (ACRS), most capital purchases were depreciated using a straight line technique, that allowed for the depreciation of the asset over its useful life.

a. Modified Accelerated Cost Recovery System
b. 7-Eleven
c. 4-4-5 Calendar
d. 529 plan

10. Straight-line depreciation is the simplest and most-often-used technique, in which the company estimates the _____ of the asset at the end of the period during which it will be used to generate revenues (useful life) and will expense a portion of original cost in equal increments over that period. The _____ is an estimate of the value of the asset at the time it will be sold or disposed of; it may be zero or even negative. _____ is scrap value, by another name.

a. Net profit
b. Depreciation
c. Fixed investment
d. Salvage value

11. The role of the _____ is to issue accounting standards in the United Kingdom. It is recognised for that purpose under the Companies Act 1985. It took over the task of setting accounting standards from the Accounting Standards Committee (ASC) in 1990.

a. ABN Amro
b. Accounting Standards Board
c. AAB
d. A Random Walk Down Wall Street

12. The _____ is a private, not-for-profit organization whose primary purpose is to develop generally accepted accounting principles (GAAP) within the United States in the public's interest. The Securities and Exchange Commission (SEC) designated the _____ as the organization responsible for setting accounting standards for public companies in the U.S. It was created in 1973, replacing the Accounting Principles Board and the Committee on Accounting Procedure of the American Institute of Certified Public Accountants. The _____'s mission is 'to establish and improve standards of financial accounting and reporting for the guidance and education of the public, including issuers, auditors, and users of financial information.'

The _____ is not a governmental body.

a. Federal Deposit Insurance Corporation
b. Financial Accounting Standards Board
c. KPMG
d. World Congress of Accountants

13. _____ or net present worth (NPW) is defined as the total present value (PV) of a time series of cash flows. It is a standard method for using the time value of money to appraise long-term projects. Used for capital budgeting, and widely throughout economics, it measures the excess or shortfall of cash flows, in present value terms, once financing charges are met.

a. Tax shield
b. Present value of costs
c. Negative gearing
d. Net present value

14. A mutual shareholder or _____ is an individual or company (including a corporation) that legally owns one or more shares of stock in a joint stock company. A company's shareholders collectively own that company. Thus, the typical goal of such companies is to enhance shareholder value.

a. Stockholder
b. Limit order
c. Stock market bubble
d. Trading curb

Chapter 7. Making Capital Investment Decisions

15. _____ is a process by which a firm can obtain the use of a certain fixed assets for which it must pay a series of contractual, periodic, tax deductable payments. The lessee is the receiver of the services or the assets under the lease contract and the lessor is the owner of the assets. The relationship between the tenant and the landlord is called a tenancy, and can be for a fixed or an indefinite period of time (called the term of the lease).

   a. Foreign Corrupt Practices Act
   b. Quiet period
   c. Royalties
   d. Leasing

16. _____ is the value on a given date of a future payment or series of future payments, discounted to reflect the time value of money and other factors such as investment risk. _____ calculations are widely used in business and economics to provide a means to compare cash flows at different times on a meaningful 'like to like' basis.

The most commonly applied model of the time value of money is compound interest.

   a. Net present value
   b. Present value
   c. Negative gearing
   d. Present value of benefits

17. _____ is a term used in accounting, economics and finance to spread the cost of an asset over the span of several years.

In simple words we can say that _____ is the reduction in the value of an asset due to usage, passage of time, wear and tear, technological outdating or obsolescence, depletion or other such factors.

In accounting, _____ is a term used to describe any method of attributing the historical or purchase cost of an asset across its useful life, roughly corresponding to normal wear and tear.

   a. Deferred financing costs
   b. Depreciation
   c. Bottom line
   d. Matching principle

18. _____ is the planning process used to determine whether a firm's long term investments such as new machinery, replacement machinery, new plants, new products, and research development projects are worth pursuing. It is budget for major capital, or investment, expenditures.

Many formal methods are used in _____, including the techniques such as

- Net present value
- Profitability index
- Internal rate of return
- Modified Internal Rate of Return
- Equivalent annuity

These methods use the incremental cash flows from each potential investment, or project. Techniques based on accounting earnings and accounting rules are sometimes used - though economists consider this to be improper - such as the accounting rate of return, and 'return on investment.' Simplified and hybrid methods are used as well, such as payback period and discounted payback period.

a. Shareholder value
b. Capital budgeting
c. Financial distress
d. Preferred stock

19. _____ is a fee paid on borrowed assets. It is the price paid for the use of borrowed money, or, money earned by deposited funds. Assets that are sometimes lent with _____ include money, shares, consumer goods through hire purchase, major assets such as aircraft, and even entire factories in finance lease arrangements.

a. A Random Walk Down Wall Street
b. Insolvency
c. AAB
d. Interest

20. An _____ is the price a borrower pays for the use of money they do not own, and the return a lender receives for deferring the use of funds, by lending it to the borrower. _____s are normally expressed as a percentage rate over the period of one year.

_____s targets are also a vital tool of monetary policy and are used to control variables like investment, inflation, and unemployment.

a. AAB
b. A Random Walk Down Wall Street
c. ABN Amro
d. Interest rate

21. In finance and economics _____ refers to the rate of interest before adjustment for inflation (in contrast with the real interest rate); or, for interest balls stated' without adjustment for the full effect of compounding (also referred to as the nominal annual rate.) An interest rate is called nominal if the frequency of compounding (e.g. a month) is not identical to the basic time unit (normally a year.)

The real interest rate includes compensation for the lender's lost value due to inflation, whereas the _____ excludes inflation.

a. Nominal interest rate
b. Cash accumulation equation
c. Shanghai Interbank Offered Rate
d. SIBOR

22. The '_____' is approximately the nominal interest rate minus the inflation rate Since the inflation rate over the course of a loan is not known initially, volatility in inflation represents a risk to both the lender and the borrower.

In economics and finance, an individual who lends money for repayment at a later point in time expects to be compensated for the time value of money, or not having the use of that money while it is lent.

a. 4-4-5 Calendar
b. 529 plan
c. 7-Eleven
d. Real interest rate

23. The terms _____, nominal _____, and effective _____ describe the interest rate for a whole year (annualized), rather than just a monthly fee/rate, as applied on a loan, mortgage, credit card, etc. Those terms have formal, legal definitions in some countries or legal jurisdictions, but in general:

- The nominal _____ is the simple-interest rate (for a year.)
- The effective _____ is the fee+compound interest rate (calculated across a year.)

The nominal _____ is calculated as: the rate, for a payment period, multiplied by the number of payment periods in a year. However, the exact legal definition of 'effective _____' can vary greatly in each jurisdiction, depending on the type of fees included, such as participation fees, loan origination fees, monthly service charges, or late fees. The effective _____ has been called the 'mathematically-true' interest rate for each year. The computation for the effective _____, as the fee+compound interest rate, can also vary depending on whether the up-front fees, such as origination or participation fees, are added to the entire amount, or treated as a short-term loan due in the first payment.

a. Annual percentage rate
b. A Random Walk Down Wall Street
c. ABN Amro
d. AAB

24. _____ relates to the cost of borrowing money. It is the price that a lender charges a borrower for the use of the lender's money. _____ is different from OPEX and CAPEX, for it relates to the capital structure of a company.
a. Interest expense
b. AAB
c. A Random Walk Down Wall Street
d. ABN Amro

25. A '_____' is a 'Charge' that is paid to obtain the right to delay a payment. Essentially, the payer purchases the right to make a given payment in the future instead of in the Present. The '_____', or 'Charge' that must be paid to delay the payment, is simply the difference between what the payment amount would be if it were paid in the present and what the payment amount would be paid if it were paid in the future.
a. Risk aversion
b. Discount
c. Risk modeling
d. Value at risk

26. _____ is a term in Corporate Finance used to indicate a condition when promises to creditors of a company are broken or honored with difficulty. Sometimes _____ can lead to bankruptcy. _____ is usually associated with some costs to the company and these are known as Costs of _____.
a. Commercial paper
b. Financial distress
c. Capital structure
d. Cashflow matching

27. A _____ is the reduction in income taxes that results from taking an allowable deduction from taxable income. For example, because interest on debt is a tax-deductible expense, taking on debt creates a _____. Since a _____ is a way to save cash flows, it increases the value of the business, and it is an important aspect of business valuation.
a. Tax shield
b. Present value of costs
c. Present value of benefits
d. Refinancing risk

28. In business and finance, a _____ (also referred to as equity _____) of stock means a _____ of ownership in a corporation (company.) In the plural, stocks is often used as a synonym for _____s especially in the United States, but it is less commonly used that way outside of North America.

In the United Kingdom, South Africa, and Australia, stock can also refer to completely different financial instruments such as government bonds or, less commonly, to all kinds of marketable securities.

a. Share
b. Margin
c. Procter ' Gamble
d. Bucket shop

Chapter 7. Making Capital Investment Decisions

29. In finance the _____ is the cost per year of owning and operating an asset over its entire lifespan.

_____ is often used as a decision making tool in capital budgeting when comparing investment projects of unequal lifespans. For example if project A has an expected lifetime of 7 years, and project B has an expected lifetime of 11 years it would be improper to simply compare the net present values (NPVs) of the two projects, unless neither project could be repeated.

   a. Indirect costs   b. AAB
   c. Equivalent annual cost   d. A Random Walk Down Wall Street

30. In economics, a _____ is a mechanism that allows people to easily buy and sell (trade) financial securities (such as stocks and bonds), commodities (such as precious metals or agricultural goods), and other fungible items of value at low transaction costs and at prices that reflect the efficient-market hypothesis.

_____s have evolved significantly over several hundred years and are undergoing constant innovation to improve liquidity.

Both general markets (where many commodities are traded) and specialized markets (where only one commodity is traded) exist.

   a. Delta hedging   b. Secondary market
   c. Financial market   d. Cost of carry

Chapter 8. Risk Analysis, Real Options, and Capital Budgeting

1. _____ is basically the process of generating a book of investor demand for the shares during an IPO for efficient price discovery. Usually, the issuer appoints a major investment bank to act as a book runner.

   _____ is a common practice in developed countries and has recently been making inroads into emerging markets as well, including India.

   a. Gross profit
   b. Preferred stock
   c. Book building
   d. Gross profit margin

2. _____ are a class of computational algorithms that rely on repeated random sampling to compute their results. _____ are often used when simulating physical and mathematical systems. Because of their reliance on repeated computation and random or pseudo-random numbers, _____ are most suited to calculation by a computer.

   _____ in finance are often used to calculate the value of companies, to evaluate investments in projects at corporate level or to evaluate financial derivatives. The method is intended for financial analysts who want to construct stochastic or probabilistic financial models as opposed to the traditional static and deterministic models.

   a. Correlation
   b. Sample size
   c. Monte Carlo methods
   d. Semivariance

3. _____ is the study of how the variation (uncertainty) in the output of a mathematical model can be apportioned, qualitatively or quantitatively, to different sources of variation in the input of a model.

   In more general terms uncertainty and sensitivity analyses investigate the robustness of a study when the study includes some form of mathematical modelling. While uncertainty analysis studies the overall uncertainty in the conclusions of the study, _____ tries to identify what source of uncertainty weights more on the study's conclusions.

   a. Proxy fight
   b. Sensitivity analysis
   c. Golden parachute
   d. Synthetic CDO

4. In business, _____ is income that a company receives from its normal business activities, usually from the sale of goods and services to customers. Some companies also receive _____ from interest, dividends or royalties paid to them by other companies. _____ may refer to business income in general, or it may refer to the amount, in a monetary unit, received during a period of time, as in 'Last year, Company X had _____ of $32 million.'

   In many countries, including the UK, _____ is referred to as turnover.

   a. Bottom line
   b. Revenue
   c. Furniture, Fixtures and Equipment
   d. Matching principle

5. _____ are business expenses that are not dependent on the level of production or sales. They tend to be time-related, such as salaries or rents being paid per month. This is in contrast to Variable costs, which are volume-related (and are paid per quantity.)

   a. Sliding scale fees
   b. Transaction cost
   c. Marginal cost
   d. Fixed costs

6. _____ are expenses that change in proportion to the activity of a business. In other words, _____ are the sum of marginal costs. It can also be considered normal costs. Along with fixed costs, _____ make up the two components of total cost. Direct Costs, however, are costs that can be associated with a particular cost object.

    a. Fixed costs   b. Transaction cost
    c. Cost accounting   d. Variable costs

7. In economics, business, and accounting, a _____ is the value of money that has been used up to produce something, and hence is not available for use anymore. In business, the _____ may be one of acquisition, in which case the amount of money expended to acquire it is counted as _____. In this case, money is the input that is gone in order to acquire the thing.

    a. Sliding scale fees   b. Fixed costs
    c. Marginal cost   d. Cost

8. In economics and business, specifically cost accounting, the _____ is the point at which cost or expenses and revenue are equal: there is no net loss or gain, and one has 'broken even'. A profit or a loss has not been made, although opportunity costs have been paid, and capital has received the risk-adjusted, expected return.

For example, if the business sells less than 200 tables each month, it will make a loss, if it sells more, it will be a profit.

    a. Fixed asset turnover   b. Defined contribution plan
    c. Market microstructure   d. Break-even point

9. _____ is a process of analyzing possible future events by considering alternative possible outcomes (scenarios.) The analysis is designed to allow improved decision-making by allowing consideration of outcomes and their implications.

For example, in economics and finance, a financial institution might attempt to forecast several possible scenarios for the economy (e.g. rapid growth, moderate growth, slow growth) and it might also attempt to forecast financial market returns (for bonds, stocks and cash) in each of those scenarios.

    a. Scenario analysis   b. 4-4-5 Calendar
    c. 529 plan   d. Detection Risk

10. In cost-volume-profit analysis, a form of management accounting, _____ is the marginal profit per unit sale. It is a useful quantity in carrying out various calculations, and can be used as a measure of operating leverage.

The Total _____ is Total Revenue (TR, or Sales) minus Total Variable Cost (TVC):

    TContribution margin = TR >− TVC

The Unit _____ (C) is Unit Revenue (Price, P) minus Unit Variable Cost (V):

    C = P >− V

Chapter 8. Risk Analysis, Real Options, and Capital Budgeting

The _____ Ratio is the percentage of Contribution over Total Revenue, which can be calculated from the unit contribution over unit price or total contribution over Total Revenue:

For instance, if the price is $10 and the unit variable cost is $2, then the unit _____ is $8, and the _____ ratio is $8/$10 = 80%.

a. 7-Eleven
b. 529 plan
c. 4-4-5 Calendar
d. Contribution margin

11. In finance, a _____ is collateral that the holder of a position in securities, options, or futures contracts has to deposit to cover the credit risk of his counterparty (most often his broker.) This risk can arise if the holder has done any of the following:

- borrowed cash from the counterparty to buy securities or options,
- sold securities or options short, or
- entered into a futures contract.

The collateral can be in the form of cash or securities, and it is deposited in a _____ account. On U.S. futures exchanges, '_____' was formally called performance bond.

_____ buying is buying securities with cash borrowed from a broker, using other securities as collateral.

a. Procter ' Gamble
b. Credit
c. Share
d. Margin

12. _____ is the planning process used to determine whether a firm's long term investments such as new machinery, replacement machinery, new plants, new products, and research development projects are worth pursuing. It is budget for major capital, or investment, expenditures.

Many formal methods are used in _____, including the techniques such as

- Net present value
- Profitability index
- Internal rate of return
- Modified Internal Rate of Return
- Equivalent annuity

These methods use the incremental cash flows from each potential investment, or project. Techniques based on accounting earnings and accounting rules are sometimes used - though economists consider this to be improper - such as the accounting rate of return, and 'return on investment.' Simplified and hybrid methods are used as well, such as payback period and discounted payback period.

a. Preferred stock
b. Shareholder value
c. Capital budgeting
d. Financial distress

13. _____ is the value on a given date of a future payment or series of future payments, discounted to reflect the time value of money and other factors such as investment risk. _____ calculations are widely used in business and economics to provide a means to compare cash flows at different times on a meaningful 'like to like' basis.

The most commonly applied model of the time value of money is compound interest.

a. Present value of benefits
b. Net present value
c. Negative gearing
d. Present value

14. In corporate finance, _____ analysis applies put option and call option valuation techniques to capital budgeting decisions. A _____ itself, is the right--but not the obligation--to undertake some business decision; typically the option to make, or abandon, a capital investment. For example, the opportunity to invest in the expansion of a firm's factory, or alternatively to sell the factory, is a _____.

a. Book building
b. Real option
c. Capital budgeting
d. Cash flow

15. An _____ is a contract written by a seller that conveys to the buyer the right -- but not the obligation -- to buy (in the case of a call _____) or to sell (in the case of a put _____) a particular asset, such as a piece of property such as, among others, a futures contract. In return for granting the _____, the seller collects a payment (the premium) from the buyer.

For example, buying a call _____ provides the right to buy a specified quantity of a security at a set strike price at some time on or before expiration, while buying a put _____ provides the right to sell.

a. Amortization
b. AT'T Mobility LLC
c. Annuity
d. Option

16. A _____ is a decision support tool that uses a tree-like graph or model of decisions and their possible consequences, including chance event outcomes, resource costs, and utility. _____s are commonly used in operations research, specifically in decision analysis, to help identify a strategy most likely to reach a goal. Another use of _____s is as a descriptive means for calculating conditional probabilities.

a. 529 plan
b. Decision tree
c. 7-Eleven
d. 4-4-5 Calendar

Chapter 9. Risk and Return: Lessons from Market History

1. A _____ is a profit that results from investments into a capital asset, such as stocks, bonds or real estate, which exceeds the purchase price. It is the difference between a higher selling price and a lower purchase price, resulting in a financial gain for the seller. Conversely, a capital loss arises if the proceeds from the sale of a capital asset are less than the purchase price.
   - a. Tax brackets
   - b. Capital gains tax
   - c. Payroll tax
   - d. Capital gain

2. _____ is the difference between a lower selling price and a higher purchase price, resulting in a financial loss for the seller. Pursuant to IRS TAX TIP 2009-35 'If your _____ exceeds your capital gain, the excess can be deducted on your tax return, up to an annual limit of $3,000 ($1,500 if you are married filing separately.)'.
   - a. 7-Eleven
   - b. Capital loss
   - c. 4-4-5 Calendar
   - d. 529 plan

3. A _____ is a payment made by a corporation to its shareholder members. When a corporation earns a profit or surplus, that money can be put to two uses: it can either be re-invested in the business (called retained earnings), or it can be paid to the shareholders as a _____. Many corporations retain a portion of their earnings and pay the remainder as a _____.
   - a. Dividend yield
   - b. Dividend puzzle
   - c. Special dividend
   - d. Dividend

4. _____, refers to consumption opportunity gained by an entity within a specified time frame, which is generally expressed in monetary terms. However, for households and individuals, '_____ is the sum of all the wages, salaries, profits, interests payments, rents and other forms of earnings received... in a given period of time.' For firms, _____ generally refers to net-profit: what remains of revenue after expenses have been subtracted.
   - a. Accrual
   - b. OIBDA
   - c. Annual report
   - d. Income

5. The _____ on a portfolio of investments takes into account not only the capital appreciation on the portfolio, but also the income received on the portfolio. The income typically consists of interest, dividends, and securities lending fees. This contrasts with the price return, which takes into account only the capital gain on an investment.
   - a. Global tactical asset allocation
   - b. Profitability index
   - c. Capitalization rate
   - d. Total return

6. In finance, _____ is a measurement of return on an asset or portfolio. It is one of the simplest measures of investment performance.

   _____ is the percentage by which the value of a portfolio (or asset) has grown for a particular period.
   - a. Market integration
   - b. Creditor
   - c. Holding period return
   - d. Stock market index option

7. In economic models, the _____ time frame assumes no fixed factors of production. Firms can enter or leave the marketplace, and the cost (and availability) of land, labor, raw materials, and capital goods can be assumed to vary. In contrast, in the short-run time frame, certain factors are assumed to be fixed, because there is not sufficient time for them to change.

a. 4-4-5 Calendar
b. 529 plan
c. Short-run
d. Long-run

8. _____ mature in one year or less. Like zero-coupon bonds, they do not pay interest prior to maturity; instead they are sold at a discount of the par value to create a positive yield to maturity. Many regard _____ as the least risky investment available to U.S. investors.
   a. Treasury Inflation Protected Securities
   b. Treasury bills
   c. Treasury securities
   d. 4-4-5 Calendar

9. In finance, a _____ is a debt security, in which the authorized issuer owes the holders a debt and, depending on the terms of the _____, is obliged to pay interest (the coupon) and/or to repay the principal at a later date, termed maturity.

Thus a _____ is a loan: the issuer is the borrower, the _____ holder is the lender, and the coupon is the interest. _____s provide the borrower with external funds to finance long-term investments, or, in the case of government _____s, to finance current expenditure.

   a. Catastrophe bonds
   b. Puttable bond
   c. Bond
   d. Convertible bond

10. _____ is a form of corporation equity ownership represented in the securities. It is dangerous in comparison to preferred shares and some other investment options, in that in the event of bankruptcy, _____ investors receive their funds after preferred stockholders, bondholders, creditors, etc. On the other hand, common shares on average perform better than preferred shares or bonds over time.
    a. Common stock
    b. Stop-limit order
    c. Stock market bubble
    d. Stock split

11. A _____ is a bond issued by a corporation. The term is usually applied to longer-term debt instruments, generally with a maturity date falling at least a year after their issue date. (The term 'commercial paper' is sometimes used for instruments with a shorter maturity.)
    a. Brady bonds
    b. Government bond
    c. Serial bond
    d. Corporate bond

12. A _____ is a bond issued by a national government denominated in the country's own currency. Bonds issued by national governments in foreign currencies are normally referred to as sovereign bonds. The first ever _____ was issued by the British government in 1693 to raise money to fund a war against France.
    a. Zero-coupon bond
    b. Collateralized debt obligations
    c. Municipal bond
    d. Government bond

13. In business and finance, a _____ (also referred to as equity _____) of stock means a _____ of ownership in a corporation (company.) In the plural, stocks is often used as a synonym for _____s especially in the United States, but it is less commonly used that way outside of North America.

In the United Kingdom, South Africa, and Australia, stock can also refer to completely different financial instruments such as government bonds or, less commonly, to all kinds of marketable securities.

Chapter 9. Risk and Return: Lessons from Market History 63

a. Margin
c. Bucket shop
b. Procter ' Gamble
d. Share

14. In statistics, a _____ is a tabulation of the values that one or more variables take in a sample.

Univariate _____s are often presented as lists ordered by quantity showing the number of times each value appears. For example, if 100 people rate a five-point Likert scale assessing their agreement with a statement on a scale on which 1 denotes strong agreement and 5 strong disagreement, the _____ of their responses might look like:

This simple tabulation has two drawbacks.

a. Covariance
c. Variance
b. Random variables
d. Frequency distribution

15. _____ is a mathematical science pertaining to the collection, analysis, interpretation or explanation, and presentation of data. It also provides tools for prediction and forecasting based on data. It is applicable to a wide variety of academic disciplines, from the natural and social sciences to the humanities, government and business.

a. Mean
c. Sample size
b. Statistics
d. Covariance

16. _____ is the planning process used to determine whether a firm's long term investments such as new machinery, replacement machinery, new plants, new products, and research development projects are worth pursuing. It is budget for major capital, or investment, expenditures.

Many formal methods are used in _____, including the techniques such as

- Net present value
- Profitability index
- Internal rate of return
- Modified Internal Rate of Return
- Equivalent annuity

These methods use the incremental cash flows from each potential investment, or project. Techniques based on accounting earnings and accounting rules are sometimes used - though economists consider this to be improper - such as the accounting rate of return, and 'return on investment.' Simplified and hybrid methods are used as well, such as payback period and discounted payback period.

a. Financial distress
c. Shareholder value
b. Preferred stock
d. Capital budgeting

17. A _____ is a measure of the average price of consumer goods and services purchased by households. The _____ can be used to index (i.e., adjust for the effects of inflation) wages, salaries, pensions, or regulated or contracted prices. The _____ is, along with the population census and the National Income and Product Accounts, one of the most closely watched national economic statistics.

a. 529 plan
c. Consumer Price Index
b. Divisia index
d. 4-4-5 Calendar

18. A _____ is a normalized average (typically a weighted average) of prices for a given class of goods or services in a given region, during a given interval of time. It is a statistic designed to help to compare how these prices, taken as a whole, differ between time periods or geographical locations.
a. Price Index
c. Price discrimination
b. Discounts and allowances
d. Transfer pricing

19. _____ is a risk-adjusted measure of the so-called active return on an investment. It is the return in excess of the compensation for the risk borne, and thus commonly used to assess active managers' performances. Often, the return of a benchmark is subtracted in order to consider relative performance, which yields Jensen's _____.
a. Amortization
c. Option
b. Annuity
d. Alpha

20.

In finance, the _____ can be the expected rate of return above the risk-free interest rate. When measuring risk, a common sense approach is to compare the risk-free return on T-bills and the very risky return on other investments. The difference between these two returns can be interpreted as a measure of the excess return on the average risky asset. This excess return is known as the _____.

a. Risk aversion
c. Risk adjusted return on capital
b. Risk modeling
d. Risk premium

21. In business and accounting, _____s are everything of value that is owned by a person or company. The balance sheet of a firm records the monetary value of the _____s owned by the firm. The two major _____ classes are tangible _____s and intangible _____s.
a. EBITDA
c. Asset
b. Accounts payable
d. Income

22. The phrase _____ refers to the aspect of corporate strategy, corporate finance and management dealing with the buying, selling and combining of different companies that can aid, finance, or help a growing company in a given industry grow rapidly without having to create another business entity.

An acquisition, also known as a takeover, is the buying of one company (the 'target') by another. An acquisition may be friendly or hostile.

a. 4-4-5 Calendar
c. 529 plan
b. Mergers and acquisitions
d. 7-Eleven

23. Under a secondary market offering or seasoned equity offering of shares to raise money, a company can opt for a _____ to raise capital. The _____ is a special form of shelf offering or shelf registration. With the issued rights, existing shareholders have the privilege to buy a specified number of new shares from the firm at a specified price within a specified time.

Chapter 9. Risk and Return: Lessons from Market History

a. Rights issue
c. Corporate finance
b. Market for corporate control
d. Tender offer

24. In probability and statistics, the _____ of a collection of numbers is a measure of the dispersion of the numbers from their expected (mean) value. It can apply to a probability distribution, a random variable, a population or a data set. The _____ is usually denoted with the letter σ (lowercase sigma.)
   a. Mean
   c. Kurtosis
   b. Standard deviation
   d. Sample size

25. In probability theory and statistics, the _____ of a random variable, probability distribution averaging the squared distance of its possible values from the expected value (mean.) Whereas the mean is a way to describe the location of a distribution, the _____ is a way to capture its scale or degree of being spread out. The unit of _____ is the square of the unit of the original variable.
   a. Semivariance
   c. Harmonic mean
   b. Monte Carlo methods
   d. Variance

26. The _____ is an important family of continuous probability distributions, applicable in many fields. Each member of the family may be defined by two parameters, location and scale: the mean and variance respectively. The standard _____ is the _____ with a mean of zero and a variance of one
   a. Random variables
   c. Normal distribution
   b. Correlation
   d. Probability distribution

27. _____, in bookkeeping, refers to assets, liabilities, income, and expenses recorded on individual pages of the so called book of final entry or ledger. Changes in _____ value are made by chronologically posting debit (DR) and credit (CR) entries to its page. Examples of _____s are cash, _____s receivable, mortgages, loans, land and buildings, common stock, sales, services provided, wages, and payroll overhead.
   a. Option
   c. Account
   b. Alpha
   d. Accretion

Chapter 10. Return and Risk: The Capital Asset Pricing Model (CAPM)

1. In probability theory and statistics, _____ indicates the strength and direction of a linear relationship between two random variables. That is in contrast with the usage of the term in colloquial speech, which denotes any relationship, not necessarily linear. In general statistical usage, _____ or co-relation refers to the departure of two random variables from independence.
   - a. Correlation
   - b. Variance
   - c. Probability distribution
   - d. Geometric mean

2. In probability theory and statistics, _____ is a measure of how much two variables change together (variance is a special case of the _____ when the two variables are identical.)

   If two variables tend to vary together (that is, when one of them is above its expected value, then the other variable tends to be above its expected value too), then the _____ between the two variables will be positive. On the other hand, when one of them is above its expected value the other variable tends to be below its expected value, then the _____ between the two variables will be negative.
   - a. Frequency distribution
   - b. Covariance
   - c. Probability distribution
   - d. Stratified sampling

3. The _____ is the weighted-average most likely outcome in gambling, probability theory, economics or finance.

   In gambling and probability theory, there is usually a discrete set of possible outcomes. In this case, _____ is a measure of the relative balance of win or loss weighted by their chances of occurring.
   - a. Expected return
   - b. ABN Amro
   - c. A Random Walk Down Wall Street
   - d. AAB

4. In probability and statistics, the _____ of a collection of numbers is a measure of the dispersion of the numbers from their expected (mean) value. It can apply to a probability distribution, a random variable, a population or a data set. The _____ is usually denoted with the letter σ (lowercase sigma.)
   - a. Kurtosis
   - b. Sample size
   - c. Standard deviation
   - d. Mean

5. In probability theory and statistics, the _____ of a random variable, probability distribution averaging the squared distance of its possible values from the expected value (mean.) Whereas the mean is a way to describe the location of a distribution, the _____ is a way to capture its scale or degree of being spread out. The unit of _____ is the square of the unit of the original variable.
   - a. Monte Carlo methods
   - b. Harmonic mean
   - c. Semivariance
   - d. Variance

6. In business and accounting, _____s are everything of value that is owned by a person or company. The balance sheet of a firm records the monetary value of the _____s owned by the firm. The two major _____ classes are tangible _____s and intangible _____s.
   - a. Accounts payable
   - b. Asset
   - c. Income
   - d. EBITDA

Chapter 10. Return and Risk: The Capital Asset Pricing Model (CAPM)

7. In finance, _____ is the process of estimating the potential market value of a financial asset or liability. they can be done on assets (for example, investments in marketable securities such as stocks, options, business enterprises, or intangible assets such as patents and trademarks) or on liabilities (e.g., Bonds issued by a company.) _____s are required in many contexts including investment analysis, capital budgeting, merger and acquisition transactions, financial reporting, taxable events to determine the proper tax liability, and in litigation.

   a. Procter ' Gamble
   b. Share
   c. Margin
   d. Valuation

8. The term _____ has three unrelated technical definitions, and is also used in a variety of non-technical ways.

   - In financial economics, it refers to any asset used to make money, as opposed to assets used for personal enjoyment or consumption. This is an important distinction because two people can disagree sharply about the value of personal assets, one person might think a sports car is more valuable than a pickup truck, another person might have the opposite taste. But if an asset is held for the purpose of making money, taste has nothing to do with it, only differences of opinion about how much money the asset will produce. With the further assumption that people agree on the probability distribution of future cash flows, it is possible to have an objective _____ pricing model. Even without the assumption of agreement, it is possible to set rational limits on _____ value.
   - In governmental accounting, it is defined as any asset used in operations with an initial useful life extending beyond one reporting period. Generally, government managers have a 'stewardship' duty to maintain _____s under their control. See International Public Sector Accounting Standards for details.
   - In US tax accounting, it is defined as any property other than a list of exceptions. The main exceptions are anything held for sale, and any real estate or depreciable property used in business. Almost everything you own and use for personal purposes, pleasure or investment is a _____. If something is a _____ for tax purposes, gains or losses on sale or disposition are capital gains or capital losses. For individuals, however, capital losses on property held for personal use are generally not deductible. See the IRS publication Tax Facts about Capital Gains and Losses for details.

   A well-known financial accounting textbook advises that the term be avoided except in tax accounting because it is used in so many different senses, not all of them well-defined. For example it is often used as a synonym for fixed assets or for investments in securities.

   A common non-technical usage occurs when people ask that employees or the environment or something else be treated as a _____.

   a. Solvency
   b. Settlement date
   c. Political risk
   d. Capital asset

9. In finance, the _____ is used to determine a theoretically appropriate required rate of return of an asset, if that asset is to be added to an already well-diversified portfolio, given that asset's non-diversifiable risk. The model takes into account the asset's sensitivity to non-diversifiable risk (also known as systemic risk or market risk), often represented by the quantity beta (β) in the financial industry, as well as the expected return of the market and the expected return of a theoretical risk-free asset.

The model was introduced by Jack Treynor (1961, 1962), William Sharpe (1964), John Lintner (1965a,b) and Jan Mossin (1966) independently, building on the earlier work of Harry Markowitz on diversification and modern portfolio theory.

a. Hull-White model
c. Cox-Ingersoll-Ross model
b. Random walk hypothesis
d. Capital asset pricing model

10. A _____ is a fungible, negotiable instrument representing financial value. They are broadly categorized into debt securities (such as banknotes, bonds and debentures), and equity securities; e.g., common stocks. The company or other entity issuing the _____ is called the issuer.

a. Securities lending
c. Book entry
b. Security
d. Tracking stock

11. _____ is the risk that the value of an investment will decrease due to moves in market factors. The five standard _____ factors are:

- Equity risk, the risk that stock prices will change.
- Interest rate risk, the risk that interest rates will change.
- Currency risk, the risk that foreign exchange rates will change.
- Commodity risk, the risk that commodity prices (e.g. grains, metals) will change.

As with other forms of risk, _____ may be measured in a number of ways. Traditionally, this is done using a Value at Risk methodology. Value at risk is well established as a risk management technique, but it contains a number of limiting assumptions that constrain its accuracy.

a. Market risk
c. Currency risk
b. Tracking error
d. Transaction risk

12. In finance, _____ is that risk which is common to an entire market and not to any individual entity or component thereof. It should be distinguished from systemic risk which is the risk that the entire financial system will collapse as a result of some catastrophic event.

Risks can be reduced in four main ways: Avoidance, Reduction, Retention and Transfer.

a. Conglomerate merger
c. Primary market
b. Systematic risk
d. Capital surplus

13. A _____ is a portfolio consisting of a weighted sum of every asset in the market, with weights in the proportions that they exist in the market (with the necessary assumption that these assets are infinitely divisible.)

Neha Tyagi's critique (1977) states that this is only a theoretical concept, as to create a _____ for investment purposes in practice would necessarily include every single possible available asset, including real estate, precious metals, stamp collections, jewelry, and anything with any worth, as the theoretical market being referred to would be the world market. As a result, proxies for the market are used in practice by investors.

a. Delta neutral
c. Market price
b. Central Securities Depository
d. Market portfolio

Chapter 10. Return and Risk: The Capital Asset Pricing Model (CAPM)

14. In economics and finance, _____ is the practice of taking advantage of a price differential between two or more markets: striking a combination of matching deals that capitalize upon the imbalance, the profit being the difference between the market prices. When used by academics, an _____ is a transaction that involves no negative cash flow at any probabilistic or temporal state and a positive cash flow in at least one state; in simple terms, a risk-free profit.
    a. Initial margin
    b. Efficient-market hypothesis
    c. Arbitrage
    d. Issuer

15. _____ , in finance, is a general theory of asset pricing, that has become influential in the pricing of stocks.

    _____ holds that the expected return of a financial asset can be modeled as a linear function of various macro-economic factors or theoretical market indices, where sensitivity to changes in each factor is represented by a factor-specific beta coefficient. The model-derived rate of return will then be used to price the asset correctly - the asset price should equal the expected end of period price discounted at the rate implied by model.

    a. ABN Amro
    b. AAB
    c. A Random Walk Down Wall Street
    d. Arbitrage pricing theory

16. In Modern Portfolio Theory, the _____ is the graphical representation of the Capital Asset Pricing Model. It displays the expected rate of return for an overall market as a function of systematic (non-diversifiable) risk (beta.)

    The Y-Intercept (beta=0) of the _____ is equal to the risk-free interest rate.

    a. Certificate in Investment Performance Measurement
    b. Divestment
    c. Security market line
    d. Rebalancing

17. The _____ is the market for securities, where companies and governments can raise longterm funds. The _____ includes the stock market and the bond market. Financial regulators, such as the U.S. Securities and Exchange Commission, oversee the _____ s in their designated countries to ensure that investors are protected against fraud.
    a. Capital market
    b. Forward market
    c. Delta neutral
    d. Spot rate

18. _____ proposes how rational investors will use diversification to optimize their portfolios, and how a risky asset should be priced. The basic concepts of the theory are Markowitz diversification, the efficient frontier, capital asset pricing model, the alpha and beta coefficients, the Capital Market Line and the Securities Market Line.

    _____ models an asset's return as a random variable, and models a portfolio as a weighted combination of assets so that the return of a portfolio is the weighted combination of the assets' returns.

    a. Payback period
    b. Consumer basket
    c. Modern portfolio theory
    d. Market value

19. _____ , in bookkeeping, refers to assets, liabilities, income, and expenses recorded on individual pages of the so called book of final entry or ledger. Changes in _____ value are made by chronologically posting debit (DR) and credit (CR) entries to its page. Examples of _____ s are cash, _____ s receivable, mortgages, loans, land and buildings, common stock, sales, services provided, wages, and payroll overhead.

a. Option
b. Alpha
c. Accretion
d. Account

1. In business and accounting, _____s are everything of value that is owned by a person or company. The balance sheet of a firm records the monetary value of the _____s owned by the firm. The two major _____ classes are tangible _____s and intangible _____s.

   a. Accounts payable
   b. EBITDA
   c. Income
   d. Asset

2. In finance, _____ is the process of estimating the potential market value of a financial asset or liability. they can be done on assets (for example, investments in marketable securities such as stocks, options, business enterprises, or intangible assets such as patents and trademarks) or on liabilities (e.g., Bonds issued by a company.) _____s are required in many contexts including investment analysis, capital budgeting, merger and acquisition transactions, financial reporting, taxable events to determine the proper tax liability, and in litigation.

   a. Share
   b. Procter ' Gamble
   c. Margin
   d. Valuation

3. The _____ is the weighted-average most likely outcome in gambling, probability theory, economics or finance.

   In gambling and probability theory, there is usually a discrete set of possible outcomes. In this case, _____ is a measure of the relative balance of win or loss weighted by their chances of occurring.

   a. AAB
   b. A Random Walk Down Wall Street
   c. ABN Amro
   d. Expected return

4. In finance, _____ is that risk which is common to an entire market and not to any individual entity or component thereof. It should be distinguished from systemic risk which is the risk that the entire financial system will collapse as a result of some catastrophic event.

   Risks can be reduced in four main ways: Avoidance, Reduction, Retention and Transfer.

   a. Primary market
   b. Capital surplus
   c. Conglomerate merger
   d. Systematic risk

5. _____ is the risk that the value of an investment will decrease due to moves in market factors. The five standard _____ factors are:

   - Equity risk, the risk that stock prices will change.
   - Interest rate risk, the risk that interest rates will change.
   - Currency risk, the risk that foreign exchange rates will change.
   - Commodity risk, the risk that commodity prices (e.g. grains, metals) will change.

   As with other forms of risk, _____ may be measured in a number of ways. Traditionally, this is done using a Value at Risk methodology. Value at risk is well established as a risk management technique, but it contains a number of limiting assumptions that constrain its accuracy.

   a. Currency risk
   b. Tracking error
   c. Market risk
   d. Transaction risk

Chapter 11. An Alternative View of Risk and Return: The Arbitrage Pricing Theory

6. In economics and finance, _____ is the practice of taking advantage of a price differential between two or more markets: striking a combination of matching deals that capitalize upon the imbalance, the profit being the difference between the market prices. When used by academics, an _____ is a transaction that involves no negative cash flow at any probabilistic or temporal state and a positive cash flow in at least one state; in simple terms, a risk-free profit.

   a. Issuer
   b. Efficient-market hypothesis
   c. Initial margin
   d. Arbitrage

7. _____ , in finance, is a general theory of asset pricing, that has become influential in the pricing of stocks.

   _____ holds that the expected return of a financial asset can be modeled as a linear function of various macro-economic factors or theoretical market indices, where sensitivity to changes in each factor is represented by a factor-specific beta coefficient. The model-derived rate of return will then be used to price the asset correctly - the asset price should equal the expected end of period price discounted at the rate implied by model.

   a. A Random Walk Down Wall Street
   b. ABN Amro
   c. Arbitrage pricing theory
   d. AAB

8. A _____ is a portfolio consisting of a weighted sum of every asset in the market, with weights in the proportions that they exist in the market (with the necessary assumption that these assets are infinitely divisible.)

   Neha Tyagi's critique (1977) states that this is only a theoretical concept, as to create a _____ for investment purposes in practice would necessarily include every single possible available asset, including real estate, precious metals, stamp collections, jewelry, and anything with any worth, as the theoretical market being referred to would be the world market. As a result, proxies for the market are used in practice by investors.

   a. Market price
   b. Delta neutral
   c. Central Securities Depository
   d. Market portfolio

Chapter 11. An Alternative View of Risk and Return: The Arbitrage Pricing Theory

9. The term _____ has three unrelated technical definitions, and is also used in a variety of non-technical ways.

   - In financial economics, it refers to any asset used to make money, as opposed to assets used for personal enjoyment or consumption. This is an important distinction because two people can disagree sharply about the value of personal assets, one person might think a sports car is more valuable than a pickup truck, another person might have the opposite taste. But if an asset is held for the purpose of making money, taste has nothing to do with it, only differences of opinion about how much money the asset will produce. With the further assumption that people agree on the probability distribution of future cash flows, it is possible to have an objective _____ pricing model. Even without the assumption of agreement, it is possible to set rational limits on _____ value.
   - In governmental accounting, it is defined as any asset used in operations with an initial useful life extending beyond one reporting period. Generally, government managers have a 'stewardship' duty to maintain _____s under their control. See International Public Sector Accounting Standards for details.
   - In US tax accounting, it is defined as any property other than a list of exceptions. The main exceptions are anything held for sale, and any real estate or depreciable property used in business. Almost everything you own and use for personal purposes, pleasure or investment is a _____. If something is a _____ for tax purposes, gains or losses on sale or disposition are capital gains or capital losses. For individuals, however, capital losses on property held for personal use are generally not deductible. See the IRS publication Tax Facts about Capital Gains and Losses for details.

   A well-known financial accounting textbook advises that the term be avoided except in tax accounting because it is used in so many different senses, not all of them well-defined. For example it is often used as a synonym for fixed assets or for investments in securities.

   A common non-technical usage occurs when people ask that employees or the environment or something else be treated as a _____.

   a. Settlement date
   c. Political risk
   b. Solvency
   d. Capital asset

10. In finance, _____ are stocks that appreciate in value and yield a high return on equity (ROE.) Analysts compute ROE by taking the company's net income and dividing it by the company's equity. To be classified as a growth stock, analysts expect to see at least 15 percent return on equity.
    a. Growth stocks
    c. Stock valuation
    b. 4-4-5 Calendar
    d. Security Analysis

11. A _____ is a professionally managed type of collective investment scheme that pools money from many investors and invests it in stocks, bonds, short-term money market instruments, and/or other securities. The _____ will have a fund manager that trades the pooled money on a regular basis. Currently, the worldwide value of all _____s totals more than $26 trillion.

    Since 1940, there have been three basic types of investment companies in the United States: open-end funds, also known in the US as _____s; unit investment trusts (UITs); and closed-end funds.

    a. Financial intermediary
    c. Net asset value
    b. Trust company
    d. Mutual fund

Chapter 12. Risk, Cost of Capital, and Capital Budgeting

1. In economics, business, and accounting, a _____ is the value of money that has been used up to produce something, and hence is not available for use anymore. In business, the _____ may be one of acquisition, in which case the amount of money expended to acquire it is counted as _____. In this case, money is the input that is gone in order to acquire the thing.
   a. Marginal cost
   b. Sliding scale fees
   c. Cost
   d. Fixed costs

2. The _____ is an expected return that the provider of capital plans to earn on their investment.

   Capital (money) used for funding a business should earn returns for the capital providers who risk their capital. For an investment to be worthwhile, the expected return on capital must be greater than the _____.

   a. Weighted average cost of capital
   b. 4-4-5 Calendar
   c. Capital intensity
   d. Cost of capital

3. A '_____' is a 'Charge' that is paid to obtain the right to delay a payment. Essentially, the payer purchases the right to make a given payment in the future instead of in the Present. The '_____', or 'Charge' that must be paid to delay the payment, is simply the difference between what the payment amount would be if it were paid in the present and what the payment amount would be paid if it were paid in the future.
   a. Risk aversion
   b. Risk modeling
   c. Value at risk
   d. Discount

4. The _____ is an interest rate a central bank charges depository institutions that borrow reserves from it.

   The term _____ has two meanings:

   - the same as interest rate; the term 'discount' does not refer to the meaning of the word, but to the purpose of using the quantity, such as computations of present value, e.g. net present value / discounted cash flow

   - the annual effective _____, which is the annual interest divided by the capital including that interest; this rate is lower than the interest rate; it corresponds to using the value after a year as the nominal value, and seeing the initial value as the nominal value minus a discount; it is used for Treasury Bills and similar financial instruments

   The annual effective _____ is the annual interest divided by the capital including that interest, which is the interest rate divided by 100% plus the interest rate. It is the annual discount factor to be applied to the future cash flow, to find the discount, subtracted from a future value to find the value one year earlier.

   For example, suppose there is a government bond that sells for $95 and pays $100 in a year's time.

   a. Stochastic volatility
   b. Discount rate
   c. Black-Scholes
   d. Fisher equation

5. The _____ is the weighted-average most likely outcome in gambling, probability theory, economics or finance.

Chapter 12. Risk, Cost of Capital, and Capital Budgeting 75

In gambling and probability theory, there is usually a discrete set of possible outcomes. In this case, _____ is a measure of the relative balance of win or loss weighted by their chances of occurring.

a. ABN Amro
c. A Random Walk Down Wall Street
b. AAB
d. Expected return

6. _____ are a class of computational algorithms that rely on repeated random sampling to compute their results. _____ are often used when simulating physical and mathematical systems. Because of their reliance on repeated computation and random or pseudo-random numbers, _____ are most suited to calculation by a computer.

_____ in finance are often used to calculate the value of companies, to evaluate investments in projects at corporate level or to evaluate financial derivatives. The method is intended for financial analysts who want to construct stochastic or probabilistic financial models as opposed to the traditional static and deterministic models.

a. Monte Carlo methods
c. Semivariance
b. Correlation
d. Sample size

7. In economics and finance, _____ is the practice of taking advantage of a price differential between two or more markets: striking a combination of matching deals that capitalize upon the imbalance, the profit being the difference between the market prices. When used by academics, an _____ is a transaction that involves no negative cash flow at any probabilistic or temporal state and a positive cash flow in at least one state; in simple terms, a risk-free profit.

a. Arbitrage
c. Initial margin
b. Efficient-market hypothesis
d. Issuer

8. _____ , in finance, is a general theory of asset pricing, that has become influential in the pricing of stocks.

_____ holds that the expected return of a financial asset can be modeled as a linear function of various macro-economic factors or theoretical market indices, where sensitivity to changes in each factor is represented by a factor-specific beta coefficient. The model-derived rate of return will then be used to price the asset correctly - the asset price should equal the expected end of period price discounted at the rate implied by model.

a. AAB
c. A Random Walk Down Wall Street
b. ABN Amro
d. Arbitrage pricing theory

9. _____ is the planning process used to determine whether a firm's long term investments such as new machinery, replacement machinery, new plants, new products, and research development projects are worth pursuing. It is budget for major capital, or investment, expenditures.

Many formal methods are used in _____, including the techniques such as

- Net present value
- Profitability index
- Internal rate of return
- Modified Internal Rate of Return
- Equivalent annuity

These methods use the incremental cash flows from each potential investment, or project. Techniques based on accounting earnings and accounting rules are sometimes used - though economists consider this to be improper - such as the accounting rate of return, and 'return on investment.' Simplified and hybrid methods are used as well, such as payback period and discounted payback period.

a. Shareholder value
b. Preferred stock
c. Financial distress
d. Capital budgeting

10. _____ is a form of corporation equity ownership represented in the securities. It is dangerous in comparison to preferred shares and some other investment options, in that in the event of bankruptcy, _____ investors receive their funds after preferred stockholders, bondholders, creditors, etc. On the other hand, common shares on average perform better than preferred shares or bonds over time.

a. Stock split
b. Stock market bubble
c. Stop-limit order
d. Common stock

11. A _____ is a fungible, negotiable instrument representing financial value. They are broadly categorized into debt securities (such as banknotes, bonds and debentures), and equity securities; e.g., common stocks. The company or other entity issuing the _____ is called the issuer.

a. Tracking stock
b. Securities lending
c. Book entry
d. Security

12. In business and accounting, _____s are everything of value that is owned by a person or company. The balance sheet of a firm records the monetary value of the _____s owned by the firm. The two major _____ classes are tangible _____s and intangible _____s.

a. Income
b. Accounts payable
c. EBITDA
d. Asset

13. The _____ is a measure of how revenue growth translates into growth in operating income. It is a measure of leverage, and of how risky (volatile) a company's operating income is.

There are various measures of _____, which can be interpreted analogously to financial leverage.

a. Invested capital
b. Average accounting return
c. Asset turnover
d. Operating leverage

Chapter 12. Risk, Cost of Capital, and Capital Budgeting

14. In finance, _____ (or gearing) is borrowing money to supplement existing funds for investment in such a way that the potential positive or negative outcome is magnified and/or enhanced. It generally refers to using borrowed funds, or debt, so as to attempt to increase the returns to equity. Deleveraging is the action of reducing borrowings.
   a. Pension fund
   b. Leverage
   c. Financial endowment
   d. Limited partnership

15. In business, _____ is income that a company receives from its normal business activities, usually from the sale of goods and services to customers. Some companies also receive _____ from interest, dividends or royalties paid to them by other companies. _____ may refer to business income in general, or it may refer to the amount, in a monetary unit, received during a period of time, as in 'Last year, Company X had _____ of $32 million.'

In many countries, including the UK, _____ is referred to as turnover.

   a. Revenue
   b. Matching principle
   c. Furniture, Fixtures and Equipment
   d. Bottom line

16. In financial and business accounting, _____ is a measure of a firm's profitability that excludes interest and income tax expenses.

EBIT = Operating Revenue - Operating Expenses (OPEX) + Non-operating Income

Operating Income = Operating Revenue - Operating Expenses

Operating income is the difference between operating revenues and operating expenses, but it is also sometimes used as a synonym for EBIT and operating profit. This is true if the firm has no non-operating income.

   a. AAB
   b. ABN Amro
   c. A Random Walk Down Wall Street
   d. Earnings before interest and taxes

17. _____ is a fee paid on borrowed assets. It is the price paid for the use of borrowed money , or, money earned by deposited funds . Assets that are sometimes lent with _____ include money, shares, consumer goods through hire purchase, major assets such as aircraft, and even entire factories in finance lease arrangements.
   a. Insolvency
   b. A Random Walk Down Wall Street
   c. AAB
   d. Interest

18. The institution most often referenced by the word '_____' is a public or publicly traded _____, the shares of which are traded on a public stock exchange (e.g., the New York Stock Exchange or Nasdaq in the United States) where shares of stock of _____s are bought and sold by and to the general public. Most of the largest businesses in the world are publicly traded _____s. However, the majority of _____s are said to be closely held, privately held or close _____s, meaning that no ready market exists for the trading of shares.
   a. Protect
   b. Federal Home Loan Mortgage Corporation
   c. Corporation
   d. Depository Trust Company

19. The _____ is the rate of return that must be met for a company to undertake a particular project. The _____ is usually determined by evaluating existing opportunities in operations expansion, rate of return for investments, and other factors deemed relevant by management. A risk premium can also be attached to the _____ if management feels that specific opportunities inherently contain more risk than others that could be pursued with the same resources.
   a. Capital structure
   b. Hurdle rate
   c. Gross profit
   d. Corporate finance

20. The _____ is a capital budgeting metric used by firms to decide whether they should make investments. It is an indicator of the efficiency or quality of an investment, as opposed to net present value (NPV), which indicates value or magnitude.

The IRR is the annualized effective compounded return rate which can be earned on the invested capital, i.e., the yield on the investment.

   a. A Random Walk Down Wall Street
   b. ABN Amro
   c. AAB
   d. Internal rate of return

21. In Modern Portfolio Theory, the _____ is the graphical representation of the Capital Asset Pricing Model. It displays the expected rate of return for an overall market as a function of systematic (non-diversifiable) risk (beta.)

The Y-Intercept (beta=0) of the _____ is equal to the risk-free interest rate.

   a. Certificate in Investment Performance Measurement
   b. Rebalancing
   c. Security market line
   d. Divestment

22. A _____ is a type of business entity in which partners (owners) share with each other the profits or losses of the business undertaking in which all have invested. _____s are often favored over corporations for taxation purposes, as the _____ structure does not generally incur a tax on profits before it is distributed to the partners (i.e. there is no dividend tax levied.) However, depending on the _____ structure and the jurisdiction in which it operates, owners of a _____ may be exposed to greater personal liability than they would as shareholders of a corporation.
   a. Clayton Antitrust Act
   b. Fiduciary
   c. National Securities Markets Improvement Act of 1996
   d. Partnership

23. _____ is a business valuation method. _____ is the net present value of a project if financed solely by ownership equity plus the present value of all the benefits of financing. Usually, the main benefit is a tax shield resulted from tax deductibility of interest payments. Another one can be a subsidized borrowing.
   a. AAB
   b. A Random Walk Down Wall Street
   c. ABN Amro
   d. Adjusted present value

24. _____ is that which is owed; usually referencing assets owed, but the term can cover other obligations. In the case of assets, _____ is a means of using future purchasing power in the present before a summation has been earned. Some companies and corporations use _____ as a part of their overall corporate finance strategy.
   a. Debt
   b. Credit cycle
   c. Partial Payment
   d. Cross-collateralization

Chapter 12. Risk, Cost of Capital, and Capital Budgeting

25. The _____ is the rate that a company is expected to pay to finance its assets. WACC is the minimum return that a company must earn on existing asset base to satisfy its creditors, owners, and other providers of capital.

Companies raise money from a number of sources: common equity, preferred equity, straight debt, convertible debt, exchangeable debt, warrants, options, pension liabilities, executive stock options, governmental subsidies, and so on.

a. 4-4-5 Calendar
b. Weighted average cost of capital
c. Cost of capital
d. Capital intensity

26. _____ are costs incurred on the purchase of land, buildings, construction and equipment to be used in the production of goods or the rendering of services. In other words, the total cost needed to bring a project to a commercially operable status. However, _____ are not limited to the initial construction of a factory or other business.

a. Defined contribution plan
b. Trade-off
c. Capital costs
d. Capital outflow

27. In finance, the _____ is the minimum rate of return a firm must offer shareholders to compensate for waiting for their returns, and for bearing some risk.

The _____ capital for a particular company is the rate of return on investment that is required by the company's ordinary shareholders. The return consists both of dividend and capital gains, e.g. increases in the share price.

a. Residual value
b. Round-tripping
c. Net pay
d. Cost of equity

28. A _____ or market-based mechanism is any of a wide variety of ways to match up buyers and sellers.

An example of a _____ uses announced bid and ask prices. Generally speaking, when two parties wish to engage in a trade, the purchaser will announce a price he is willing to pay (the bid price) and seller will announce a price he is willing to accept (the ask price).

a. Price mechanism
b. 4-4-5 Calendar
c. 529 plan
d. 7-Eleven

29. The _____ for securities is the difference between the price quoted by a market maker for an immediate sale and an immediate purchase The size of the bid-offer spread in a given commodity is a measure of the liquidity of the market.

The trader initiating the transaction is said to demand liquidity, and the other party to the transaction supplies liquidity.

a. Bid/offer spread
b. Capital outflow
c. Trade-off
d. Defined contribution plan

30. _____ is a measure of the ability of a debtor to pay their debts as and when they fall due. It is usually expressed as a ratio or a percentage of current liabilities.

For a corporation with a published balance sheet there are various ratios used to calculate a measure of liquidity.

   a. Accounting liquidity
   c. Invested capital
   b. Operating leverage
   d. Operating profit margin

31. The _____ is a stock exchange based in New York City, New York. It is the largest stock exchange in the world by dollar value of its listed companies securities. As of October 2008, the combined capitalization of all domestic _____ listed companies was $10.1 trillion.
   a. 529 plan
   c. 4-4-5 Calendar
   b. 7-Eleven
   d. New York Stock Exchange

32. A _____, securities exchange or (in Europe) bourse is a corporation or mutual organization which provides 'trading' facilities for stock brokers and traders, to trade stocks and other securities. _____s also provide facilities for the issue and redemption of securities as well as other financial instruments and capital events including the payment of income and dividends. The securities traded on a _____ include: shares issued by companies, unit trusts and other pooled investment products and bonds.
   a. 4-4-5 Calendar
   c. Stock Exchange
   b. 7-Eleven
   d. 529 plan

33. The phrase _____ refers to the aspect of corporate strategy, corporate finance and management dealing with the buying, selling and combining of different companies that can aid, finance, or help a growing company in a given industry grow rapidly without having to create another business entity.

An acquisition, also known as a takeover, is the buying of one company (the 'target') by another. An acquisition may be friendly or hostile.

   a. 7-Eleven
   c. Mergers and acquisitions
   b. 529 plan
   d. 4-4-5 Calendar

Chapter 13. Corporate Financing Decisions and Efficient Capital Markets

1. _____ or financing is to provide capital (funds), which means money for a project, a person, a business or any other private or public institutions.

Those funds can be allocated for either short term or long term purposes. The health fund is a new way of _____ private healthcare centers.

   a. Product life cycle
   b. Funding
   c. Synthetic CDO
   d. Proxy fight

2. _____ are a class of computational algorithms that rely on repeated random sampling to compute their results. _____ are often used when simulating physical and mathematical systems. Because of their reliance on repeated computation and random or pseudo-random numbers, _____ are most suited to calculation by a computer.

   _____ in finance are often used to calculate the value of companies, to evaluate investments in projects at corporate level or to evaluate financial derivatives. The method is intended for financial analysts who want to construct stochastic or probabilistic financial models as opposed to the traditional static and deterministic models.

   a. Monte Carlo methods
   b. Sample size
   c. Semivariance
   d. Correlation

3. In economics, business, and accounting, a _____ is the value of money that has been used up to produce something, and hence is not available for use anymore. In business, the _____ may be one of acquisition, in which case the amount of money expended to acquire it is counted as _____. In this case, money is the input that is gone in order to acquire the thing.
   a. Marginal cost
   b. Cost
   c. Sliding scale fees
   d. Fixed costs

4. A _____ is a fungible, negotiable instrument representing financial value. They are broadly categorized into debt securities (such as banknotes, bonds and debentures), and equity securities; e.g., common stocks. The company or other entity issuing the _____ is called the issuer.
   a. Securities lending
   b. Tracking stock
   c. Book entry
   d. Security

5. A _____, securities exchange or (in Europe) bourse is a corporation or mutual organization which provides 'trading' facilities for stock brokers and traders, to trade stocks and other securities. _____s also provide facilities for the issue and redemption of securities as well as other financial instruments and capital events including the payment of income and dividends. The securities traded on a _____ include: shares issued by companies, unit trusts and other pooled investment products and bonds.
   a. Stock exchange
   b. 4-4-5 Calendar
   c. 529 plan
   d. 7-Eleven

6. The _____ is the market for securities, where companies and governments can raise longterm funds. The _____ includes the stock market and the bond market. Financial regulators, such as the U.S. Securities and Exchange Commission, oversee the _____s in their designated countries to ensure that investors are protected against fraud.
   a. Spot rate
   b. Forward market
   c. Capital market
   d. Delta neutral

Chapter 13. Corporate Financing Decisions and Efficient Capital Markets

7. _____ means regulating, adapting or settling in a variety of contexts:

In commercial law, _____ means the settlement of a loss incurred on insured goods. The calculation of the amounts of compensation to be paid by or to the several interests is a complicated matter. It involves much detail and arithmetic, and requires a full and accurate knowledge of the principles of the subject.

   a. Intelligent investor
   b. Asset recovery
   c. Equity method
   d. Adjustment

8. _____ is the provision of resources (such as granting a loan) by one party to another party where that second party does not reimburse the first party immediately, thereby generating a debt, and instead arranges either to repay or return those resources (or material(s) of equal value) at a later date. The first party is called a creditor, also known as a lender, while the second party is called a debtor, also known as a borrower.

Movements of financial capital are normally dependent on either _____ or equity transfers.

   a. Warrant
   b. Comparable
   c. Clearing house
   d. Credit

9. _____, also called fair price (in a commonplace conflation of the two distinct concepts), is a concept used in finance and economics, defined as a rational and unbiased estimate of the potential market price of a good, service, or asset, taking into account such objective factors as:

   - acquisition/production/distribution costs, replacement costs, or costs of close substitutes
   - actual utility at a given level of development of social productive capability
   - supply vs. demand

and subjective factors such as

   - risk characteristics
   - cost of capital
   - individually perceived utility

In accounting, _____ is used as an estimate of the market value of an asset (or liability) for which a market price cannot be determined (usually because there is no established market for the asset.) Under GAAP (FAS 157), _____ is the amount at which the asset could be bought or sold in a current transaction between willing parties, or transferred to an equivalent party, other than in a liquidation sale. This is used for assets whose carrying value is based on mark-to-market valuations; for assets carried at historical cost, the _____ of the asset is not used. One example of where _____ is an issue is a College kitchen with a cost of $2 million which was built 5 years ago.

   a. 7-Eleven
   b. 4-4-5 Calendar
   c. 529 plan
   d. Fair value

Chapter 13. Corporate Financing Decisions and Efficient Capital Markets

10. A _____ is the price of a single share of a no. of saleable stocks of the company. Once the stock is purchased, the owner becomes a shareholder of the company that issued the share.
    a. Trading curb
    b. Whisper numbers
    c. Stock split
    d. Share price

11. In economics and finance, _____ is the practice of taking advantage of a price differential between two or more markets: striking a combination of matching deals that capitalize upon the imbalance, the profit being the difference between the market prices. When used by academics, an _____ is a transaction that involves no negative cash flow at any probabilistic or temporal state and a positive cash flow in at least one state; in simple terms, a risk-free profit.
    a. Initial margin
    b. Issuer
    c. Arbitrage
    d. Efficient-market hypothesis

12. A _____, is a mathematical formalization of a trajectory that consists of taking successive random steps. The results of _____ analysis have been applied to computer science, physics, ecology, economics and a number of other fields as a fundamental model for random processes in time. For example, the path traced by a molecule as it travels in a liquid or a gas, the search path of a foraging animal, the price of a fluctuating stock and the financial status of a gambler can all be modeled as _____s.
    a. Random walk
    b. 529 plan
    c. 4-4-5 Calendar
    d. 7-Eleven

13. In probability theory and statistics, _____ indicates the strength and direction of a linear relationship between two random variables. That is in contrast with the usage of the term in colloquial speech, which denotes any relationship, not necessarily linear. In general statistical usage, _____ or co-relation refers to the departure of two random variables from independence.
    a. Probability distribution
    b. Correlation
    c. Geometric mean
    d. Variance

14. A mutual shareholder or _____ is an individual or company (including a corporation) that legally owns one or more shares of stock in a joint stock company. A company's shareholders collectively own that company. Thus, the typical goal of such companies is to enhance shareholder value.
    a. Stock market bubble
    b. Trading curb
    c. Limit order
    d. Stockholder

15. In finance, an _____ is the difference between the expected return of a security and the actual return. _____s are sometimes triggered by 'events.' Events can include mergers, dividend announcements, company earning announcements, interest rate increases, lawsuits, etc. all which can contribute to an _____.
    a. ABN Amro
    b. AAB
    c. Abnormal return
    d. A Random Walk Down Wall Street

16. An _____ is a statistical method to assess the impact of an event on the value of a firm. For example, the announcement of a merger between two firms can be analyzed to see whether investors believe the merger will create or destroy value. Event studies have been used in a large variety of studies, including [mergers and acquisitions], earnings announcements, debt or equity issues, corporate reorganisations, investment decisions and corporate social responsibility (MacKinlay 1997; McWilliams ' Siegel, 1997).

Chapter 13. Corporate Financing Decisions and Efficient Capital Markets

a. AAB
b. ABN Amro
c. Event study
d. A Random Walk Down Wall Street

17. A _____ is a professionally managed type of collective investment scheme that pools money from many investors and invests it in stocks, bonds, short-term money market instruments, and/or other securities. The _____ will have a fund manager that trades the pooled money on a regular basis. Currently, the worldwide value of all _____s totals more than $26 trillion.

Since 1940, there have been three basic types of investment companies in the United States: open-end funds, also known in the US as _____s; unit investment trusts (UITs); and closed-end funds.

a. Trust company
b. Financial intermediary
c. Net asset value
d. Mutual fund

18. _____ is the trading of a corporation's stock or other securities (e.g. bonds or stock options) by individuals with potential access to non-public information about the company. In most countries, trading by corporate insiders such as officers, key employees, directors, and large shareholders may be legal, if this trading is done in a way that does not take advantage of non-public information. However, the term is frequently used to refer to a practice in which an insider or a related party trades based on material non-public information obtained during the performance of the insider's duties at the corporation, or otherwise in breach of a fiduciary duty or other relationship of trust and confidence or where the non-public information was misappropriated from the company.

a. Equity investment
b. Open outcry
c. Insider trading
d. Intellidex

19. The U.S. _____ is an independent agency of the United States government which holds primary responsibility for enforcing the federal securities laws and regulating the securities industry, the nation's stock and options exchanges, and other electronic securities markets. The SEC was created by section 4 of the SEC of 1934 (now codified as 15 U.S.C. § 78d and commonly referred to as the 1934 Act.)

a. 4-4-5 Calendar
b. Securities and Exchange Commission
c. 7-Eleven
d. 529 plan

20. In business, investment, and accounting, the principle or convention of _____ has at least two meanings.

In investment and finance, it is a strategy which aims at long-term capital appreciation with low risk. It can be characterized as moderate or cautious and is the opposite of aggressive behavior.

a. Debt-snowball method
b. Barcampbank
c. Duration gap
d. Conservatism

21. Behavioral economics and _____ are closely related fields that have evolved to be a separate branch of economic and financial analysis which applies scientific research on human and social, cognitive and emotional factors to better understand economic decisions by, say, consumers, borrowers, investors, and how they affect market prices, returns and the allocation of resources.

The field is primarily concerned with the bounds of rationality (selfishness, self-control) of economic agents. Behavioral models typically integrate insights from psychology with neo-classical economic theory.

Chapter 13. Corporate Financing Decisions and Efficient Capital Markets

a. Recession
c. Market structure
b. Medium of exchange
d. Behavioral finance

22. _____ is a theory which assumes that restrictions placed upon funds, that would ordinarily be used by rational traders to arbitrage away pricing inefficiencies, leave prices in a non-equilibrium state for protracted periods of time.

The efficient market hypothesis assumes that whenever mispricing of a publicly-traded stock occurs as a result of an over-reaction to news, or some similar event, an opportuntity for low-risk profit is created for rational traders. The low-risk profit opportunity exists through the tool of arbitrage, which, briefly, is buying and selling differently priced items of the same value, and pocketing the difference.

a. Market anomaly
c. Delta hedging
b. Limits to Arbitrage
d. Forward market

23. In finance, _____ are stocks that appreciate in value and yield a high return on equity (ROE.) Analysts compute ROE by taking the company's net income and dividing it by the company's equity. To be classified as a growth stock, analysts expect to see at least 15 percent return on equity.

a. Stock valuation
c. 4-4-5 Calendar
b. Growth stocks
d. Security Analysis

24. In business and finance, a _____ (also referred to as equity _____) of stock means a _____ of ownership in a corporation (company.) In the plural, stocks is often used as a synonym for _____s especially in the United States, but it is less commonly used that way outside of North America.

In the United Kingdom, South Africa, and Australia, stock can also refer to completely different financial instruments such as government bonds or, less commonly, to all kinds of marketable securities.

a. Margin
c. Procter ' Gamble
b. Share
d. Bucket shop

25. A _____ is a private or public market for the trading of company stock and derivatives of company stock at an agreed price; these are securities listed on a stock exchange as well as those only traded privately.

The size of the world _____ is estimated at about $36.6 trillion US at the beginning of October 2008 . The world derivatives market has been estimated at about $480 trillion face or nominal value, 12 times the size of the entire world economy.

a. Anton Gelonkin
c. Adolph Coors
b. Andrew Tobias
d. Stock market

26. Two primary _____, cash and accrual basis, and their combination, called modified cash basis, are used in recognizing income (revenues) and expenses in bookkeeping in order to measure net income for a specified time interval (accounting period.) Both methods differ on such recognition leading to varying income recordings, which may be subject to error or - manipulation. Many financial scandals involved accounting manipulations.

Chapter 13. Corporate Financing Decisions and Efficient Capital Markets

a. Outstanding balance
b. Accounting equation
c. Asset
d. Accounting methods

27. _____ or First In, First Out, is an abstraction in ways of organizing and manipulation of data relative to time and prioritization. This expression describes the principle of a queue processing technique or servicing conflicting demands by ordering process by first-come, first-served (FCFS) behaviour: what comes in first is handled first, what comes in next waits until the first is finished, etc.

Thus it is analogous to the behaviour of persons queueing (or 'standing in line', in common American parlance), where the persons leave the queue in the order they arrive, or waiting one's turn at a traffic control signal.

a. 4-4-5 Calendar
b. Risk management
c. Penny stock
d. FIFO

28. _____ is an acronym which stands for last in, first out. In computer science and queueing theory this refers to the way items stored in some types of data structures are processed. By definition, in a _____ structured linear list, elements can be added or taken off from only one end, called the 'top'.

a. 7-Eleven
b. 4-4-5 Calendar
c. LIFO
d. 529 plan

29. In finance, a _____ is a type of bond that can be converted into shares of stock in the issuing company, usually at some pre-announced ratio. It is a hybrid security with debt- and equity-like features. Although it typically has a low coupon rate, the holder is compensated with the ability to convert the bond to common stock, usually at a substantial discount to the stock's market value.

a. Bond fund
b. Gilts
c. Corporate bond
d. Convertible bond

30. _____ are those dividends paid out in form of additional stock shares of the issuing corporation or other corporation They are usually issued in proportion to shares owned (for example for every 100 shares of stock owned, 5% stock dividend will yield 5 extra shares). If this payment involves the issue of new shares, this is very similar to a stock split in that it increases the total number of shares while lowering the price of each share and does not change the market capitalization or the total value of the shares held

a. Database auditing
b. Stock or scrip dividends
c. The Hong Kong Securities Institute
d. Time-based currency

31. In finance, a _____ is a debt security, in which the authorized issuer owes the holders a debt and, depending on the terms of the _____, is obliged to pay interest (the coupon) and/or to repay the principal at a later date, termed maturity.

Thus a _____ is a loan: the issuer is the borrower, the _____ holder is the lender, and the coupon is the interest. _____s provide the borrower with external funds to finance long-term investments, or, in the case of government _____s, to finance current expenditure.

a. Puttable bond
b. Convertible bond
c. Catastrophe bonds
d. Bond

Chapter 13. Corporate Financing Decisions and Efficient Capital Markets

32. A _____ is a payment made by a corporation to its shareholder members. When a corporation earns a profit or surplus, that money can be put to two uses: it can either be re-invested in the business (called retained earnings), or it can be paid to the shareholders as a _____. Many corporations retain a portion of their earnings and pay the remainder as a _____.
   - a. Dividend yield
   - b. Dividend puzzle
   - c. Special dividend
   - d. Dividend

33. _____ (in a financial context) is the assumption of the risk of loss, in return for the uncertain possibility of a reward. Only if one may safely say that a particular position involves no risk may one say, strictly speaking, that such a position represents an 'investment.' Financial _____ involves the buying, holding, selling, and short-selling of stocks, bonds, commodities, currencies, collectibles, real estate, derivatives, or any valuable financial instrument to profit from fluctuations in its price as opposed to buying it for use or for income via methods such as dividends or interest. _____ represents one of four market roles in Western financial markets, distinct from hedging, long- or short-term investing, and arbitrage.
   - a. Central Securities Depository
   - b. Speculation
   - c. Market anomaly
   - d. Forward market

34. A _____ is a financial contract whose value is derived from the value of something else (known as the underlying.) The underlying on which a _____ is based can be an asset, weather conditions bonds or other forms of credit.
   - a. 7-Eleven
   - b. 529 plan
   - c. 4-4-5 Calendar
   - d. Derivative

35. _____ is an economic concept with commonplace familiarity. It is the price that a good or service is offered at, or will fetch, in the marketplace. It is of interest mainly in the study of microeconomics.
   - a. Convertible arbitrage
   - b. Market price
   - c. Central Securities Depository
   - d. Delta hedging

36. _____, in bookkeeping, refers to assets, liabilities, income, and expenses recorded on individual pages of the so called book of final entry or ledger. Changes in _____ value are made by chronologically posting debit (DR) and credit (CR) entries to its page. Examples of _____s are cash, _____s receivable, mortgages, loans, land and buildings, common stock, sales, services provided, wages, and payroll overhead.
   - a. Account
   - b. Alpha
   - c. Accretion
   - d. Option

Chapter 14. Long-Term Financing: An Introduction

1. _____ is a form of corporation equity ownership represented in the securities. It is dangerous in comparison to preferred shares and some other investment options, in that in the event of bankruptcy, _____ investors receive their funds after preferred stockholders, bondholders, creditors, etc. On the other hand, common shares on average perform better than preferred shares or bonds over time.
    a. Stop-limit order
    b. Stock split
    c. Stock market bubble
    d. Common stock

2. In economic models, the _____ time frame assumes no fixed factors of production. Firms can enter or leave the marketplace, and the cost (and availability) of land, labor, raw materials, and capital goods can be assumed to vary. In contrast, in the short-run time frame, certain factors are assumed to be fixed, because there is not sufficient time for them to change.
    a. 529 plan
    b. 4-4-5 Calendar
    c. Short-run
    d. Long-run

3. _____, in finance and accounting, means stated value or face value. From this comes the expressions at par (at the _____), over par (over _____) and under par (under _____.)

    The term '_____' has several meanings depending on context and geography.

    a. Global Squeeze
    b. Par value
    c. Sinking fund
    d. FIDC

4. In finance, a _____ is a debt security, in which the authorized issuer owes the holders a debt and, depending on the terms of the _____, is obliged to pay interest (the coupon) and/or to repay the principal at a later date, termed maturity.

    Thus a _____ is a loan: the issuer is the borrower, the _____ holder is the lender, and the coupon is the interest. _____s provide the borrower with external funds to finance long-term investments, or, in the case of government _____s, to finance current expenditure.

    a. Convertible bond
    b. Catastrophe bonds
    c. Bond
    d. Puttable bond

5. The phrase _____ refers to the aspect of corporate strategy, corporate finance and management dealing with the buying, selling and combining of different companies that can aid, finance, or help a growing company in a given industry grow rapidly without having to create another business entity.

    An acquisition, also known as a takeover, is the buying of one company (the 'target') by another. An acquisition may be friendly or hostile.

    a. 7-Eleven
    b. 4-4-5 Calendar
    c. 529 plan
    d. Mergers and acquisitions

6. The _____ are the primary rules governing the management of a corporation in the United States and Canada, and are filed with a state or other regulatory agency. The equivalent in the United Kingdom and various other countries is Articles of Association.

A corporation's _____ generally provide information such as:

- The corporation's name, which has to be unique from any other corporation in that jurisdiction. As part of the corporation's name, certain words such as 'incorporated', 'limited', 'corporation', (or their abbreviations) or some equivalent term in countries whose language is not English, are usually required as part of the name as a 'flag' to indicate to persons doing business with the organization that it is a corporation as opposed to an individual or partnership (with unlimited liability.) In some cases, certain types of names are prohibited except by special permission, such as words implying the corporation is a government agency or has powers to act in ways it is not otherwise allowed.
- The name of the person(s) organizing the corporation (usually members of the board of directors.)
- Whether the corporation is a stock corporation or a non-stock corporation.
- Whether the corporation's existence is permanent or limited for a specific period of time. Generally the rule is that a corporation existence is forever, or until (1) it stops paying the yearly corporate renewal fees or otherwise fails to do something required to continue its existence such as file certain paperwork each year; or (2) it files a request to 'wind up and dissolve.'
- In some cases, a corporation must state the purposes for which it is formed. Some jurisdictions permit a general statement such as 'any lawful purpose' but some require explicit specifications.
- If a non-stock corporation, whether it is for profit or non-profit. However, some jurisdictions differentiate by 'for profit' or 'non profit' and some by 'stock or non-stock'.
- In the United States, if a corporation is to be organized as a non-profit, to be recognized as such by the Internal Revenue Service, such as for eligibility for tax exemption, certain specific wording must be included stating no part of the assets of the corporation are to benefit the members.
- If a stock corporation, the number of shares the corporation is authorized to issue, or the maximum amount in a specific currency of stock that may be issued, e.g. a maximum of $25,000.
- The number and names of the corporation's initial Board of Directors (though this is optional in most cases.)
- The initial director(s) of the corporation (in some cases the incorporator or the registered agent must be a director, if not an attorney or another corporation.)
- The location of the corporation's 'registered office' - the location at which legal papers can be served to the corporation if necessary. Some states further require the designation of a Registered Agent: a person to whom such papers could be delivered.

Most states permit a corporation to be formed by one person; in some cases (such as non-profit corporations) it may require three or five or more. This change has come about as a result of Delaware liberalizing its corporation rules to allow corporations to be formed by one person, and states not wanting to lose corporate charters to Delaware had to revise their rules as a result.

   a. Expedited Funds Availability Act   b. Articles of incorporation
   c. Articles of Partnership   d. External risks

   7. In accounting, _____ or *Carrying value* is the value of an asset according to its balance sheet account balance. For assets, the value is based on the original cost of the asset less any depreciation, amortization or impairment costs made against the asset. A company's _____ is its total assets minus intangible assets and liabilities.

a. Retained earnings
b. Book value
c. Pro forma
d. Current liabilities

8. _____ is an accounting term which frequently appears as a balance sheet item as a component of shareholders' equity. _____ is used to account for any funds the issuing firm has received over and above the par value of the common stock. It may also be used to account for any gains the firm may derive from selling treasury stock, although this is less commonly seen.
   a. Flight-to-quality
   b. Capital surplus
   c. Commercial finance
   d. Stock market index option

9. The institution most often referenced by the word '_____' is a public or publicly traded _____, the shares of which are traded on a public stock exchange (e.g., the New York Stock Exchange or Nasdaq in the United States) where shares of stock of _____s are bought and sold by and to the general public. Most of the largest businesses in the world are publicly traded _____s. However, the majority of _____s are said to be closely held, privately held or close _____s, meaning that no ready market exists for the trading of shares.
   a. Depository Trust Company
   b. Protect
   c. Federal Home Loan Mortgage Corporation
   d. Corporation

10. The free _____ of a public company is an estimate of the proportion of shares that are not held by large owners and that are not stock with sales restrictions (restricted stock that cannot be sold until they become unrestricted stock.)

The free _____ or a public _____ is usually defined as being all shares held by investors other than:

- shares held by owners owning more than 5% of all shares (those could be institutional investors, 'strategic shareholders,' founders, executives, and other insiders' holdings)
- restricted stocks (granted to executives that can be, but don't have to be, registered insiders)
- insider holdings (it is assumed that insiders hold stock for the very long term)

The free _____ is an important criterion in quoting a share on the stock market.

To _____ a company means to list its shares on a public stock exchange through an initial public offering (or 'flotation'.)

- Open market
- Outstanding shares
- Market capitalization
- Public _____ *loat*
- Reverse takeover

a. Synthetic CDO
b. Golden parachute
c. Trade finance
d. Float

Chapter 14. Long-Term Financing: An Introduction

11. In accounting, _____ refers to the portion of net income which is retained by the corporation rather than distributed to its owners as dividends. Similarly, if the corporation makes a loss, then that loss is retained and called variously retained losses, accumulated losses or accumulated deficit. _____ and losses are cumulative from year to year with losses offsetting earnings.
   a. Matching principle
   b. Historical cost
   c. Generally Accepted Accounting Principles
   d. Retained earnings

12. _____ is the price at which an asset would trade in a competitive Walrasian auction setting. _____ is often used interchangeably with open _____, fair value or fair _____, although these terms have distinct definitions in different standards, and may differ in some circumstances.

   International Valuation Standards defines _____ as 'the estimated amount for which a property should exchange on the date of valuation between a willing buyer and a willing seller in an arm'e;s-length transaction after proper marketing wherein the parties had each acted knowledgeably, prudently, and without compulsion.'

   _____ is a concept distinct from market price, which is 'e;the price at which one can transact'e;, while _____ is 'e;the true underlying value'e; according to theoretical standards.

   a. Market value
   b. T-Model
   c. Debt restructuring
   d. Wrap account

13. _____ is typically a higher ranking stock than voting shares, and its terms are negotiated between the corporation and the investor.

   _____ usually carry no voting rights, but may carry superior priority over common stock in the payment of dividends and upon liquidation. _____ may carry a dividend that is paid out prior to any dividends to common stock holders.

   a. Follow-on offering
   b. Second lien loan
   c. Trade-off theory
   d. Preferred stock

14. A _____ or reacquired stock is stock which is bought back by the issuing company, reducing the amount of outstanding stock on the open market ('open market' including insiders' holdings.)

   Stock repurchases are often used as a tax-efficient method to put cash into shareholders' hands, rather than pay dividends. Sometimes, companies do this when they feel that their stock is undervalued on the open market.

   a. Treasury stock
   b. Current asset
   c. Generally Accepted Accounting Principles
   d. Trial balance

15. _____ is a multiple-winner voting system intended to promote proportional representation while also being simple to understand.

_____ is used frequently in corporate governance, where it is mandated by many U.S. states, and it was used to elect the Illinois House of Representatives from 1870 until its repeal in 1980. It was used in England in the late 19th century to elect school boards.

    a. 7-Eleven
    b. Cumulative voting
    c. 4-4-5 Calendar
    d. 529 plan

16. In finance, _____ occurs when a debtor has not met its legal obligations according to the debt contract, e.g. it has not made a scheduled payment, or has violated a loan covenant (condition) of the debt contract. _____ may occur if the debtor is either unwilling or unable to pay their debt. This can occur with all debt obligations including bonds, mortgages, loans, and promissory notes.
    a. Credit crunch
    b. Default
    c. Vendor finance
    d. Debt validation

17. A _____ is a payment made by a corporation to its shareholder members. When a corporation earns a profit or surplus, that money can be put to two uses: it can either be re-invested in the business (called retained earnings), or it can be paid to the shareholders as a _____. Many corporations retain a portion of their earnings and pay the remainder as a _____.
    a. Dividend
    b. Dividend puzzle
    c. Dividend yield
    d. Special dividend

18. _____ is a term in Corporate Finance used to indicate a condition when promises to creditors of a company are broken or honored with difficulty. Sometimes _____ can lead to bankruptcy. _____ is usually associated with some costs to the company and these are known as Costs of _____.
    a. Cashflow matching
    b. Commercial paper
    c. Capital structure
    d. Financial distress

19. A _____ is a right to acquire certain property in preference to any other person. It usually refers to property newly coming into existence. A right to acquire existing property in preference to any other person is usually referred to as a right of first refusal.

In practice, the most common form of _____ is the right of existing shareholders to acquire newly issued shares issued by a company in a rights issue, a usually but not always public offering.

    a. Court of Audit of Belgium
    b. Fraud deterrence
    c. Down payment
    d. Pre-emption right

20. _____ is commonly used in corporations for voting by members or shareholders, because it allows members who have confidence in the judgment of other members to vote for them and allows the assembly to have a quorum of votes when it is difficult for all members to attend, or there are too many members for all of them to conveniently meet and deliberate.
    a. 529 plan
    b. 4-4-5 Calendar
    c. 7-Eleven
    d. Proxy voting

Chapter 14. Long-Term Financing: An Introduction

21. In finance, a _____ is the party in a loan agreement which receives money or other instrument from a lender and promises to repay the lender in a specified time.
    a. Borrower
    b. Cash credit
    c. Debt management plan
    d. Line of credit

22. A _____ is a party (e.g. person, organization, company, or government) that has a claim to the services of a second party. The first party, in general, has provided some property or service to the second party under the assumption (usually enforced by contract) that the second party will return an equivalent property or service. The second party is frequently called a debtor or borrower.
    a. Redemption value
    b. False billing
    c. Creditor
    d. NOPLAT

23. _____ is that which is owed; usually referencing assets owed, but the term can cover other obligations. In the case of assets, _____ is a means of using future purchasing power in the present before a summation has been earned. Some companies and corporations use _____ as a part of their overall corporate finance strategy.
    a. Debt
    b. Cross-collateralization
    c. Credit cycle
    d. Partial Payment

24. In economics a _____ is simply an entity that owes a debt to someone else, the entity could be an individual, a firm, a government, or an organization. The counterparty of this arrangement is called a creditor. When the counterparty of this debt arrangement is a bank, the _____ is more often referred to as a borrower.
    a. Biweekly Mortgage
    b. Financial rand
    c. Tick size
    d. Debtor

25. _____ is a fee paid on borrowed assets. It is the price paid for the use of borrowed money , or, money earned by deposited funds . Assets that are sometimes lent with _____ include money, shares, consumer goods through hire purchase, major assets such as aircraft, and even entire factories in finance lease arrangements.
    a. AAB
    b. Insolvency
    c. Interest
    d. A Random Walk Down Wall Street

26. The coupon or _____ of a bond is the amount of interest paid per year expressed as a percentage of the face value of the bond.

For example if you hold $10,000 nominal of a bond described as a 4.5% loan stock, you will receive $450 in interest each year (probably in two installments of $225 each.)

Not all bonds have coupons.

    a. Revenue bonds
    b. Coupon rate
    c. Puttable bond
    d. Zero-coupon bond

27. A _____ is defined as a certificate of agreement of loans which is given under the company's stamp and carries an undertaking that the _____ holder will get a fixed return (fixed on the basis of interest rates) and the principal amount whenever the _____ matures.

In finance, a _____ is a long-term debt instrument used by governments and large companies to obtain funds. It is defined as 'a debt secured only by the debtor's earning power, not by a lien on any specific asset.' It is similar to a bond except the securitization conditions are different.

    a. Collection agency   b. Collateral Management
    c. Partial Payment   d. Debenture

28. In law, _____ refers to the process by which a company (or part of a company) is brought to an end, and the assets and property of the company redistributed. _____ can also be referred to as winding-up or dissolution, although dissolution technically refers to the last stage of _____. The process of _____ also arises when customs, an authority or agency in a country responsible for collecting and safeguarding customs duties, determines the final computation or ascertainment of the duties or drawback accruing on an entry.

    a. Liquidation   b. 529 plan
    c. Debt settlement   d. 4-4-5 Calendar

29. _____ is a life of security. It may also refer to the final payment date of a loan or other financial instrument, at which point all remaining interest and principal is due to be paid.

1, 3, 6 months _____ band can be calculated by using 30-day per month periods.

    a. Replacement cost   b. Primary market
    c. False billing   d. Maturity

30. In economics, the concept of the _____ refers to the decision-making time frame of a firm in which at least one factor of production is fixed. Costs which are fixed in the _____ have no impact on a firms decisions. For example a firm can raise output by increasing the amount of labour through overtime.

    a. Long-run   b. 4-4-5 Calendar
    c. 529 plan   d. Short-run

31. A _____ is a document that indicates that the bearer of the document has title to property, such as shares or bonds. They differ from normal registered instruments, in that no records are kept of who owns the underlying property, or of the transactions involving transfer of ownership. Whoever physically holds the bearer bond papers owns the property.

    a. Securities lending   b. Book entry
    c. Marketable   d. Bearer instrument

32. A '_____' is a 'Charge' that is paid to obtain the right to delay a payment. Essentially, the payer purchases the right to make a given payment in the future instead of in the Present. The '_____', or 'Charge' that must be paid to delay the payment, is simply the difference between what the payment amount would be if it were paid in the present and what the payment amount would be paid if it were paid in the future.

    a. Discount   b. Value at risk
    c. Risk modeling   d. Risk aversion

Chapter 14. Long-Term Financing: An Introduction

33. _____ is the process of decreasing an amount over a period of time. The word comes from Middle English amortisen to kill, alienate in mortmain, from Anglo-French amorteser, alteration of amortir, from Vulgar Latin admortire to kill, from Latin ad- + mort-, mors death. Particular instances of the term include:

- _____ (business), the allocation of a lump sum amount to different time periods, particularly for loans and other forms of finance, including related interest or other finance charges.
  - _____ schedule, a table detailing each periodic payment on a loan (typically a mortgage), as generated by an _____ calculator.
  - Negative _____, an _____ schedule where the loan amount actually increases through not paying the full interest
- Amortized analysis, analyzing the execution cost of algorithms over a sequence of operations.
- _____ of capital expenditures of certain assets under accounting rules, particularly intangible assets, in a manner analogous to depreciation.
- _____ (tax law)

_____ is also used in the context of zoning regulations and describes the time in which a property owner has to relocate when the property's use constitutes a preexisting nonconforming use under zoning regulations.

- Depreciation

a. AT'T Inc.
b. Option
c. Intrinsic value
d. Amortization

34. _____ is a type of bond that allows the issuer of the bond to retain the privilege of redeeming the bond at some point before the bond reaches the date of maturity. In other words, on the call dates, the issuer has the right, but not the obligation, to buy back the bonds from the bond holders at the call price. Technically speaking, the bonds are not really bought and held by the issuer but cancelled immediately.

a. Coupon rate
b. Gilts
c. Bond fund
d. Callable bond

35. _____ are a form of British government bond (gilt), dating originally from the 18th century. _____ are one of the rare examples of an actual perpetuity: although they may be redeemed by the British government, they are unlikely to do so in the foreseeable future.

In 1752, the Chancellor of the Exchequer and Prime Minister Sir Henry Pelham converted all outstanding issues of redeemable government stock into one bond, Consolidated 3.5% Annuities, in order to reduce the coupon rate paid on the government debt.

a. Brady bonds
b. Revenue bonds
c. Serial bond
d. Consols

36. A _____ is a fungible, negotiable instrument representing financial value. They are broadly categorized into debt securities (such as banknotes, bonds and debentures), and equity securities; e.g., common stocks. The company or other entity issuing the _____ is called the issuer.

a. Security
c. Securities lending
b. Book entry
d. Tracking stock

37. A _____ is a fund established by a government agency or business for the purpose of reducing debt.

The _____ was first used in Great Britain in the 18th century to reduce national debt. While used by Robert Walpole in 1716 and effectively in the 1720s and early 1730s, it originated in the commercial tax syndicates of the Italian peninsula of the 14th century to retire redeemable public debt of those cities.

a. Modern portfolio theory
c. Security interest
b. Debtor
d. Sinking fund

38. In finance, _____ is debt which ranks after other debts should a company fall into receivership or be closed.

Such debt is referred to as subordinate, because the debt providers have subordinate status in relationship to the normal debt. A typical example for this would be when a promoter of a company invests money in the form of debt, rather than in the form of stock.

a. Participation loan
c. Subordinated debt
b. Cross-collateralization
d. Credit rating

39. A _____, in its most general sense, is a solemn promise to engage in or refrain from a specified action.

More specifically, a _____, in contrast to a contract, is a one-way agreement whereby the _____er is the only party bound by the promise. A _____ may have conditions and prerequisites that qualify the undertaking, including the actions of second or third parties, but there is no inherent agreement by such other parties to fulfill those requirements.

a. Federal Trade Commission Act
c. Clayton Antitrust Act
b. Partnership
d. Covenant

40. In financial accounting, _____s are precautions for which the amount or probability of occurrence are not known. Typical examples are _____s for warranty costs and _____ for taxes the term reserve is used instead of term _____; such a use, however, is inconsistent with the terminology suggested by International Accounting Standards Board.

a. Momentum Accounting and Triple-Entry Bookkeeping
c. Petty cash
b. Money measurement concept
d. Provision

41. In the global money market, _____ is an unsecured promissory note with a fixed maturity of one to 270 days. _____ is a money-market security issued (sold) by large banks and corporations to get money to meet short term debt obligations (for example, payroll), and is only backed by an issuing bank or corporation's promise to pay the face amount on the maturity date specified on the note. Since it is not backed by collateral, only firms with excellent credit ratings from a recognized rating agency will be able to sell their _____ at a reasonable price.

a. Trade-off theory
b. Commercial paper
c. Book building
d. Financial distress

42. _____ is a financial ratio that indicates the percentage of a company's assets are provided via debt. It is the ratio of total debt (the sum of current liabilities and long-term liabilities) and total assets (the sum of current assets, fixed assets, and other assets such as 'goodwill'.)

>

or alternatively:

>

For example, a company with $2 million in total assets and $500,000 in total liabilities would have a _____ of 25%

Like all financial ratios, a company's _____ should be compared with their industry average or other competing firms.

a. Debt ratio
b. Capitalization rate
c. Cash management
d. Cash concentration

Chapter 15. Capital Structure: Basic Concepts

1. In finance, _____ refers to the way a corporation finances its assets through some combination of equity, debt, or hybrid securities. A firm's _____ is then the composition or 'structure' of its liabilities. For example, a firm that sells $20 billion in equity and $80 billion in debt is said to be 20% equity-financed and 80% debt-financed.
   - a. Book building
   - b. Rights issue
   - c. Market for corporate control
   - d. Capital structure

2. _____ is that which is owed; usually referencing assets owed, but the term can cover other obligations. In the case of assets, _____ is a means of using future purchasing power in the present before a summation has been earned. Some companies and corporations use _____ as a part of their overall corporate finance strategy.
   - a. Cross-collateralization
   - b. Credit cycle
   - c. Partial Payment
   - d. Debt

3. _____ is a term in Corporate Finance used to indicate a condition when promises to creditors of a company are broken or honored with difficulty. Sometimes _____ can lead to bankruptcy. _____ is usually associated with some costs to the company and these are known as Costs of _____.
   - a. Commercial paper
   - b. Capital structure
   - c. Cashflow matching
   - d. Financial distress

4. _____ is the corporate management term for the act of reorganizing the legal, ownership, operational, or other structures of a company for the purpose of making it more profitable or better organized for its present needs. Alternate reasons for restructing include a change of ownership or ownership structure, demerger repositioning debt _____ and financial _____.
   - a. Day trading
   - b. Concentrated stock
   - c. Cross-border leasing
   - d. Restructuring

5. _____ is a fee paid on borrowed assets. It is the price paid for the use of borrowed money , or, money earned by deposited funds . Assets that are sometimes lent with _____ include money, shares, consumer goods through hire purchase, major assets such as aircraft, and even entire factories in finance lease arrangements.
   - a. Interest
   - b. AAB
   - c. Insolvency
   - d. A Random Walk Down Wall Street

6. In business and accounting, _____s are everything of value that is owned by a person or company. The balance sheet of a firm records the monetary value of the _____s owned by the firm. The two major _____ classes are tangible _____s and intangible _____s.
   - a. Accounts payable
   - b. EBITDA
   - c. Income
   - d. Asset

7. The term _____ is often used to refer to the investment management of collective investments, (not necessarily) whilst the more generic fund management may refer to all forms of institutional investment as well as investment management for private investors. Investment managers who specialize in advisory or discretionary management on behalf of (normally wealthy) private investors may often refer to their services as wealth management or portfolio management often within the context of so-called 'private banking'.

The provision of 'investment management services' includes elements of financial analysis, asset selection, stock selection, plan implementation and ongoing monitoring of investments.

Chapter 15. Capital Structure: Basic Concepts

a. Asset management
c. ABN Amro
b. AAB
d. A Random Walk Down Wall Street

8. _____ are the earnings returned on the initial investment amount.

In the US, the Financial Accounting Standards Board (FASB) requires companies' income statements to report _____ for each of the major categories of the income statement: continuing operations, discontinued operations, extraordinary items, and net income.

The _____ formula does not include preferred dividends for categories outside of continued operations and net income.

a. Earnings per share
c. Average accounting return
b. Assets turnover
d. Inventory turnover

9. In finance, _____ (or gearing) is borrowing money to supplement existing funds for investment in such a way that the potential positive or negative outcome is magnified and/or enhanced. It generally refers to using borrowed funds, or debt, so as to attempt to increase the returns to equity. Deleveraging is the action of reducing borrowings.

a. Financial endowment
c. Limited partnership
b. Pension fund
d. Leverage

10. The phrase _____ refers to the aspect of corporate strategy, corporate finance and management dealing with the buying, selling and combining of different companies that can aid, finance, or help a growing company in a given industry grow rapidly without having to create another business entity.

An acquisition, also known as a takeover, is the buying of one company (the 'target') by another. An acquisition may be friendly or hostile.

a. 7-Eleven
c. 529 plan
b. 4-4-5 Calendar
d. Mergers and acquisitions

11. In business and finance, a _____ (also referred to as equity _____) of stock means a _____ of ownership in a corporation (company.) In the plural, stocks is often used as a synonym for _____s especially in the United States, but it is less commonly used that way outside of North America.

In the United Kingdom, South Africa, and Australia, stock can also refer to completely different financial instruments such as government bonds or, less commonly, to all kinds of marketable securities.

a. Margin
c. Bucket shop
b. Procter ' Gamble
d. Share

Chapter 15. Capital Structure: Basic Concepts

12. In finance, a _____ is collateral that the holder of a position in securities, options, or futures contracts has to deposit to cover the credit risk of his counterparty (most often his broker.) This risk can arise if the holder has done any of the following:

- borrowed cash from the counterparty to buy securities or options,
- sold securities or options short, or
- entered into a futures contract.

The collateral can be in the form of cash or securities, and it is deposited in a _____ account. On U.S. futures exchanges, '_____' was formally called performance bond.

_____ buying is buying securities with cash borrowed from a broker, using other securities as collateral.

a. Procter ' Gamble	b. Credit
c. Share	d. Margin

13. A _____ is a payment made by a corporation to its shareholder members. When a corporation earns a profit or surplus, that money can be put to two uses: it can either be re-invested in the business (called retained earnings), or it can be paid to the shareholders as a _____. Many corporations retain a portion of their earnings and pay the remainder as a _____.

a. Dividend yield	b. Dividend puzzle
c. Dividend	d. Special dividend

14. _____ refers to a tax levied by various jurisdictions on the profits made by companies or associations. It is a tax on the value of the corporation's profits.

The measure of taxable profits varies from country to country.

a. First-mover advantage	b. Trade finance
c. Proxy fight	d. Corporate tax

15. _____ is the value on a given date of a future payment or series of future payments, discounted to reflect the time value of money and other factors such as investment risk. _____ calculations are widely used in business and economics to provide a means to compare cash flows at different times on a meaningful 'like to like' basis.

The most commonly applied model of the time value of money is compound interest.

a. Present value	b. Net present value
c. Negative gearing	d. Present value of benefits

16. A _____ is the reduction in income taxes that results from taking an allowable deduction from taxable income. For example, because interest on debt is a tax-deductible expense, taking on debt creates a _____. Since a _____ is a way to save cash flows, it increases the value of the business, and it is an important aspect of business valuation.

a. Present value of benefits	b. Refinancing risk
c. Present value of costs	d. Tax shield

Chapter 15. Capital Structure: Basic Concepts

17. The _____ is the weighted-average most likely outcome in gambling, probability theory, economics or finance.

In gambling and probability theory, there is usually a discrete set of possible outcomes. In this case, _____ is a measure of the relative balance of win or loss weighted by their chances of occurring.

a. A Random Walk Down Wall Street
b. ABN Amro
c. AAB
d. Expected return

18. In economics, business, and accounting, a _____ is the value of money that has been used up to produce something, and hence is not available for use anymore. In business, the _____ may be one of acquisition, in which case the amount of money expended to acquire it is counted as _____. In this case, money is the input that is gone in order to acquire the thing.

a. Cost
b. Sliding scale fees
c. Marginal cost
d. Fixed costs

19. The _____ is an expected return that the provider of capital plans to earn on their investment.

Capital (money) used for funding a business should earn returns for the capital providers who risk their capital. For an investment to be worthwhile, the expected return on capital must be greater than the _____.

a. Capital intensity
b. Weighted average cost of capital
c. 4-4-5 Calendar
d. Cost of capital

20. The _____ is the rate that a company is expected to pay to finance its assets. WACC is the minimum return that a company must earn on existing asset base to satisfy its creditors, owners, and other providers of capital.

Companies raise money from a number of sources: common equity, preferred equity, straight debt, convertible debt, exchangeable debt, warrants, options, pension liabilities, executive stock options, governmental subsidies, and so on.

a. Capital intensity
b. Cost of capital
c. 4-4-5 Calendar
d. Weighted average cost of capital

21. A _____ is the price of a single share of a no. of saleable stocks of the company. Once the stock is purchased, the owner becomes a shareholder of the company that issued the share.

a. Trading curb
b. Share price
c. Whisper numbers
d. Stock split

Chapter 16. Capital Structure: Limits to the Use of Debt

1. _____ is a legally declared inability or impairment of ability of an individual or organization to pay their creditors. Creditors may file a _____ petition against a debtor ('involuntary _____') in an effort to recoup a portion of what they are owed or initiate a restructuring. In the majority of cases, however, _____ is initiated by the debtor (a 'voluntary _____' that is filed by the bankrupt individual or organization.)
   a. Debt settlement
   b. 529 plan
   c. Bankruptcy
   d. 4-4-5 Calendar

2. In finance, _____ refers to the way a corporation finances its assets through some combination of equity, debt, or hybrid securities. A firm's _____ is then the composition or 'structure' of its liabilities. For example, a firm that sells $20 billion in equity and $80 billion in debt is said to be 20% equity-financed and 80% debt-financed.
   a. Market for corporate control
   b. Book building
   c. Rights issue
   d. Capital structure

3. _____ is a term in Corporate Finance used to indicate a condition when promises to creditors of a company are broken or honored with difficulty. Sometimes _____ can lead to bankruptcy. _____ is usually associated with some costs to the company and these are known as Costs of _____.
   a. Capital structure
   b. Commercial paper
   c. Cashflow matching
   d. Financial distress

4. In economics, business, and accounting, a _____ is the value of money that has been used up to produce something, and hence is not available for use anymore. In business, the _____ may be one of acquisition, in which case the amount of money expended to acquire it is counted as _____. In this case, money is the input that is gone in order to acquire the thing.
   a. Sliding scale fees
   b. Cost
   c. Fixed costs
   d. Marginal cost

5. _____ is that which is owed; usually referencing assets owed, but the term can cover other obligations. In the case of assets, _____ is a means of using future purchasing power in the present before a summation has been earned. Some companies and corporations use _____ as a part of their overall corporate finance strategy.
   a. Cross-collateralization
   b. Partial Payment
   c. Credit cycle
   d. Debt

6. _____ is the capital that a business raises by taking out a loan. It is a loan made to a company that is normally repaid at some future date. _____ differs from equity or share capital because subscribers to _____ do not become part owners of the business, but are merely creditors, and the suppliers of _____ usually receive a contractually fixed annual percentage return on their loan, and this is known as the coupon rate.
   a. Risk-return spectrum
   b. Floating charge
   c. Financial assistance
   d. Debt Capital

7. In finance, a _____ (non-investment grade bond, speculative grade bond or junk bond) is a bond that is rated below investment grade at the time of purchase. These bonds have a higher risk of default or other adverse credit events, but typically pay higher yields than better quality bonds in order to make them attractive to investors.
   a. Sharpe ratio
   b. Volatility
   c. Private equity
   d. High yield bond

Chapter 16. Capital Structure: Limits to the Use of Debt

8. In finance, a _____ is a debt security, in which the authorized issuer owes the holders a debt and, depending on the terms of the _____, is obliged to pay interest (the coupon) and/or to repay the principal at a later date, termed maturity.

Thus a _____ is a loan: the issuer is the borrower, the _____ holder is the lender, and the coupon is the interest. _____s provide the borrower with external funds to finance long-term investments, or, in the case of government _____s, to finance current expenditure.

a. Convertible bond
b. Puttable bond
c. Catastrophe bonds
d. Bond

9. _____ are expenses that change in proportion to the activity of a business. In other words, _____ are the sum of marginal costs. It can also be considered normal costs. Along with fixed costs, _____ make up the two components of total cost. Direct Costs, however, are costs that can be associated with a particular cost object.

a. Cost accounting
b. Fixed costs
c. Transaction cost
d. Variable costs

10. _____ is the price at which an asset would trade in a competitive Walrasian auction setting. _____ is often used interchangeably with open _____, fair value or fair _____, although these terms have distinct definitions in different standards, and may differ in some circumstances.

International Valuation Standards defines _____ as 'the estimated amount for which a property should exchange on the date of valuation between a willing buyer and a willing seller in an arm'e;s-length transaction after proper marketing wherein the parties had each acted knowledgeably, prudently, and without compulsion.'

_____ is a concept distinct from market price, which is 'e;the price at which one can transact'e;, while _____ is 'e;the true underlying value'e; according to theoretical standards.

a. T-Model
b. Debt restructuring
c. Wrap account
d. Market value

11. _____ are costs that are not directly accountable to a particular function or product. _____ may be either fixed or variable. _____ include taxes, administration, personnel and security costs, and are also known as overhead.

a. Equivalent annual cost
b. AAB
c. A Random Walk Down Wall Street
d. Indirect costs

12. An _____ is an economic concept that relates to the cost incurred by an entity (such as organizations) associated with problems such as divergent management-shareholder objectives and information asymmetry. The costs consist of two main sources:

1. The costs inherently associated with using an agent (e.g., the risk that agents will use organizational resource for their own benefit) and
2. The costs of techniques used to mitigate the problems associated with using an agent (e.g., the costs of producing financial statements or the use of stock options to align executive interests to shareholder interests.)

Though effects of _____ are present in any agency relationship, the term is most used in business contexts.

Chapter 16. Capital Structure: Limits to the Use of Debt

The information asymmetry that exists between shareholders and the Chief Executive Officer is generally considered to be a classic example of a principal-agent problem. The agent (the manager) is working on behalf of the principal (the shareholders), who does not observe the actions of the agent.

a. ABN Amro
c. AAB
b. Agency cost
d. A Random Walk Down Wall Street

13. In finance, the _____ between two currencies specifies how much one currency is worth in terms of the other. For example an _____ of 102 Japanese yen to the United States dollar means that JPY 102 is worth the same as USD 1. The foreign exchange market is one of the largest markets in the world.

a. AAB
c. ABN Amro
b. A Random Walk Down Wall Street
d. Exchange rate

14. _____ is a form of risk that arises from the change in price of one currency against another. Whenever investors or companies have assets or business operations across national borders, they face _____ if their positions are not hedged.

- Transaction risk is the risk that exchange rates will change unfavourably over time. It can be hedged against using forward currency contracts;
- Translation risk is an accounting risk, proportional to the amount of assets held in foreign currencies. Changes in the exchange rate over time will render a report inaccurate, and so assets are usually balanced by borrowings in that currency.

The exchange risk associated with a foreign denominated instrument is a key element in foreign investment. This risk flows from differential monetary policy and growth in real productivity, which results in differential inflation rates.

a. Credit risk
c. Tracking error
b. Market risk
d. Currency risk

15. A _____, in its most general sense, is a solemn promise to engage in or refrain from a specified action.

More specifically, a _____, in contrast to a contract, is a one-way agreement whereby the _____er is the only party bound by the promise. A _____ may have conditions and prerequisites that qualify the undertaking, including the actions of second or third parties, but there is no inherent agreement by such other parties to fulfill those requirements.

a. Partnership
c. Federal Trade Commission Act
b. Clayton Antitrust Act
d. Covenant

16. _____ or amalgamation is the act of merging many things into one. In business, it often refers to the mergers or acquisitions of many smaller companies into much larger ones. The financial accounting term of _____ refers to the aggregated financial statements of a group company as consolidated account.

a. Consolidation
b. Cost of goods sold
c. Write-off
d. Retained earnings

17. A _____ is a contract entered into between which regulates the terms of a loan. they usually relate to loans of cash, but market specific contracts are also used to regulate securities lending.

They are usually in written form, but there is no legal reason why a _____ cannot be a purely oral contract (although in some countries this may be limited by the Statute of frauds or equivalent legislation).

a. Lien
b. Royalties
c. Loan agreement
d. Foreclosure

18. A _____ is a fungible, negotiable instrument representing financial value. They are broadly categorized into debt securities (such as banknotes, bonds and debentures), and equity securities; e.g., common stocks. The company or other entity issuing the _____ is called the issuer.
a. Tracking stock
b. Book entry
c. Securities lending
d. Security

19. _____ refers to a tax levied by various jurisdictions on the profits made by companies or associations. It is a tax on the value of the corporation's profits.

The measure of taxable profits varies from country to country.

a. Proxy fight
b. First-mover advantage
c. Corporate tax
d. Trade finance

20. A _____ is a situation that involves losing one quality or aspect of something in return for gaining another quality or aspect. It implies a decision to be made with full comprehension of both the upside and downside of a particular choice.

In economics the term is expressed as opportunity cost, referring the most preferred alternative given up.

a. Capital outflow
b. Total revenue
c. Break-even point
d. Trade-off

21. The _____ of Capital Structure refers to the idea that a company chooses how much debt finance and how much equity finance to use by balancing the costs and benefits. The classical version of the hypothesis goes back to Kraus and Litzenberger who considered a balance between the dead-weight costs of bankruptcy and the tax saving benefits of debt. Often agency costs are also included in the balance.
a. Financial distress
b. Trade-off theory
c. Firm commitment
d. Rights issue

22. _____ are securities that can be easily converted into cash. Such securities will generally have highly liquid markets allowing the security to be sold at a reasonable price very quickly. This is a usual feature in real estate .
a. Securities lending
b. Book entry
c. Tracking stock
d. Marketable

Chapter 16. Capital Structure: Limits to the Use of Debt

23. A _____ is a payment made by a corporation to its shareholder members. When a corporation earns a profit or surplus, that money can be put to two uses: it can either be re-invested in the business (called retained earnings), or it can be paid to the shareholders as a _____. Many corporations retain a portion of their earnings and pay the remainder as a _____.

   a. Special dividend
   b. Dividend yield
   c. Dividend puzzle
   d. Dividend

24. _____ is the provision of resources (such as granting a loan) by one party to another party where that second party does not reimburse the first party immediately, thereby generating a debt, and instead arranges either to repay or return those resources (or material(s) of equal value) at a later date. The first party is called a creditor, also known as a lender, while the second party is called a debtor, also known as a borrower.

   Movements of financial capital are normally dependent on either _____ or equity transfers.

   a. Comparable
   b. Warrant
   c. Clearing house
   d. Credit

25. In finance, the _____ is the minimum rate of return a firm must offer shareholders to compensate for waiting for their returns, and for bearing some risk.

   The _____ capital for a particular company is the rate of return on investment that is required by the company's ordinary shareholders. The return consists both of dividend and capital gains, e.g. increases in the share price.

   a. Net pay
   b. Round-tripping
   c. Residual value
   d. Cost of equity

26. In finance, _____ (or gearing) is borrowing money to supplement existing funds for investment in such a way that the potential positive or negative outcome is magnified and/or enhanced. It generally refers to using borrowed funds, or debt, so as to attempt to increase the returns to equity. Deleveraging is the action of reducing borrowings.

   a. Limited partnership
   b. Pension fund
   c. Leverage
   d. Financial endowment

27. A _____ occurs when a financial sponsor acquires a controlling interest in a company's equity and where a significant percentage of the purchase price is financed through leverage (borrowing.) The assets of the acquired company are used as collateral for the borrowed capital, sometimes with assets of the acquiring company. The bonds or other paper issued for _____s are commonly considered not to be investment grade because of the significant risks involved.

   a. Pension fund
   b. Limited partnership
   c. Leverage
   d. Leveraged buyout

28. In finance, a _____ or accounting ratio is a ratio of two selected numerical values taken from an enterprise's financial statements. There are many standard ratios used to try to evaluate the overall financial condition of a corporation or other organization. They may be used by managers within a firm, by current and potential shareholders (owners) of a firm, and by a firm's creditors. Security analysts use these to compare the strengths and weaknesses in various companies.

Chapter 16. Capital Structure: Limits to the Use of Debt

a. Return on capital employed
c. Sustainable growth rate
b. Price/cash flow ratio
d. Financial ratio

29. The institution most often referenced by the word '_____' is a public or publicly traded _____, the shares of which are traded on a public stock exchange (e.g., the New York Stock Exchange or Nasdaq in the United States) where shares of stock of _____s are bought and sold by and to the general public. Most of the largest businesses in the world are publicly traded _____s. However, the majority of _____s are said to be closely held, privately held or close _____s, meaning that no ready market exists for the trading of shares.

a. Protect
c. Depository Trust Company
b. Federal Home Loan Mortgage Corporation
d. Corporation

30. _____ is the planning process used to determine whether a firm's long term investments such as new machinery, replacement machinery, new plants, new products, and research development projects are worth pursuing. It is budget for major capital, or investment, expenditures.

Many formal methods are used in _____, including the techniques such as

- Net present value
- Profitability index
- Internal rate of return
- Modified Internal Rate of Return
- Equivalent annuity

These methods use the incremental cash flows from each potential investment, or project. Techniques based on accounting earnings and accounting rules are sometimes used - though economists consider this to be improper - such as the accounting rate of return, and 'return on investment.' Simplified and hybrid methods are used as well, such as payback period and discounted payback period.

a. Financial distress
c. Preferred stock
b. Shareholder value
d. Capital budgeting

Chapter 17. Valuation and Capital Budgeting for the Levered Firm

1. _____ is a business valuation method. _____ is the net present value of a project if financed solely by ownership equity plus the present value of all the benefits of financing. Usually, the main benefit is a tax shield resulted from tax deductibility of interest payments. Another one can be a subsidized borrowing.

   a. ABN Amro
   b. A Random Walk Down Wall Street
   c. Adjusted present value
   d. AAB

2. In business and accounting, _____s are everything of value that is owned by a person or company. The balance sheet of a firm records the monetary value of the _____s owned by the firm. The two major _____ classes are tangible _____s and intangible _____s.

   a. Asset
   b. Income
   c. Accounts payable
   d. EBITDA

3. The term _____ is often used to refer to the investment management of collective investments, (not necessarily) whilst the more generic fund management may refer to all forms of institutional investment as well as investment management for private investors. Investment managers who specialize in advisory or discretionary management on behalf of (normally wealthy) private investors may often refer to their services as wealth management or portfolio management often within the context of so-called 'private banking'.

   The provision of 'investment management services' includes elements of financial analysis, asset selection, stock selection, plan implementation and ongoing monitoring of investments.

   a. AAB
   b. ABN Amro
   c. A Random Walk Down Wall Street
   d. Asset management

4. _____ is the planning process used to determine whether a firm's long term investments such as new machinery, replacement machinery, new plants, new products, and research development projects are worth pursuing. It is budget for major capital, or investment, expenditures.

   Many formal methods are used in _____, including the techniques such as

   - Net present value
   - Profitability index
   - Internal rate of return
   - Modified Internal Rate of Return
   - Equivalent annuity

   These methods use the incremental cash flows from each potential investment, or project. Techniques based on accounting earnings and accounting rules are sometimes used - though economists consider this to be improper - such as the accounting rate of return, and 'return on investment.' Simplified and hybrid methods are used as well, such as payback period and discounted payback period.

   a. Financial distress
   b. Preferred stock
   c. Shareholder value
   d. Capital budgeting

5. _____ is the value on a given date of a future payment or series of future payments, discounted to reflect the time value of money and other factors such as investment risk. _____ calculations are widely used in business and economics to provide a means to compare cash flows at different times on a meaningful 'like to like' basis.

Chapter 17. Valuation and Capital Budgeting for the Levered Firm 109

The most commonly applied model of the time value of money is compound interest.

   a. Present value of benefits
   b. Negative gearing
   c. Net present value
   d. Present value

6. The phrase _____ refers to the aspect of corporate strategy, corporate finance and management dealing with the buying, selling and combining of different companies that can aid, finance, or help a growing company in a given industry grow rapidly without having to create another business entity.

An acquisition, also known as a takeover, is the buying of one company (the 'target') by another. An acquisition may be friendly or hostile.

   a. Mergers and acquisitions
   b. 4-4-5 Calendar
   c. 529 plan
   d. 7-Eleven

7. _____ are a class of computational algorithms that rely on repeated random sampling to compute their results. _____ are often used when simulating physical and mathematical systems. Because of their reliance on repeated computation and random or pseudo-random numbers, _____ are most suited to calculation by a computer.

_____ in finance are often used to calculate the value of companies, to evaluate investments in projects at corporate level or to evaluate financial derivatives. The method is intended for financial analysts who want to construct stochastic or probabilistic financial models as opposed to the traditional static and deterministic models.

   a. Monte Carlo methods
   b. Semivariance
   c. Sample size
   d. Correlation

8. In economics, business, and accounting, a _____ is the value of money that has been used up to produce something, and hence is not available for use anymore. In business, the _____ may be one of acquisition, in which case the amount of money expended to acquire it is counted as _____. In this case, money is the input that is gone in order to acquire the thing.

   a. Fixed costs
   b. Cost
   c. Sliding scale fees
   d. Marginal cost

9. The _____ is an expected return that the provider of capital plans to earn on their investment.

Capital (money) used for funding a business should earn returns for the capital providers who risk their capital. For an investment to be worthwhile, the expected return on capital must be greater than the _____.

   a. 4-4-5 Calendar
   b. Cost of capital
   c. Capital intensity
   d. Weighted average cost of capital

10. The _____ is the rate that a company is expected to pay to finance its assets. WACC is the minimum return that a company must earn on existing asset base to satisfy its creditors, owners, and other providers of capital.

Companies raise money from a number of sources: common equity, preferred equity, straight debt, convertible debt, exchangeable debt, warrants, options, pension liabilities, executive stock options, governmental subsidies, and so on.

a. Capital intensity
b. 4-4-5 Calendar
c. Cost of capital
d. Weighted average cost of capital

11. A '_____' is a 'Charge' that is paid to obtain the right to delay a payment. Essentially, the payer purchases the right to make a given payment in the future instead of in the Present. The '_____', or 'Charge' that must be paid to delay the payment, is simply the difference between what the payment amount would be if it were paid in the present and what the payment amount would be paid if it were paid in the future.

a. Risk modeling
b. Value at risk
c. Risk aversion
d. Discount

12. The _____ is an interest rate a central bank charges depository institutions that borrow reserves from it.

The term _____ has two meanings:

- the same as interest rate; the term 'discount' does not refer to the meaning of the word, but to the purpose of using the quantity, such as computations of present value, e.g. net present value / discounted cash flow

- the annual effective _____, which is the annual interest divided by the capital including that interest; this rate is lower than the interest rate; it corresponds to using the value after a year as the nominal value, and seeing the initial value as the nominal value minus a discount; it is used for Treasury Bills and similar financial instruments

The annual effective _____ is the annual interest divided by the capital including that interest, which is the interest rate divided by 100% plus the interest rate. It is the annual discount factor to be applied to the future cash flow, to find the discount, subtracted from a future value to find the value one year earlier.

For example, suppose there is a government bond that sells for $95 and pays $100 in a year's time.

a. Fisher equation
b. Black-Scholes
c. Discount rate
d. Stochastic volatility

13. _____, is when a company issues common stock or shares to the public for the first time. They are often issued by smaller, younger companies seeking capital to expand, but can also be done by large privately-owned companies looking to become publicly traded.

In an _____ the issuer may obtain the assistance of an underwriting firm, which helps it determine what type of security to issue (common or preferred), best offering price and time to bring it to market.

a. Initial public offering
b. Asian Financial Crisis
c. Insolvency
d. Interest

14. _____ refers to a tax levied by various jurisdictions on the profits made by companies or associations. It is a tax on the value of the corporation's profits.

The measure of taxable profits varies from country to country.

a. First-mover advantage
b. Proxy fight
c. Trade finance
d. Corporate tax

15. In finance, _____ (or gearing) is borrowing money to supplement existing funds for investment in such a way that the potential positive or negative outcome is magnified and/or enhanced. It generally refers to using borrowed funds, or debt, so as to attempt to increase the returns to equity. Deleveraging is the action of reducing borrowings.

a. Leverage
b. Financial endowment
c. Pension fund
d. Limited partnership

16. A _____ occurs when a financial sponsor acquires a controlling interest in a company's equity and where a significant percentage of the purchase price is financed through leverage (borrowing.) The assets of the acquired company are used as collateral for the borrowed capital, sometimes with assets of the acquiring company. The bonds or other paper issued for _____s are commonly considered not to be investment grade because of the significant risks involved.

a. Limited partnership
b. Pension fund
c. Leverage
d. Leveraged buyout

Chapter 18. Dividends and Other Payouts

1. In finance, a _____ is a type of bond that can be converted into shares of stock in the issuing company, usually at some pre-announced ratio. It is a hybrid security with debt- and equity-like features. Although it typically has a low coupon rate, the holder is compensated with the ability to convert the bond to common stock, usually at a substantial discount to the stock's market value.
   - a. Gilts
   - b. Convertible bond
   - c. Bond fund
   - d. Corporate bond

2. A _____ is a payment made by a corporation to its shareholder members. When a corporation earns a profit or surplus, that money can be put to two uses: it can either be re-invested in the business (called retained earnings), or it can be paid to the shareholders as a _____. Many corporations retain a portion of their earnings and pay the remainder as a _____.
   - a. Dividend yield
   - b. Special dividend
   - c. Dividend
   - d. Dividend puzzle

3. _____ is a payment of a dividend to stockholders that exceeds the company's retained earnings. Once retained earnings is depleted, capital accounts such as additional paid-in capital are decreased to make up for the remaining dividend to be paid to stockholders. When a _____ occurs, it is considered to be a return of investment instead of profits.
   - a. Liquidating dividend
   - b. Stock market index option
   - c. Revolving credit
   - d. Securities offering

4. _____ are those dividends paid out in form of additional stock shares of the issuing corporation or other corporation They are usually issued in proportion to shares owned (for example for every 100 shares of stock owned, 5% stock dividend will yield 5 extra shares). If this payment involves the issue of new shares, this is very similar to a stock split in that it increases the total number of shares while lowering the price of each share and does not change the market capitalization or the total value of the shares held
   - a. Database auditing
   - b. Time-based currency
   - c. The Hong Kong Securities Institute
   - d. Stock or scrip dividends

5. A _____ is the price of a single share of a no. of saleable stocks of the company. Once the stock is purchased, the owner becomes a shareholder of the company that issued the share.
   - a. Stock split
   - b. Share price
   - c. Whisper numbers
   - d. Trading curb

6. In finance, a _____ is a debt security, in which the authorized issuer owes the holders a debt and, depending on the terms of the _____, is obliged to pay interest (the coupon) and/or to repay the principal at a later date, termed maturity.

   Thus a _____ is a loan: the issuer is the borrower, the _____ holder is the lender, and the coupon is the interest. _____s provide the borrower with external funds to finance long-term investments, or, in the case of government _____s, to finance current expenditure.
   - a. Catastrophe bonds
   - b. Convertible bond
   - c. Puttable bond
   - d. Bond

7. The _____ on a company stock is the company's annual dividend payments divided by its market cap, or the dividend per share divided by the price per share. It is often expressed as a percentage.

Chapter 18. Dividends and Other Payouts

Dividend payments on preferred shares are stipulated by the prospectus.

a. Special dividend
b. Dividend reinvestment plan
c. Dividend imputation
d. Dividend yield

8. The key date to remember for dividend paying stocks is the _____. The _____ is different from the record date. The _____ is typically two trading days before the record date.

In order to receive the upcoming dividend payment payout, you must already own or you must purchase the stock prior to the _____. It is important to note that in most countries, when you buy or sell any stock, there is a three trading-day settlement period on your order.

a. Index number
b. Asian Financial Crisis
c. Insolvency
d. Ex-dividend date

9. In business and finance, a _____ (also referred to as equity _____) of stock means a _____ of ownership in a corporation (company.) In the plural, stocks is often used as a synonym for _____s especially in the United States, but it is less commonly used that way outside of North America.

In the United Kingdom, South Africa, and Australia, stock can also refer to completely different financial instruments such as government bonds or, less commonly, to all kinds of marketable securities.

a. Margin
b. Procter ' Gamble
c. Share
d. Bucket shop

10. In finance, the term _____ describes the amount in cash that returns to the owners of a security. Normally it does not include the price variations, at the difference of the total return. _____ applies to various stated rates of return on stocks (common and preferred, and convertible), fixed income instruments (bonds, notes, bills, strips, zero coupon), and some other investment type insurance products (e.g. annuities.)

a. Yield to maturity
b. Macaulay duration
c. 4-4-5 Calendar
d. Yield

11. _____ is the balance of the amounts of cash being received and paid by a business during a defined period of time, sometimes tied to a specific project. Measurement of _____ can be used

- to evaluate the state or performance of a business or project.
- to determine problems with liquidity. Being profitable does not necessarily mean being liquid. A company can fail because of a shortage of cash, even while profitable.
- to generate project rate of returns. The time of _____s into and out of projects are used as inputs to financial models such as internal rate of return, and net present value.
- to examine income or growth of a business when it is believed that accrual accounting concepts do not represent economic realities. Alternately, _____ can be used to 'validate' the net income generated by accrual accounting.

Chapter 18. Dividends and Other Payouts

_____ as a generic term may be used differently depending on context, and certain _____ definitions may be adapted by analysts and users for their own uses. Common terms include operating _____ and free _____.

_____s can be classified into:

1. Operational _____s: Cash received or expended as a result of the company's core business activities.
2. Investment _____s: Cash received or expended through capital expenditure, investments or acquisitions.
3. Financing _____s: Cash received or expended as a result of financial activities, such as interests and dividends.

All three together - the net _____ - are necessary to reconcile the beginning cash balance to the ending cash balance. Loan draw downs or equity injections, that is just shifting of capital but no expenditure as such, are not considered in the net _____.

a. Corporate finance
b. Shareholder value
c. Real option
d. Cash flow

12. In finance, _____ is the process of estimating the potential market value of a financial asset or liability. they can be done on assets (for example, investments in marketable securities such as stocks, options, business enterprises, or intangible assets such as patents and trademarks) or on liabilities (e.g., Bonds issued by a company.) _____s are required in many contexts including investment analysis, capital budgeting, merger and acquisition transactions, financial reporting, taxable events to determine the proper tax liability, and in litigation.

a. Margin
b. Valuation
c. Share
d. Procter ' Gamble

13. An _____ is any government regulation or law that encourages or discourages foreign investment in the local economy, e.g. currency exchange limits.

As globalization integrates the economies of neighboring and of trading states, they are typically forced to trade off such rules as part of a common tax, tariff and trade regime, e.g. as defined by a free trade pact. _____ favoring local investors over global ones is typically discouraged in such pacts, and the idea of a separate _____ rapidly becomes a fiction or fantasy, as real decisions reflect the real need for nations to compete for investment, even from their own local investors.

a. ABN Amro
b. AAB
c. A Random Walk Down Wall Street
d. Investment policy

14. _____ is a type of bond that allows the issuer of the bond to retain the privilege of redeeming the bond at some point before the bond reaches the date of maturity. In other words, on the call dates, the issuer has the right, but not the obligation, to buy back the bonds from the bond holders at the call price. Technically speaking, the bonds are not really bought and held by the issuer but cancelled immediately.

Chapter 18. Dividends and Other Payouts

a. Gilts
c. Coupon rate
b. Bond fund
d. Callable bond

15. _____ is a corporate finance term denoting a type of takeover bid. The _____ is a public, open offer or invitation (usually announced in a newspaper advertisement) by a prospective acquirer to all stockholders of a publicly traded corporation (the target corporation) to tender their stock for sale at a specified price during a specified time, subject to the tendering of a minimum and maximum number of shares. In a _____, the bidder contacts shareholders directly; the directors of the company may or may not have endorsed the _____ proposal.
   a. Cash is king
   c. Shareholder value
   b. Follow-on offering
   d. Tender offer

16. _____ refers to a business or organization attempting to acquire goods or services to accomplish the goals of the enterprise. Though there are several organizations that attempt to set standards in the _____ process, processes can vary greatly between organizations. Typically the word '_____' is not used interchangeably with the word 'procurement', since procurement typically includes Expediting, Supplier Quality, and Traffic and Logistics (T'L) in addition to _____.
   a. 4-4-5 Calendar
   c. 7-Eleven
   b. 529 plan
   d. Purchasing

17. A _____ is an agreement between a company and an employee (usually upper executive) specifying that the employee will receive certain significant benefits if employment is terminated. Sometimes, certain conditions, typically a change in company ownership, must be met, but often the cause of termination is unspecified. These benefits may include severance pay, cash bonuses, stock options, or other benefits.
   a. Golden parachute
   c. Market capitalization
   b. Trade finance
   d. Debtor-in-possession financing

18. The phrase _____ refers to the aspect of corporate strategy, corporate finance and management dealing with the buying, selling and combining of different companies that can aid, finance, or help a growing company in a given industry grow rapidly without having to create another business entity.

An acquisition, also known as a takeover, is the buying of one company (the 'target') by another. An acquisition may be friendly or hostile.

   a. 4-4-5 Calendar
   c. 7-Eleven
   b. 529 plan
   d. Mergers and acquisitions

19. In business and accounting, _____s are everything of value that is owned by a person or company. The balance sheet of a firm records the monetary value of the _____s owned by the firm. The two major _____ classes are tangible _____s and intangible _____s.
   a. Income
   c. Asset
   b. EBITDA
   d. Accounts payable

20. In business, _____ is income that a company receives from its normal business activities, usually from the sale of goods and services to customers. Some companies also receive _____ from interest, dividends or royalties paid to them by other companies. _____ may refer to business income in general, or it may refer to the amount, in a monetary unit, received during a period of time, as in 'Last year, Company X had _____ of $32 million.'

Chapter 18. Dividends and Other Payouts

In many countries, including the UK, _____ is referred to as turnover.

a. Revenue
c. Bottom line
b. Furniture, Fixtures and Equipment
d. Matching principle

21. A _____ is a fungible, negotiable instrument representing financial value. They are broadly categorized into debt securities (such as banknotes, bonds and debentures), and equity securities; e.g., common stocks. The company or other entity issuing the _____ is called the issuer.

a. Tracking stock
c. Securities lending
b. Book entry
d. Security

22. The U.S. _____ is an independent agency of the United States government which holds primary responsibility for enforcing the federal securities laws and regulating the securities industry, the nation's stock and options exchanges, and other electronic securities markets. The SEC was created by section 4 of the SEC of 1934 (now codified as 15 U.S.C. Â§ 78d and commonly referred to as the 1934 Act.)

a. 529 plan
c. Securities and Exchange Commission
b. 4-4-5 Calendar
d. 7-Eleven

23. _____ is a process by which a firm can obtain the use of a certain fixed assets for which it must pay a series of contractual, periodic, tax deductable payments. The lessee is the receiver of the services or the assets under the lease contract and the lessor is the owner of the assets. The relationship between the tenant and the landlord is called a tenancy, and can be for a fixed or an indefinite period of time (called the term of the lease).

a. Leasing
c. Quiet period
b. Foreign Corrupt Practices Act
d. Royalties

24. _____, refers to consumption opportunity gained by an entity within a specified time frame, which is generally expressed in monetary terms. However, for households and individuals, '_____ is the sum of all the wages, salaries, profits, interests payments, rents and other forms of earnings received... in a given period of time.' For firms, _____ generally refers to net-profit: what remains of revenue after expenses have been subtracted.

a. Accrual
c. OIBDA
b. Income
d. Annual report

25. An _____ is an economic concept that relates to the cost incurred by an entity (such as organizations) associated with problems such as divergent management-shareholder objectives and information asymmetry. The costs consist of two main sources:

1. The costs inherently associated with using an agent (e.g., the risk that agents will use organizational resource for their own benefit) and
2. The costs of techniques used to mitigate the problems associated with using an agent (e.g., the costs of producing financial statements or the use of stock options to align executive interests to shareholder interests.)

Though effects of _____ are present in any agency relationship, the term is most used in business contexts.

The information asymmetry that exists between shareholders and the Chief Executive Officer is generally considered to be a classic example of a principal-agent problem. The agent (the manager) is working on behalf of the principal (the shareholders), who does not observe the actions of the agent.

 a. ABN Amro   b. AAB
 c. A Random Walk Down Wall Street   d. Agency cost

26. In economics, business, and accounting, a _____ is the value of money that has been used up to produce something, and hence is not available for use anymore. In business, the _____ may be one of acquisition, in which case the amount of money expended to acquire it is counted as _____. In this case, money is the input that is gone in order to acquire the thing.
 a. Sliding scale fees   b. Marginal cost
 c. Cost   d. Fixed costs

27. _____ is the provision of resources (such as granting a loan) by one party to another party where that second party does not reimburse the first party immediately, thereby generating a debt, and instead arranges either to repay or return those resources (or material(s) of equal value) at a later date. The first party is called a creditor, also known as a lender, while the second party is called a debtor, also known as a borrower.

Movements of financial capital are normally dependent on either _____ or equity transfers.

 a. Comparable   b. Credit
 c. Warrant   d. Clearing house

28. _____ represents the impact on the stock price that investors would cause in reaction to a change in policy of a company.
 a. Trade date   b. Clientele effect
 c. Volatility clustering   d. Bonus share

29. In statistics and image processing, to smooth a data set is to create an approximating function that attempts to capture important patterns in the data, while leaving out noise or other fine-scale structures/rapid phenomena. Many different algorithms are used in _____. One of the most common algorithms is the 'moving average', often used to try to capture important trends in repeated statistical surveys.
 a. Smoothing   b. 529 plan
 c. 7-Eleven   d. 4-4-5 Calendar

30. A _____ or stock divide increases or decreases the number of shares in a public company. The price is adjusted such that the before and after market capitalization of the company remains the same and dilution does not occur. Options and warrants are included.
 a. Stock split   b. Stop price
 c. Contract for difference   d. Stop order

31. In finance, a _____ is a security that entitles the holder to buy stock of the company that issued it at a specified price, which is usually higher than the stock price at time of issue.

Chapter 18. Dividends and Other Payouts

_____s are frequently attached to bonds or preferred stock as a sweetener, allowing the issuer to pay lower interest rates or dividends. They can be used to enhance the yield of the bond, and make them more attractive to potential buyers.

a. Clearing house
b. Warrant
c. Credit
d. Clearing

32. On a stock exchange, a _____ is the opposite of a stock split, i.e. a stock merge - a reduction in the number of shares and an accompanying increase in the share price. The ratio is also reversed: 1-for-2, 1-for-3 and so on.

There is a stigma attached to doing this so it is not initiated without very good reason.

a. Conglomerate merger
b. Correlation trading
c. Trade date
d. Reverse stock split

Chapter 19. Issuing Securities to the Public

1. _____, is when a company issues common stock or shares to the public for the first time. They are often issued by smaller, younger companies seeking capital to expand, but can also be done by large privately-owned companies looking to become publicly traded.

In an _____ the issuer may obtain the assistance of an underwriting firm, which helps it determine what type of security to issue (common or preferred), best offering price and time to bring it to market.

   a. Initial public offering
   b. Insolvency
   c. Interest
   d. Asian Financial Crisis

2. In finance, _____ is an asset class consisting of equity securities in operating companies that are not publicly traded on a stock exchange. Investments in _____ most often involve either an investment of capital into an operating company or the acquisition of an operating company. Capital for _____ is raised primarily from institutional investors.
   a. Currency swap
   b. Pecking order theory
   c. Private equity
   d. Stock valuation

3. A _____ is a fungible, negotiable instrument representing financial value. They are broadly categorized into debt securities (such as banknotes, bonds and debentures), and equity securities; e.g., common stocks. The company or other entity issuing the _____ is called the issuer.
   a. Securities lending
   b. Book entry
   c. Security
   d. Tracking stock

4. The _____ of 1934 is a law governing the secondary trading of securities (stocks, bonds, and debentures) in the United States of America. The Act, 48 Stat. 881 (enacted June 6, 1934), codified at 15 U.S.C. § 78a et seq., was a sweeping piece of legislation. The Act and related statutes form the basis of regulation of the financial markets and their participants in the United States.
   a. 7-Eleven
   b. 529 plan
   c. 4-4-5 Calendar
   d. Securities Exchange Act

5. The U.S. _____ is an independent agency of the United States government which holds primary responsibility for enforcing the federal securities laws and regulating the securities industry, the nation's stock and options exchanges, and other electronic securities markets. The SEC was created by section 4 of the SEC of 1934 (now codified as 15 U.S.C. § 78d and commonly referred to as the 1934 Act.)
   a. 4-4-5 Calendar
   b. 7-Eleven
   c. 529 plan
   d. Securities and Exchange Commission

6. In finance, a _____ is a debt security, in which the authorized issuer owes the holders a debt and, depending on the terms of the _____, is obliged to pay interest (the coupon) and/or to repay the principal at a later date, termed maturity.

Thus a _____ is a loan: the issuer is the borrower, the _____ holder is the lender, and the coupon is the interest. _____s provide the borrower with external funds to finance long-term investments, or, in the case of government _____s, to finance current expenditure.

   a. Catastrophe bonds
   b. Convertible bond
   c. Puttable bond
   d. Bond

Chapter 19. Issuing Securities to the Public

7. A _____ is a private or public market for the trading of company stock and derivatives of company stock at an agreed price; these are securities listed on a stock exchange as well as those only traded privately.

The size of the world _____ is estimated at about $36.6 trillion US at the beginning of October 2008 . The world derivatives market has been estimated at about $480 trillion face or nominal value, 12 times the size of the entire world economy.

a. Stock market
b. Anton Gelonkin
c. Adolph Coors
d. Andrew Tobias

8. The term _____, also known as a waiting period is a period extended from the time a company files a registration statement with the SEC until SEC staff declared the registration statement effective. During that period, the federal securities laws limited what information a company and related parties can release to the public.'

Under the rules of the Securities Act of 1933, as modified June 29, 2005, electronic communications, including electronic road shows and information located on or hyperlinked to an issuer's website are also governed. The rules changes of June 29, 2005 also included various changes which 'liberalize permitted offering activity and communications to allow more information' for certain qualifying organizations.

a. Lien
b. Duty of loyalty
c. Quiet period
d. Leasing

9. The phrase _____ refers to the aspect of corporate strategy, corporate finance and management dealing with the buying, selling and combining of different companies that can aid, finance, or help a growing company in a given industry grow rapidly without having to create another business entity.

An acquisition, also known as a takeover, is the buying of one company (the 'target') by another. An acquisition may be friendly or hostile.

a. 7-Eleven
b. 529 plan
c. 4-4-5 Calendar
d. Mergers and acquisitions

10. A _____, also known by its legal title as an 'over-allotment option' (the only way it can be referred to in a prospectus), gives underwriters the right to sell additional shares in a registered securities offering if demand for the securities is in excess of the original amount offered. The _____ can vary in size up to 15% of the original number of shares offered.

The _____ option is popular because it is the only SEC-permitted means for an underwriter to stabilize the price of a new issue post-pricing.

a. Green Shoe
b. Business valuation standards
c. Supply and demand
d. Foreign Language and Area Studies

11. Under a secondary market offering or seasoned equity offering of shares to raise money, a company can opt for a _____ to raise capital. The _____ is a special form of shelf offering or shelf registration. With the issued rights, existing shareholders have the privilege to buy a specified number of new shares from the firm at a specified price within a specified time.
    a. Corporate finance
    b. Rights issue
    c. Market for corporate control
    d. Tender offer

12. A _____ is a payment made by a corporation to its shareholder members. When a corporation earns a profit or surplus, that money can be put to two uses: it can either be re-invested in the business (called retained earnings), or it can be paid to the shareholders as a _____. Many corporations retain a portion of their earnings and pay the remainder as a _____.
    a. Dividend
    b. Dividend puzzle
    c. Dividend yield
    d. Special dividend

13. In financial accounting, _____s are precautions for which the amount or probability of occurrence are not known. Typical examples are _____s for warranty costs and _____ for taxes the term reserve is used instead of term _____; such a use, however, is inconsistent with the terminology suggested by International Accounting Standards Board.
    a. Momentum Accounting and Triple-Entry Bookkeeping
    b. Money measurement concept
    c. Petty cash
    d. Provision

14. In the _____ contract the underwriter agrees to sell as many shares as possible at the agreed-upon price.

Under the all-or-none contract the underwriter agrees either to sell the entire offering or to cancel the deal.

Stand-by underwriting, also known as strict underwriting or old-fashioned underwriting is a form of stock insurance: the issuer contracts the underwriter for the latter to purchase the shares the issuer failed to sell under stockholders' subscription and applications.

   a. Book building
   b. Real option
   c. Best efforts
   d. Follow-on offering

15. A '_____' is a 'Charge' that is paid to obtain the right to delay a payment. Essentially, the payer purchases the right to make a given payment in the future instead of in the Present. The '_____', or 'Charge' that must be paid to delay the payment, is simply the difference between what the payment amount would be if it were paid in the present and what the payment amount would be paid if it were paid in the future.
    a. Risk modeling
    b. Value at risk
    c. Discount
    d. Risk aversion

16. A _____ is a type of auction where the auctioneer begins with a high asking price which is lowered until some participant is willing to accept the auctioneer's price, or a predetermined reserve price (the seller's minimum acceptable price) is reached. The winning participant pays the last announced price. This is also known as a 'clock auction' or an open-outcry descending-price auction.

a. 529 plan
b. 4-4-5 Calendar
c. 7-Eleven
d. Dutch auction

17. In the _____ contract the underwriter guarantees the sale of the issued stock at the agreed-upon price. For the issuer, it is the safest but the most expensive type of the contracts, since the underwriter takes the risk of sale.

In the best efforts contract the underwriter agrees to sell as many shares as possible at the agreed-upon price.

a. Firm commitment
b. Participating preferred stock
c. Rights issue
d. Special purpose entity

18. A _____ or bank is a financial institution whose primary activity is to act as a payment agent for customers and to borrow and lend money.

The first modern bank was founded in Italy in Genoa in 1406, its name was Banco di San Giorgio (Bank of St. George.)

Many other financial activities were added over time.

a. Bought deal
b. Black Sea Trade and Development Bank
c. 4-4-5 Calendar
d. Banker

19. The _____ is the financial market where previously issued securities and financial instruments such as stock, bonds, options, and futures are bought and sold. The term '_____' is also used refer to the market for any used goods or assets, or an alternative use for an existing product or asset where the customer base is the second market

With primary issuances of securities or financial instruments, or the primary market, investors purchase these securities directly from issuers such as corporations issuing shares in an IPO or private placement, or directly from the federal government in the case of treasuries.

a. Secondary market
b. Financial market
c. Delta neutral
d. Performance attribution

20. In economics, business, and accounting, a _____ is the value of money that has been used up to produce something, and hence is not available for use anymore. In business, the _____ may be one of acquisition, in which case the amount of money expended to acquire it is counted as _____. In this case, money is the input that is gone in order to acquire the thing.

a. Marginal cost
b. Cost
c. Sliding scale fees
d. Fixed costs

21. _____ is the provision of resources (such as granting a loan) by one party to another party where that second party does not reimburse the first party immediately, thereby generating a debt, and instead arranges either to repay or return those resources (or material(s) of equal value) at a later date. The first party is called a creditor, also known as a lender, while the second party is called a debtor, also known as a borrower.

Movements of financial capital are normally dependent on either _____ or equity transfers.

Chapter 19. Issuing Securities to the Public

a. Clearing house
b. Credit
c. Warrant
d. Comparable

22. A _____ is a right to acquire certain property in preference to any other person. It usually refers to property newly coming into existence. A right to acquire existing property in preference to any other person is usually referred to as a right of first refusal.

In practice, the most common form of _____ is the right of existing shareholders to acquire newly issued shares issued by a company in a rights issue, a usually but not always public offering.

a. Fraud deterrence
b. Court of Audit of Belgium
c. Down payment
d. Pre-emption right

23. The term _____ refers to three closely related concepts:

- The _____ model is a mathematical model of the market for an equity, in which the equity's price is a stochastic process.
- The _____ PDE is a partial differential equation which (in the model) must be satisfied by the price of a derivative on the equity.
- The _____ formula is the result obtained by solving the _____ PDE for a European call option.

Fischer Black and Myron Scholes first articulated the _____ formula in their 1973 paper, 'The Pricing of Options and Corporate Liabilities.' The foundation for their research relied on work developed by scholars such as Jack L. Treynor, Paul Samuelson, A. James Boness, Sheen T. Kassouf, and Edward O. Thorp. The fundamental insight of _____ is that the option is implicitly priced if the stock is traded.

Robert C. Merton was the first to publish a paper expanding the mathematical understanding of the options pricing model and coined the term '_____' options pricing model.

a. Perpetuity
b. Stochastic volatility
c. Modified Internal Rate of Return
d. Black-Scholes

24. In corporate finance, _____ analysis applies put option and call option valuation techniques to capital budgeting decisions. A _____ itself, is the right--but not the obligation--to undertake some business decision; typically the option to make, or abandon, a capital investment. For example, the opportunity to invest in the expansion of a firm's factory, or alternatively to sell the factory, is a _____.

a. Book building
b. Capital budgeting
c. Cash flow
d. Real option

25. In business and finance, a _____ (also referred to as equity _____) of stock means a _____ of ownership in a corporation (company.) In the plural, stocks is often used as a synonym for _____s especially in the United States, but it is less commonly used that way outside of North America.

In the United Kingdom, South Africa, and Australia, stock can also refer to completely different financial instruments such as government bonds or, less commonly, to all kinds of marketable securities.

a. Procter ' Gamble
c. Bucket shop
b. Margin
d. Share

26. An _____ is a contract written by a seller that conveys to the buyer the right -- but not the obligation -- to buy (in the case of a call _____) or to sell (in the case of a put _____) a particular asset, such as a piece of property such as, among others, a futures contract. In return for granting the _____, the seller collects a payment (the premium) from the buyer.

For example, buying a call _____ provides the right to buy a specified quantity of a security at a set strike price at some time on or before expiration, while buying a put _____ provides the right to sell.

a. Amortization
c. Annuity
b. AT'T Mobility LLC
d. Option

27. In finance, a _____ is a security that entitles the holder to buy stock of the company that issued it at a specified price, which is usually higher than the stock price at time of issue.

_____s are frequently attached to bonds or preferred stock as a sweetener, allowing the issuer to pay lower interest rates or dividends. They can be used to enhance the yield of the bond, and make them more attractive to potential buyers.

a. Credit
c. Clearing house
b. Clearing
d. Warrant

28. In financial accounting, a _____ or statement of financial position is a summary of a person's or organization's balances. Assets, liabilities and ownership equity are listed as of a specific date, such as the end of its financial year. A _____ is often described as a snapshot of a company's financial condition.

a. Balance sheet
c. Financial statements
b. Statement of retained earnings
d. Statement on Auditing Standards No. 70: Service Organizations

29. _____ is the standard framework of guidelines for financial accounting used in the United States of America. It includes the standards, conventions, and rules accountants follow in recording and summarizing transactions, and in the preparation of financial statements. _____ are now issued by the Financial Accounting Standards Board (FASB).

a. Revenue
c. Net income
b. Generally Accepted Accounting Principles
d. Depreciation

30. _____ is a measure of the ability of a debtor to pay their debts as and when they fall due. It is usually expressed as a ratio or a percentage of current liabilities.

For a corporation with a published balance sheet there are various ratios used to calculate a measure of liquidity.

a. Operating profit margin
c. Operating leverage
b. Invested capital
d. Accounting liquidity

31. A _____ is the price of a single share of a no. of saleable stocks of the company. Once the stock is purchased, the owner becomes a shareholder of the company that issued the share.
   a. Share price
   b. Whisper numbers
   c. Stock split
   d. Trading curb

32. In finance, a _____ is a type of bond that can be converted into shares of stock in the issuing company, usually at some pre-announced ratio. It is a hybrid security with debt- and equity-like features. Although it typically has a low coupon rate, the holder is compensated with the ability to convert the bond to common stock, usually at a substantial discount to the stock's market value.
   a. Gilts
   b. Bond fund
   c. Corporate bond
   d. Convertible bond

33. A bond is considered _____ if its credit rating is BBB- or higher by Standard and Poor's or Baa3 or higher by Moody's or BBB(low) or higher by DBRS. Generally they are bonds that are judged by the rating agency as likely enough to meet payment obligations that banks are allowed to invest in them.

Ratings play a critical role in determining how much companies and other entities that issue debt, including sovereign governments, have to pay to access credit markets, i.e., the amount of interest they pay on their issued debt.

   a. A Random Walk Down Wall Street
   b. ABN Amro
   c. AAB
   d. Investment grade

34. _____ is an arrangement with the U.S. Securities and Exchange Commission that allows a single registration document to be filed that permits the issuance of multiple securities.

_____ is a registration of a new issue which can be prepared up to two years in advance, so that the issue can be offered quickly as soon as funds are needed or market conditions are favorable.

For example, current market conditions in the housing market are not favorable for a specific firm to issue a public offering.

   a. Black Sea Trade and Development Bank
   b. Bought deal
   c. 4-4-5 Calendar
   d. Shelf registration

35. _____, adopted pursuant to the U.S. Securities Act of 1933, as amended (the 'Securities Act') provides a safe harbor from the registration requirements of the Securities Act of 1933 for certain private resales of restricted securities to QIBs (qualified institutional buyers), which generally are large institutional investors with over $100 million in investable assets. When a broker or dealer is selling securities in reliance on _____, it is subject to the condition that it may not make offers to persons other than those it reasonably believes to be QIBs.

Since its adoption, _____ has greatly increased the liquidity of the securities affected.

   a. SIPC
   b. Prudent man rule
   c. Rule 144A
   d. Securities Investor Protection Corporation

Chapter 19. Issuing Securities to the Public

36. _____ is a type of private equity capital typically provided to early-stage, high-potential, growth companies in the interest of generating a return through an eventual realization event such as an IPO or trade sale of the company. _____ investments are generally made as cash in exchange for shares in the invested company. It is typical for _____ investors to identify and back companies in high technology industries such as biotechnology and ICT.
   a. Probability distribution
   b. Tail risk
   c. Treasury Inflation-Protected Securities
   d. Venture capital

37. In the United States, a _____ is an offering of securities that are not registered with the Securities and Exchange Commission (SEC.) Such offerings exploit an exemption offered by the Securities Act of 1933 that comes with several restrictions, including a prohibition against general solicitation. This exemption allows companies to avoid quarterly reporting requirements and many of the legal liabilities associated with the Sarbanes-Oxley Act.
   a. 4-4-5 Calendar
   b. 7-Eleven
   c. Private placement
   d. 529 plan

38. The phrase _____ according to the Organization for Economic Co-operation and Development, refers to 'creative work undertaken on a systematic basis in order to increase the stock of knowledge, including knowledge of (hu)man, culture and society, and the use of this stock of knowledge to devise new applications'.

   New product design and development is more than often a crucial factor in the survival of a company. In an industry that is fast changing, firms must continually revise their design and range of products. This is necessary due to continuous technology change and development as well as other competitors and the changing preference of customers.

   a. 4-4-5 Calendar
   b. Research and Development
   c. 529 plan
   d. 7-Eleven

39. The institution most often referenced by the word '_____' is a public or publicly traded _____, the shares of which are traded on a public stock exchange (e.g., the New York Stock Exchange or Nasdaq in the United States) where shares of stock of _____s are bought and sold by and to the general public. Most of the largest businesses in the world are publicly traded _____s. However, the majority of _____s are said to be closely held, privately held or close _____s, meaning that no ready market exists for the trading of shares.
   a. Depository Trust Company
   b. Corporation
   c. Federal Home Loan Mortgage Corporation
   d. Protect

40. _____ or financing is to provide capital (funds), which means money for a project, a person, a business or any other private or public institutions.

   Those funds can be allocated for either short term or long term purposes. The health fund is a new way of _____ private healthcare centers.

   a. Funding
   b. Proxy fight
   c. Product life cycle
   d. Synthetic CDO

41. A _____ is a type of business entity in which partners (owners) share with each other the profits or losses of the business undertaking in which all have invested. _____s are often favored over corporations for taxation purposes, as the _____ structure does not generally incur a tax on profits before it is distributed to the partners (i.e. there is no dividend tax levied.) However, depending on the _____ structure and the jurisdiction in which it operates, owners of a _____ may be exposed to greater personal liability than they would as shareholders of a corporation.
   a. National Securities Markets Improvement Act of 1996   b. Clayton Antitrust Act
   c. Partnership   d. Fiduciary

42. _____, in bookkeeping, refers to assets, liabilities, income, and expenses recorded on individual pages of the so called book of final entry or ledger. Changes in _____ value are made by chronologically posting debit (DR) and credit (CR) entries to its page. Examples of _____s are cash, _____s receivable, mortgages, loans, land and buildings, common stock, sales, services provided, wages, and payroll overhead.
   a. Option   b. Accretion
   c. Alpha   d. Account

Chapter 20. Long-Term Debt

1. In finance, a _____ is a debt security, in which the authorized issuer owes the holders a debt and, depending on the terms of the _____, is obliged to pay interest (the coupon) and/or to repay the principal at a later date, termed maturity.

   Thus a _____ is a loan: the issuer is the borrower, the _____ holder is the lender, and the coupon is the interest. _____s provide the borrower with external funds to finance long-term investments, or, in the case of government _____s, to finance current expenditure.

   a. Catastrophe bonds
   b. Puttable bond
   c. Convertible bond
   d. Bond

2. In economics, the concept of the _____ refers to the decision-making time frame of a firm in which at least one factor of production is fixed. Costs which are fixed in the _____ have no impact on a firms decisions. For example a firm can raise output by increasing the amount of labour through overtime.

   a. 4-4-5 Calendar
   b. Long-run
   c. 529 plan
   d. Short-run

3. _____ is that which is owed; usually referencing assets owed, but the term can cover other obligations. In the case of assets, _____ is a means of using future purchasing power in the present before a summation has been earned. Some companies and corporations use _____ as a part of their overall corporate finance strategy.

   a. Debt
   b. Partial Payment
   c. Credit cycle
   d. Cross-collateralization

4. _____ is a life of security. It may also refer to the final payment date of a loan or other financial instrument, at which point all remaining interest and principal is due to be paid.

   1, 3, 6 months _____ band can be calculated by using 30-day per month periods.

   a. Replacement cost
   b. Maturity
   c. Primary market
   d. False billing

5. _____ (also trust indenture or deed of trust) is a legal document issued to lenders and describes key terms such as the interest rate, maturity date, convertibility, pledge, promises, representations, covenants, and other terms of the bond offering. When the Offering Memorandum is prepared in advance of marketing a Bond, the indenture will typically be summarised in the 'Description of Notes' section.

   a. Court of Audit of Belgium
   b. McFadden Act
   c. Fair Labor Standards Act
   d. Bond indenture

6. A _____ is a corporation, especially a commercial bank, organized to perform the fiduciary functions of trusts and agencies. It is normally owned by one of three types of structures: an independent partnership, a bank, or a law firm, each of which specializes in being a trustee of various kinds of trusts and in managing estates.

   a. Trust company
   b. Savings and loan association
   c. Person-to-person lending
   d. Mutual fund

Chapter 20. Long-Term Debt

7. The institution most often referenced by the word '_____' is a public or publicly traded _____, the shares of which are traded on a public stock exchange (e.g., the New York Stock Exchange or Nasdaq in the United States) where shares of stock of _____s are bought and sold by and to the general public. Most of the largest businesses in the world are publicly traded _____s. However, the majority of _____s are said to be closely held, privately held or close _____s, meaning that no ready market exists for the trading of shares.
   a. Federal Home Loan Mortgage Corporation
   b. Corporation
   c. Protect
   d. Depository Trust Company

8. The coupon or _____ of a bond is the amount of interest paid per year expressed as a percentage of the face value of the bond.

For example if you hold $10,000 nominal of a bond described as a 4.5% loan stock, you will receive $450 in interest each year (probably in two installments of $225 each.)

Not all bonds have coupons.

   a. Revenue bonds
   b. Coupon rate
   c. Puttable bond
   d. Zero-coupon bond

9. In economic models, the _____ time frame assumes no fixed factors of production. Firms can enter or leave the marketplace, and the cost (and availability) of land, labor, raw materials, and capital goods can be assumed to vary. In contrast, in the short-run time frame, certain factors are assumed to be fixed, because there is not sufficient time for them to change.
   a. Long-run
   b. Short-run
   c. 529 plan
   d. 4-4-5 Calendar

10. _____, in finance and accounting, means stated value or face value. From this comes the expressions at par (at the _____), over par (over _____) and under par (under _____.)

The term '_____' has several meanings depending on context and geography.

   a. Global Squeeze
   b. FIDC
   c. Sinking fund
   d. Par value

11. A _____ is a document that indicates that the bearer of the document has title to property, such as shares or bonds. They differ from normal registered instruments, in that no records are kept of who owns the underlying property, or of the transactions involving transfer of ownership. Whoever physically holds the bearer bond papers owns the property.
   a. Securities lending
   b. Marketable
   c. Book entry
   d. Bearer instrument

12. In finance, the _____ is the price of a bond excluding any interest that has accrued since issue or the most recent coupon payment. This is to be compared with the dirty price, which is the price of a bond including the accrued interest.

When bond prices are quoted on a Bloomberg Terminal or Reuters they are quoted using the _____.

a. Bowie bonds
b. Gilts
c. Clean price
d. Bond valuation

13. In lending agreements, _____ is a borrower's pledge of specific property to a lender, to secure repayment of a loan. The _____ serves as protection for a lender against a borrower's risk of default - that is, a borrower failing to pay the principal and interest under the terms of a loan obligation. If a borrower does default on a loan (due to insolvency or other event), that borrower forfeits (gives up) the property pledged as _____ *ollateral* - and the lender then becomes the owner of the _____.

a. Nominal value
b. Refinancing risk
c. Future-oriented
d. Collateral

14. The _____ of a bond represents the value of a bond, exclusive of any commissions or fees. The _____ is also called the 'full price.'

Bonds, as well as a variety of other fixed income securities, provide for coupon payments to be made to bond holders on a fixed schedule. The _____ of a bond will decrease on the days coupons are paid, resulting in a saw-tooth pattern for the bond value.

a. Serial bond
b. Premium bond
c. Collateralized debt obligations
d. Dirty price

15. A _____ is a fungible, negotiable instrument representing financial value. They are broadly categorized into debt securities (such as banknotes, bonds and debentures), and equity securities; e.g., common stocks. The company or other entity issuing the _____ is called the issuer.

a. Book entry
b. Tracking stock
c. Securities lending
d. Security

16. A _____ is defined as a certificate of agreement of loans which is given under the company's stamp and carries an undertaking that the _____ holder will get a fixed return (fixed on the basis of interest rates) and the principal amount whenever the _____ matures.

In finance, a _____ is a long-term debt instrument used by governments and large companies to obtain funds. It is defined as 'a debt secured only by the debtor's earning power, not by a lien on any specific asset.' It is similar to a bond except the securitization conditions are different.

a. Collection agency
b. Debenture
c. Partial Payment
d. Collateral Management

17. A _____ is a fund established by a government agency or business for the purpose of reducing debt.

The _____ was first used in Great Britain in the 18th century to reduce national debt. While used by Robert Walpole in 1716 and effectively in the 1720s and early 1730s, it originated in the commercial tax syndicates of the Italian peninsula of the 14th century to retire redeemable public debt of those cities.

Chapter 20. Long-Term Debt

a. Security interest
c. Modern portfolio theory
b. Debtor
d. Sinking fund

18. A _____, in its most general sense, is a solemn promise to engage in or refrain from a specified action.

More specifically, a _____, in contrast to a contract, is a one-way agreement whereby the _____er is the only party bound by the promise. A _____ may have conditions and prerequisites that qualify the undertaking, including the actions of second or third parties, but there is no inherent agreement by such other parties to fulfill those requirements.

a. Partnership
c. Federal Trade Commission Act
b. Clayton Antitrust Act
d. Covenant

19. The phrase _____ or bullet payment refers to one of two ways for repaying a loan; the other type is called amortizing payment or Amortization (business).

With a balloon loan, a _____ is paid back when the loan comes to its contractual maturity, e.g. reaches the deadline set to repayment at the time the loan was granted, representing the full loan amount (also called principal.) Periodic interest payments are generally made throughout the life of the loan.

a. Present value of costs
c. Future-oriented
b. Refinancing risk
d. Balloon payment

20. _____ is a type of bond that allows the issuer of the bond to retain the privilege of redeeming the bond at some point before the bond reaches the date of maturity. In other words, on the call dates, the issuer has the right, but not the obligation, to buy back the bonds from the bond holders at the call price. Technically speaking, the bonds are not really bought and held by the issuer but cancelled immediately.

a. Gilts
c. Bond fund
b. Callable bond
d. Coupon rate

21. _____, in accrual accounting, is any account where the asset or liability is not realized until a future date, e.g. annuities, charges, taxes, income, etc. The _____ item may be carried, dependent on type of deferral, as either an asset or liability. See also: accrual

_____ is also used in the university admissions process. It is the action by which a school rejects a student for early admission but still opts to review that student in the general admissions pool.

a. Net profit
c. Revenue
b. Current asset
d. Deferred

22. _____ mature in one year or less. Like zero-coupon bonds, they do not pay interest prior to maturity; instead they are sold at a discount of the par value to create a positive yield to maturity. Many regard _____ as the least risky investment available to U.S. investors.

a. 4-4-5 Calendar
c. Treasury Inflation Protected Securities
b. Treasury securities
d. Treasury bills

23. In financial accounting, _____s are precautions for which the amount or probability of occurrence are not known. Typical examples are _____s for warranty costs and _____ for taxes the term reserve is used instead of term _____; such a use, however, is inconsistent with the terminology suggested by International Accounting Standards Board.
   a. Provision
   b. Momentum Accounting and Triple-Entry Bookkeeping
   c. Petty cash
   d. Money measurement concept

24. _____ is a fee paid on borrowed assets. It is the price paid for the use of borrowed money, or, money earned by deposited funds. Assets that are sometimes lent with _____ include money, shares, consumer goods through hire purchase, major assets such as aircraft, and even entire factories in finance lease arrangements.
   a. A Random Walk Down Wall Street
   b. Insolvency
   c. AAB
   d. Interest

25. An _____ is the price a borrower pays for the use of money they do not own, and the return a lender receives for deferring the use of funds, by lending it to the borrower. _____s are normally expressed as a percentage rate over the period of one year.

    _____s targets are also a vital tool of monetary policy and are used to control variables like investment, inflation, and unemployment.

   a. AAB
   b. ABN Amro
   c. A Random Walk Down Wall Street
   d. Interest rate

26. _____ occurs when an entity that has issued callable bonds calls those debt securities from the debt holders with the express purpose of reissuing new debt at a lower coupon rate. In essence, the issue of new, lower-interest debt allows the company to prematurely refund the older, higher-interest debt.

    On the contrary, NonRefundable Bonds may be callable but they cannot be re-issued with a lower coupon rate.

   a. Market neutral
   b. No-arbitrage bounds
   c. Systematic risk
   d. Refunding

27. The terms _____, nominal _____, and effective _____ describe the interest rate for a whole year (annualized), rather than just a monthly fee/rate, as applied on a loan, mortgage, credit card, etc. Those terms have formal, legal definitions in some countries or legal jurisdictions, but in general:

   - The nominal _____ is the simple-interest rate (for a year.)
   - The effective _____ is the fee+compound interest rate (calculated across a year.)

Chapter 20. Long-Term Debt

The nominal _____ is calculated as: the rate, for a payment period, multiplied by the number of payment periods in a year. However, the exact legal definition of 'effective _____' can vary greatly in each jurisdiction, depending on the type of fees included, such as participation fees, loan origination fees, monthly service charges, or late fees. The effective _____ has been called the 'mathematically-true' interest rate for each year. The computation for the effective _____, as the fee+compound interest rate, can also vary depending on whether the up-front fees, such as origination or participation fees, are added to the entire amount, or treated as a short-term loan due in the first payment.

a. Annual percentage rate
c. ABN Amro

b. AAB
d. A Random Walk Down Wall Street

28. _____ refers to a tax levied by various jurisdictions on the profits made by companies or associations. It is a tax on the value of the corporation's profits.

The measure of taxable profits varies from country to country.

a. Corporate tax
c. Proxy fight

b. Trade finance
d. First-mover advantage

29. An _____ is any government regulation or law that encourages or discourages foreign investment in the local economy, e.g. currency exchange limits.

As globalization integrates the economies of neighboring and of trading states, they are typically forced to trade off such rules as part of a common tax, tariff and trade regime, e.g. as defined by a free trade pact. _____ favoring local investors over global ones is typically discouraged in such pacts, and the idea of a separate _____ rapidly becomes a fiction or fantasy, as real decisions reflect the real need for nations to compete for investment, even from their own local investors.

a. AAB
c. Investment policy

b. ABN Amro
d. A Random Walk Down Wall Street

30. The phrase _____ refers to the aspect of corporate strategy, corporate finance and management dealing with the buying, selling and combining of different companies that can aid, finance, or help a growing company in a given industry grow rapidly without having to create another business entity.

An acquisition, also known as a takeover, is the buying of one company (the 'target') by another. An acquisition may be friendly or hostile.

a. 529 plan
c. 4-4-5 Calendar

b. 7-Eleven
d. Mergers and acquisitions

31. In finance, a _____ (non-investment grade bond, speculative grade bond or junk bond) is a bond that is rated below investment grade at the time of purchase. These bonds have a higher risk of default or other adverse credit events, but typically pay higher yields than better quality bonds in order to make them attractive to investors.

a. Volatility
c. Private equity
b. Sharpe ratio
d. High yield bond

32. In finance, _____ occurs when a debtor has not met its legal obligations according to the debt contract, e.g. it has not made a scheduled payment, or has violated a loan covenant (condition) of the debt contract. _____ may occur if the debtor is either unwilling or unable to pay their debt. This can occur with all debt obligations including bonds, mortgages, loans, and promissory notes.
   a. Vendor finance
   c. Credit crunch
   b. Default
   d. Debt validation

33. In finance, a _____ is a type of bond that can be converted into shares of stock in the issuing company, usually at some pre-announced ratio. It is a hybrid security with debt- and equity-like features. Although it typically has a low coupon rate, the holder is compensated with the ability to convert the bond to common stock, usually at a substantial discount to the stock's market value.
   a. Convertible bond
   c. Bond fund
   b. Corporate bond
   d. Gilts

34. In economics, business, and accounting, a _____ is the value of money that has been used up to produce something, and hence is not available for use anymore. In business, the _____ may be one of acquisition, in which case the amount of money expended to acquire it is counted as _____. In this case, money is the input that is gone in order to acquire the thing.
   a. Sliding scale fees
   c. Marginal cost
   b. Cost
   d. Fixed costs

35. The _____ is a daily reference rate based on the interest rates at which banks borrow unsecured funds from banks in the London wholesale money market (or interbank market.) It is roughly comparable to the U.S. Federal funds rate.

During 1984 it became apparent that an increasing number of banks were trading actively in a variety of relatively new market instruments, notably interest rate swaps, foreign currency options and forward rate agreements.

   a. Risk-free interest rate
   c. Fixed interest
   b. Shanghai Interbank Offered Rate
   d. London Interbank Offered Rate

36. _____ are bonds that have a variable coupon, equal to a money market reference rate, like LIBOR or federal funds rate, plus a spread. The spread is a rate that remains constant. Almost all _____ have quarterly coupons, i.e. they pay out interest every three months, though counter examples do exist.
   a. Gordon growth model
   c. CVECAs
   b. Loan participation
   d. Floating rate notes

37. _____ are the inflation-indexed bonds issued by the U.S. Treasury. The principal is adjusted to the Consumer Price Index, the commonly used measure of inflation. The coupon rate is constant, but generates a different amount of interest when multiplied by the inflation-adjusted principal, thus protecting the holder against inflation. _____ are currently offered in 5-year, 10-year and 20-year maturities.
   a. Treasury securities
   c. 4-4-5 Calendar
   b. Treasury Inflation-Protected Securities
   d. Treasury Inflation Protected Securities

Chapter 20. Long-Term Debt

38. A _____ is a bond bought at a price lower than its face value, with the face value repaid at the time of maturity. It does not make periodic interest payments, or so-called 'coupons,' hence the term zero-coupon bond. Investors earn return from the compounded interest all paid at maturity plus the difference between the discounted price of the bond and its par value.

   a. Callable bond
   b. Municipal bond
   c. Zero coupon bond
   d. Bowie bonds

39. A '_____' is a 'Charge' that is paid to obtain the right to delay a payment. Essentially, the payer purchases the right to make a given payment in the future instead of in the Present. The '_____', or 'Charge' that must be paid to delay the payment, is simply the difference between what the payment amount would be if it were paid in the present and what the payment amount would be paid if it were paid in the future.

   a. Risk modeling
   b. Value at risk
   c. Risk aversion
   d. Discount

40. _____, refers to consumption opportunity gained by an entity within a specified time frame, which is generally expressed in monetary terms. However, for households and individuals, '_____ is the sum of all the wages, salaries, profits, interests payments, rents and other forms of earnings received... in a given period of time.' For firms, _____ generally refers to net-profit: what remains of revenue after expenses have been subtracted.

   a. Annual report
   b. OIBDA
   c. Accrual
   d. Income

41. The term _____ refers to three closely related concepts:

   - The _____ model is a mathematical model of the market for an equity, in which the equity's price is a stochastic process.
   - The _____ PDE is a partial differential equation which (in the model) must be satisfied by the price of a derivative on the equity.
   - The _____ formula is the result obtained by solving the _____ PDE for a European call option.

   Fischer Black and Myron Scholes first articulated the _____ formula in their 1973 paper, 'The Pricing of Options and Corporate Liabilities.' The foundation for their research relied on work developed by scholars such as Jack L. Treynor, Paul Samuelson, A. James Boness, Sheen T. Kassouf, and Edward O. Thorp. The fundamental insight of _____ is that the option is implicitly priced if the stock is traded.

   Robert C. Merton was the first to publish a paper expanding the mathematical understanding of the options pricing model and coined the term '_____' options pricing model.

   a. Modified Internal Rate of Return
   b. Stochastic volatility
   c. Black-Scholes
   d. Perpetuity

42. In the United States, a _____ is an offering of securities that are not registered with the Securities and Exchange Commission (SEC.) Such offerings exploit an exemption offered by the Securities Act of 1933 that comes with several restrictions, including a prohibition against general solicitation. This exemption allows companies to avoid quarterly reporting requirements and many of the legal liabilities associated with the Sarbanes-Oxley Act.

a. 529 plan
c. 4-4-5 Calendar
b. 7-Eleven
d. Private placement

43. _____ is a combination of straight bond and embedded put option. The holder of the _____ has the right, but not the obligation, to demand early repayment of the principal. The put option is usually exercisable on specified dates.
   a. Convertible bond
   c. Callable bond
   b. Brady bonds
   d. Puttable bond

44. In business and finance, a _____ (also referred to as equity _____) of stock means a _____ of ownership in a corporation (company.) In the plural, stocks is often used as a synonym for _____s especially in the United States, but it is less commonly used that way outside of North America.

In the United Kingdom, South Africa, and Australia, stock can also refer to completely different financial instruments such as government bonds or, less commonly, to all kinds of marketable securities.

   a. Procter ' Gamble
   c. Margin
   b. Bucket shop
   d. Share

45. The free _____ of a public company is an estimate of the proportion of shares that are not held by large owners and that are not stock with sales restrictions (restricted stock that cannot be sold until they become unrestricted stock.)

The free _____ or a public _____ is usually defined as being all shares held by investors other than:

- shares held by owners owning more than 5% of all shares (those could be institutional investors, 'strategic shareholders,' founders, executives, and other insiders' holdings)
- restricted stocks (granted to executives that can be, but don't have to be, registered insiders)
- insider holdings (it is assumed that insiders hold stock for the very long term)

The free _____ is an important criterion in quoting a share on the stock market.

To _____ a company means to list its shares on a public stock exchange through an initial public offering (or 'flotation'.)

- Open market
- Outstanding shares
- Market capitalization
- Public _____ *loat*
- Reverse takeover

   a. Trade finance
   c. Synthetic CDO
   b. Golden parachute
   d. Float

46. A _____ (or 'syndicated bank facility') is a large loan in which a group of banks provide funds for a borrower, usually several but without joint liability. There is usually a lead bank or group of banks (the 'Arranger/s' or 'Agent/s') that takes a percentage of the loan and syndicates or sells the rest to other banks. In contrast, a bilateral loan, only involves one borrower and one lender (often a bank or financial institution.)
- a. Debt buyer
- b. Credit score
- c. Collection agency
- d. Syndicated loan

47. _____ or financing is to provide capital (funds), which means money for a project, a person, a business or any other private or public institutions.

Those funds can be allocated for either short term or long term purposes. The health fund is a new way of _____ private healthcare centers.

- a. Synthetic CDO
- b. Proxy fight
- c. Funding
- d. Product life cycle

Chapter 21. Leasing

1. Leasing is a process by which a firm can obtain the use of a certain fixed assets for which it must pay a series of contractual, periodic, tax deductable payments. The lessee is the receiver of the services or the assets under the lease contract and the lessor is the owner of the assets. The relationship between the tenant and the landlord is called a _____, and can be for a fixed or an indefinite period of time (called the term of the lease.)
   a. Real estate investing
   b. REIT
   c. Real Estate Investment Trust
   d. Tenancy

2. An _____ is a lease whose term is short compared to the useful life of the asset or piece of equipment (an airliner, a ship etc.) being leased. An _____ is commonly used to acquire equipment on a relatively short-term basis.
   a. ABN Amro
   b. AAB
   c. A Random Walk Down Wall Street
   d. Operating lease

3. _____ are cash, evidence of an ownership interest in an entity or deliver, cash or another financial instrument.

   _____ can be categorized by form depending on whether they are cash instruments or derivative instruments:

   - Cash instruments are _____ whose value is determined directly by markets. They can be divided into securities, which are readily transferable, and other cash instruments such as loans and deposits, where both borrower and lender have to agree on a transfer.
   - Derivative instruments are _____ which derive their value from the value and characteristics of one or more underlying assets. They can be divided into exchange-traded derivatives and over-the-counter (OTC) derivatives.

   Alternatively, _____ can be categorized by 'asset class' depending on whether they are equity based (reflecting ownership of the issuing entity) or debt based (reflecting a loan the investor has made to the issuing entity). If it is debt, it can be further categorised into short term (less than one year) or long term.

   Foreign Exchange instruments and transactions are neither debt nor equity based and belong in their own category.

   a. Cost of carry
   b. Financial services
   c. Secondary market
   d. Financial instruments

4. _____ is a process by which a firm can obtain the use of a certain fixed assets for which it must pay a series of contractual, periodic, tax deductable payments. The lessee is the receiver of the services or the assets under the lease contract and the lessor is the owner of the assets. The relationship between the tenant and the landlord is called a tenancy, and can be for a fixed or an indefinite period of time (called the term of the lease).
   a. Foreign Corrupt Practices Act
   b. Royalties
   c. Quiet period
   d. Leasing

5. The role of the _____ is to issue accounting standards in the United Kingdom. It is recognised for that purpose under the Companies Act 1985. It took over the task of setting accounting standards from the Accounting Standards Committee (ASC) in 1990.
   a. AAB
   b. Accounting Standards Board
   c. ABN Amro
   d. A Random Walk Down Wall Street

Chapter 21. Leasing

6. _____ is the field of accountancy concerned with the preparation of financial statements for decision makers, such as stockholders, suppliers, banks, employees, government agencies, owners, and other stakeholders. The fundamental need for _____ is to reduce principal-agent problem by measuring and monitoring agents' performance and reporting the results to interested users.

_____ is used to prepare accounting information for people outside the organization or not involved in the day to day running of the company.

   a. 529 plan
   c. 7-Eleven
   b. 4-4-5 Calendar
   d. Financial Accounting

7. The _____ is a private, not-for-profit organization whose primary purpose is to develop generally accepted accounting principles (GAAP) within the United States in the public's interest. The Securities and Exchange Commission (SEC) designated the _____ as the organization responsible for setting accounting standards for public companies in the U.S. It was created in 1973, replacing the Accounting Principles Board and the Committee on Accounting Procedure of the American Institute of Certified Public Accountants. The _____'s mission is 'to establish and improve standards of financial accounting and reporting for the guidance and education of the public, including issuers, auditors, and users of financial information.'

The _____ is not a governmental body.

   a. World Congress of Accountants
   c. KPMG
   b. Federal Deposit Insurance Corporation
   d. Financial Accounting Standards Board

8. A _____ is a lease in which the lessor puts up some of the money required to purchase the asset and borrows the rest from a lender. The lender is given a senior secured interest on the asset and an assignment of the lease and lease payments. The lessee makes payments to the lessor, who makes payments to the lender.
   a. Leveraged lease
   c. Collection agency
   b. Guaranteed consumer funding
   d. Debt buyer

9. _____ short for sale-and-_____ is a financial transaction, where one sells an asset and leases it back for a long-term: thus one continues to be able to use the asset, but no longer owns it.

This is generally done for fixed assets, notably real estate and planes, and the purposes are varied, but include financing, accounting, and tax reasons.

After purchasing an asset, the owner enters a long-term agreement by which the property is leased back to the seller, at an agreed-to rate.

   a. 7-Eleven
   c. 4-4-5 Calendar
   b. 529 plan
   d. Leaseback,

10. The phrase _____ refers to the aspect of corporate strategy, corporate finance and management dealing with the buying, selling and combining of different companies that can aid, finance, or help a growing company in a given industry grow rapidly without having to create another business entity.

An acquisition, also known as a takeover, is the buying of one company (the 'target') by another. An acquisition may be friendly or hostile.

a. 7-Eleven
b. 529 plan
c. 4-4-5 Calendar
d. Mergers and acquisitions

11. A finance lease or _____ is a type of lease. It is a commercial arrangement where:

- the lessee (customer or borrower) will select an asset (equipment, vehicle, software);
- the lessor (finance company) will purchase that asset;
- the lessee will have use of that asset during the lease;
- the lessee will pay a series of rentals or installments for the use of that asset;
- the lessor will recover a large part or all of the cost of the asset plus earn interest from the rentals paid by the lessee;
- the lessee has the option to acquire ownership of the asset (e.g. paying the last rental, or bargain option purchase price);

The finance company is the legal owner of the asset during duration of the lease.

However the lessee has control over the asset providing them the benefits and risks of (economic) ownership.

A finance lease differs from an operating lease in that:

- in a finance lease the lessee has use of the asset over most of its economic life and beyond (generally by making small 'peppercorn' payments at the end of the lease term.)

In an operating lease the lessee only uses the asset for some of the asset's life.

- in a finance lease the lessor will recover all or most of the cost of the equipment from the rentals paid by the lessee.

In an operating lease the lessor will have a substantial investment or residual value on completion of the lease.

- in a finance lease the lessee has the benefits and risks of economic ownership of the asset (e.g. risk of obsolescence, paying for maintenance, claiming capital allowances/depreciation.)

In an operating lease the lessor has the benefits and risks of owning the asset.

The U.S. Financial Accounting Standards Board and the International Accounting Standards Board announced in 2006 a joint project to comprehensively review lease accounting standards.

a. Cash management
b. Capitalization rate
c. Cash concentration
d. Capital lease

12. An _____ is a contract written by a seller that conveys to the buyer the right -- but not the obligation -- to buy (in the case of a call _____) or to sell (in the case of a put _____) a particular asset, such as a piece of property such as, among others, a futures contract. In return for granting the _____, the seller collects a payment (the premium) from the buyer.

For example, buying a call _____ provides the right to buy a specified quantity of a security at a set strike price at some time on or before expiration, while buying a put _____ provides the right to sell.

   a. AT'T Mobility LLC   b. Annuity
   c. Option   d. Amortization

13. The phrase _____ or bullet payment refers to one of two ways for repaying a loan; the other type is called amortizing payment or Amortization (business).

With a balloon loan, a _____ is paid back when the loan comes to its contractual maturity, e.g. reaches the deadline set to repayment at the time the loan was granted, representing the full loan amount (also called principal.) Periodic interest payments are generally made throughout the life of the loan.

   a. Refinancing risk   b. Present value of costs
   c. Future-oriented   d. Balloon payment

14. In finance, a _____ is a debt security, in which the authorized issuer owes the holders a debt and, depending on the terms of the _____, is obliged to pay interest (the coupon) and/or to repay the principal at a later date, termed maturity.

Thus a _____ is a loan: the issuer is the borrower, the _____ holder is the lender, and the coupon is the interest. _____s provide the borrower with external funds to finance long-term investments, or, in the case of government _____s, to finance current expenditure.

   a. Puttable bond   b. Catastrophe bonds
   c. Convertible bond   d. Bond

15. _____ is a type of bond that allows the issuer of the bond to retain the privilege of redeeming the bond at some point before the bond reaches the date of maturity. In other words, on the call dates, the issuer has the right, but not the obligation, to buy back the bonds from the bond holders at the call price. Technically speaking, the bonds are not really bought and held by the issuer but cancelled immediately.

   a. Coupon rate   b. Bond fund
   c. Callable bond   d. Gilts

16. _____ is a fee paid on borrowed assets. It is the price paid for the use of borrowed money , or, money earned by deposited funds . Assets that are sometimes lent with _____ include money, shares, consumer goods through hire purchase, major assets such as aircraft, and even entire factories in finance lease arrangements.

   a. A Random Walk Down Wall Street   b. AAB
   c. Insolvency   d. Interest

17. _____ is the value on a given date of a future payment or series of future payments, discounted to reflect the time value of money and other factors such as investment risk. _____ calculations are widely used in business and economics to provide a means to compare cash flows at different times on a meaningful 'like to like' basis.

The most commonly applied model of the time value of money is compound interest.

   a. Present value of benefits
   b. Present value
   c. Negative gearing
   d. Net present value

18. A '_____' is a 'Charge' that is paid to obtain the right to delay a payment. Essentially, the payer purchases the right to make a given payment in the future instead of in the Present. The '_____', or 'Charge' that must be paid to delay the payment, is simply the difference between what the payment amount would be if it were paid in the present and what the payment amount would be paid if it were paid in the future.
   a. Value at risk
   b. Risk modeling
   c. Risk aversion
   d. Discount

19. The _____ is an interest rate a central bank charges depository institutions that borrow reserves from it.

The term _____ has two meanings:

   - the same as interest rate; the term 'discount' does not refer to the meaning of the word, but to the purpose of using the quantity, such as computations of present value, e.g. net present value / discounted cash flow

   - the annual effective _____, which is the annual interest divided by the capital including that interest; this rate is lower than the interest rate; it corresponds to using the value after a year as the nominal value, and seeing the initial value as the nominal value minus a discount; it is used for Treasury Bills and similar financial instruments

The annual effective _____ is the annual interest divided by the capital including that interest, which is the interest rate divided by 100% plus the interest rate. It is the annual discount factor to be applied to the future cash flow, to find the discount, subtracted from a future value to find the value one year earlier.

For example, suppose there is a government bond that sells for $95 and pays $100 in a year's time.

   a. Fisher equation
   b. Black-Scholes
   c. Stochastic volatility
   d. Discount rate

20. In financial accounting, a _____ or statement of financial position is a summary of a person's or organization's balances. Assets, liabilities and ownership equity are listed as of a specific date, such as the end of its financial year. A _____ is often described as a snapshot of a company's financial condition.
   a. Statement of retained earnings
   b. Financial statements
   c. Balance sheet
   d. Statement on Auditing Standards No. 70: Service Organizations

Chapter 21. Leasing

21. _____ is that which is owed; usually referencing assets owed, but the term can cover other obligations. In the case of assets, _____ is a means of using future purchasing power in the present before a summation has been earned. Some companies and corporations use _____ as a part of their overall corporate finance strategy.
   a. Cross-collateralization
   b. Credit cycle
   c. Partial Payment
   d. Debt

22. The _____ is a capital budgeting metric used by firms to decide whether they should make investments. It is an indicator of the efficiency or quality of an investment, as opposed to net present value (NPV), which indicates value or magnitude.

The IRR is the annualized effective compounded return rate which can be earned on the invested capital, i.e., the yield on the investment.

   a. A Random Walk Down Wall Street
   b. AAB
   c. ABN Amro
   d. Internal rate of return

23. In economic models, the _____ time frame assumes no fixed factors of production. Firms can enter or leave the marketplace, and the cost (and availability) of land, labor, raw materials, and capital goods can be assumed to vary. In contrast, in the short-run time frame, certain factors are assumed to be fixed, because there is not sufficient time for them to change.
   a. 529 plan
   b. 4-4-5 Calendar
   c. Short-run
   d. Long-run

24. _____ is one of the constituents of a leasing calculus or operation. It describes the future value of a good in terms of percentage of depreciation of its initial value.

Example: A car is sold at a list price of $20,000 today. After a usage of 36 months and 50,000 miles its value is contractually defined as 50% or $10,000. The credited amount, on which the interest is applied, thus is $20,000 present value minus $10,000 future value.

   a. Days Sales Outstanding
   b. Net pay
   c. Round-tripping
   d. Residual value

25. In economics and related disciplines, a _____ is a cost incurred in making an economic exchange. For example, most people, when buying or selling a stock, must pay a commission to their broker; that commission is a _____ of doing the stock deal. Or consider buying a banana from a store; to purchase the banana, your costs will be not only the price of the banana itself, but also the energy and effort it requires to find out which of the various banana products you prefer, where to get them and at what price, the cost of traveling from your house to the store and back, the time waiting in line, and the effort of the paying itself; the costs above and beyond the cost of the banana are the _____s.
   a. Marginal cost
   b. Variable costs
   c. Transaction cost
   d. Fixed costs

26. In economics, business, and accounting, a _____ is the value of money that has been used up to produce something, and hence is not available for use anymore. In business, the _____ may be one of acquisition, in which case the amount of money expended to acquire it is counted as _____. In this case, money is the input that is gone in order to acquire the thing.

a. Marginal cost
c. Cost
b. Fixed costs
d. Sliding scale fees

27. An _____ is the price a borrower pays for the use of money they do not own, and the return a lender receives for deferring the use of funds, by lending it to the borrower. _____s are normally expressed as a percentage rate over the period of one year.

_____s targets are also a vital tool of monetary policy and are used to control variables like investment, inflation, and unemployment.

a. Interest rate
c. AAB
b. ABN Amro
d. A Random Walk Down Wall Street

28. The _____ percentage shows how profitable a company's assets are in generating revenue.

_____ can be computed as:

$$ROA = \frac{\text{Net Income}}{\text{Total Assets}}$$

This number tells you 'what the company can do with what it's got', i.e. how many dollars of earnings they derive from each dollar of assets they control. It's a useful number for comparing competing companies in the same industry.

a. Return on assets
c. P/E ratio
b. Return on sales
d. Receivables turnover ratio

29. In business and accounting, _____s are everything of value that is owned by a person or company. The balance sheet of a firm records the monetary value of the _____s owned by the firm. The two major _____ classes are tangible _____s and intangible _____s.
a. EBITDA
c. Income
b. Accounts payable
d. Asset

30. _____, refers to consumption opportunity gained by an entity within a specified time frame, which is generally expressed in monetary terms. However, for households and individuals, '_____ is the sum of all the wages, salaries, profits, interests payments, rents and other forms of earnings received... in a given period of time.' For firms, _____ generally refers to net-profit: what remains of revenue after expenses have been subtracted.
a. Annual report
c. Income
b. OIBDA
d. Accrual

Chapter 22. Options and Corporate Finance

1. An _____ is a contract written by a seller that conveys to the buyer the right -- but not the obligation -- to buy (in the case of a call _____) or to sell (in the case of a put _____) a particular asset, such as a piece of property such as, among others, a futures contract. In return for granting the _____, the seller collects a payment (the premium) from the buyer.

   For example, buying a call _____ provides the right to buy a specified quantity of a security at a set strike price at some time on or before expiration, while buying a put _____ provides the right to sell.

   a. Amortization
   c. AT'T Mobility LLC
   b. Option
   d. Annuity

2. In options, the _____ is a key variable in a derivatives contract between two parties. Where the contract requires delivery of the underlying instrument, the trade will be at the _____, regardless of the spot price (market price) of the underlying instrument at that time.

   Definition - The fixed price at which the owner of an option can purchase, in the case of a call in the case of a put, the underlying security or commodity.

   a. Moneyness
   c. Naked put
   b. Swaption
   d. Strike price

3. In finance, _____ is the process of estimating the potential market value of a financial asset or liability. they can be done on assets (for example, investments in marketable securities such as stocks, options, business enterprises, or intangible assets such as patents and trademarks) or on liabilities (e.g., Bonds issued by a company.) _____s are required in many contexts including investment analysis, capital budgeting, merger and acquisition transactions, financial reporting, taxable events to determine the proper tax liability, and in litigation.
   a. Share
   c. Procter ' Gamble
   b. Margin
   d. Valuation

4. A _____ is a financial contract between two parties, the buyer and the seller of this type of option. Often it is simply labeled a 'call'. The buyer of the option has the right, but not the obligation to buy an agreed quantity of a particular commodity or financial instrument (the underlying instrument) from the seller of the option at a certain time (the expiration date) for a certain price (the strike price.)
   a. Call option
   c. Bear spread
   b. Bear call spread
   d. Bull spread

5. _____ is a concept whereby a person's financial liability is limited to a fixed sum, most commonly the value of a person's investment in a company or partnership with _____. A shareholder in a limited company is not personally liable for any of the debts of the company, other than for the value of his investment in that company. The same is true for the members of a _____ partnership and the limited partners in a limited partnership.
   a. Sarbanes-Oxley Act
   c. Personal property
   b. Beneficial owner
   d. Limited liability

6. A _____ is a financial contract between two parties, the seller (writer) and the buyer of the option. The put allows its buyer the right but not the obligation to sell a commodity or financial instrument (the underlying instrument) to the writer (seller) of the option at a certain time for a certain price (the strike price.) The writer (seller) has the obligation to purchase the underlying asset at that strike price, if the buyer exercises the option.

Chapter 22. Options and Corporate Finance

    a. Bear call spread
    b. Debit spread
    c. Bear spread
    d. Put option

7. In the most general sense, a _____ is anything that is a hindrance, or puts individuals at a disadvantage.

Before we discuss the financial terms, we should note that a _____ can also have a much more important slang meaning.

This is best described in an example.

    a. Covenant
    b. Limited liability
    c. McFadden Act
    d. Liability

8. In finance, a _____ is a debt security, in which the authorized issuer owes the holders a debt and, depending on the terms of the _____, is obliged to pay interest (the coupon) and/or to repay the principal at a later date, termed maturity.

Thus a _____ is a loan: the issuer is the borrower, the _____ holder is the lender, and the coupon is the interest. _____s provide the borrower with external funds to finance long-term investments, or, in the case of government _____s, to finance current expenditure.

    a. Bond
    b. Puttable bond
    c. Catastrophe bonds
    d. Convertible bond

9. The coupon or _____ of a bond is the amount of interest paid per year expressed as a percentage of the face value of the bond.

For example if you hold $10,000 nominal of a bond described as a 4.5% loan stock, you will receive $450 in interest each year (probably in two installments of $225 each.)

Not all bonds have coupons.

    a. Revenue bonds
    b. Zero-coupon bond
    c. Puttable bond
    d. Coupon rate

10. In finance, the _____ of a derivative is an asset, basket of assets, index, or even another derivative, such that the cash flows of the (former) derivative depend on the value of this _____. There must be an independent way to observe this value to avoid conflicts of interest.

For example, in a stock option to buy 100 shares of Nokia at EUR 50 in September 2006, the _____ is a Nokia share.

    a. Underlying
    b. ABN Amro
    c. A Random Walk Down Wall Street
    d. AAB

Chapter 22. Options and Corporate Finance

11. A _____ is a bond bought at a price lower than its face value, with the face value repaid at the time of maturity. It does not make periodic interest payments, or so-called 'coupons,' hence the term zero-coupon bond. Investors earn return from the compounded interest all paid at maturity plus the difference between the discounted price of the bond and its par value.
    a. Callable bond
    b. Bowie bonds
    c. Municipal bond
    d. Zero coupon bond

12. In financial mathematics, _____ defines a relationship between the price of a call option and a put option--both with the identical strike price and expiry. To derive the _____ relationship, the assumption is that the options are not exercised before expiration day, which necessarily applies to European options. _____ can be derived in a manner that is largely model independent.
    a. Put-call parity
    b. Cox-Ingersoll-Ross model
    c. Rendleman-Bartter model
    d. Hull-White model

13. A _____ is a transaction in which the seller of call options already owns the corresponding amount of the underlying instrument, such as shares of a stock or other securities. These owned shares provide the 'cover' as they can be handed over to the buyer of the options when he decides to exercise them, instead of having to buy the optioned shares at unfavorable market prices in the case of 'uncovered' or short call. Thus, the _____ limits the (potentially unlimited) loss that results from a short call when the price of the underlying stock moves above the strike price of the option.
    a. 529 plan
    b. 7-Eleven
    c. 4-4-5 Calendar
    d. Covered call

14. In economics and finance, _____ is the practice of taking advantage of a price differential between two or more markets: striking a combination of matching deals that capitalize upon the imbalance, the profit being the difference between the market prices. When used by academics, an _____ is a transaction that involves no negative cash flow at any probabilistic or temporal state and a positive cash flow in at least one state; in simple terms, a risk-free profit.
    a. Initial margin
    b. Issuer
    c. Efficient-market hypothesis
    d. Arbitrage

15. In business and accounting, _____s are everything of value that is owned by a person or company. The balance sheet of a firm records the monetary value of the _____s owned by the firm. The two major _____ classes are tangible _____s and intangible _____s.
    a. EBITDA
    b. Asset
    c. Income
    d. Accounts payable

16. The term _____ is often used to refer to the investment management of collective investments, (not necessarily) whilst the more generic fund management may refer to all forms of institutional investment as well as investment management for private investors. Investment managers who specialize in advisory or discretionary management on behalf of (normally wealthy) private investors may often refer to their services as wealth management or portfolio management often within the context of so-called 'private banking'.

The provision of 'investment management services' includes elements of financial analysis, asset selection, stock selection, plan implementation and ongoing monitoring of investments.

a. Asset management
b. A Random Walk Down Wall Street
c. AAB
d. ABN Amro

17. In finance, _____ refers to the value of a security which is intrinsic to or contained in the security itself. It is also frequently called fundamental value. It is ordinarily calculated by summing the future income generated by the asset, and discounting it to the present value.

a. Alpha
b. Intrinsic value
c. Amortization
d. Accretion

18. The phrase _____ refers to the aspect of corporate strategy, corporate finance and management dealing with the buying, selling and combining of different companies that can aid, finance, or help a growing company in a given industry grow rapidly without having to create another business entity.

An acquisition, also known as a takeover, is the buying of one company (the 'target') by another. An acquisition may be friendly or hostile.

a. 4-4-5 Calendar
b. 7-Eleven
c. Mergers and acquisitions
d. 529 plan

19. In finance, the binomial options pricing model (BOPM) provides a generalisable numerical method for the valuation of options. The _____ was first proposed by Cox, Ross and Rubinstein (1979.) Essentially, the model uses a 'discrete-time' model of the varying price over time of the underlying financial instrument.

a. Binomial model
b. Discount rate
c. Modified Internal Rate of Return
d. Perpetuity

20. The term _____ refers to three closely related concepts:

- The _____ model is a mathematical model of the market for an equity, in which the equity's price is a stochastic process.
- The _____ PDE is a partial differential equation which (in the model) must be satisfied by the price of a derivative on the equity.
- The _____ formula is the result obtained by solving the _____ PDE for a European call option.

Fischer Black and Myron Scholes first articulated the _____ formula in their 1973 paper, 'The Pricing of Options and Corporate Liabilities.' The foundation for their research relied on work developed by scholars such as Jack L. Treynor, Paul Samuelson, A. James Boness, Sheen T. Kassouf, and Edward O. Thorp. The fundamental insight of _____ is that the option is implicitly priced if the stock is traded.

Robert C. Merton was the first to publish a paper expanding the mathematical understanding of the options pricing model and coined the term '_____' options pricing model.

a. Stochastic volatility
b. Perpetuity
c. Modified Internal Rate of Return
d. Black-Scholes

21. A _____ is the price of a single share of a no. of saleable stocks of the company. Once the stock is purchased, the owner becomes a shareholder of the company that issued the share.

a. Stock split
c. Trading curb
b. Whisper numbers
d. Share price

22. _____ is a fee paid on borrowed assets. It is the price paid for the use of borrowed money , or, money earned by deposited funds . Assets that are sometimes lent with _____ include money, shares, consumer goods through hire purchase, major assets such as aircraft, and even entire factories in finance lease arrangements.
   a. A Random Walk Down Wall Street
   c. AAB
   b. Insolvency
   d. Interest

23. An _____ is the price a borrower pays for the use of money they do not own, and the return a lender receives for deferring the use of funds, by lending it to the borrower. _____s are normally expressed as a percentage rate over the period of one year.

   _____s targets are also a vital tool of monetary policy and are used to control variables like investment, inflation, and unemployment.

   a. Interest rate
   c. A Random Walk Down Wall Street
   b. ABN Amro
   d. AAB

24. The terms _____ , nominal _____, and effective _____ describe the interest rate for a whole year (annualized), rather than just a monthly fee/rate, as applied on a loan, mortgage, credit card, etc. Those terms have formal, legal definitions in some countries or legal jurisdictions, but in general:

   - The nominal _____ is the simple-interest rate (for a year.)
   - The effective _____ is the fee+compound interest rate (calculated across a year.)

   The nominal _____ is calculated as: the rate, for a payment period, multiplied by the number of payment periods in a year. However, the exact legal definition of 'effective _____' can vary greatly in each jurisdiction, depending on the type of fees included, such as participation fees, loan origination fees, monthly service charges, or late fees. The effective _____ has been called the 'mathematically-true' interest rate for each year. The computation for the effective _____, as the fee+compound interest rate, can also vary depending on whether the up-front fees, such as origination or participation fees, are added to the entire amount, or treated as a short-term loan due in the first payment.

   a. ABN Amro
   c. A Random Walk Down Wall Street
   b. AAB
   d. Annual percentage rate

25. _____ is a derivative financial instrument.

   The global market for exchange-traded _____s is notionally valued by the Bank for International Settlements at $3,075,400 million in 2005.

   a. Eurobond
   c. Education production function
   b. Economic entity
   d. Interest rate Option

26. The _____ is an important family of continuous probability distributions, applicable in many fields. Each member of the family may be defined by two parameters, location and scale: the mean and variance respectively. The standard _____ is the _____ with a mean of zero and a variance of one

a. Random variables
c. Probability distribution
b. Correlation
d. Normal distribution

27. In business and finance, a _____ (also referred to as equity _____) of stock means a _____ of ownership in a corporation (company.) In the plural, stocks is often used as a synonym for _____s especially in the United States, but it is less commonly used that way outside of North America.

In the United Kingdom, South Africa, and Australia, stock can also refer to completely different financial instruments such as government bonds or, less commonly, to all kinds of marketable securities.

a. Share
c. Bucket shop
b. Procter ' Gamble
d. Margin

28. A _____ is an exchange of promises between two or more parties to do an act which is enforceable in a court of law. It is where an unqualified offer meets a qualified acceptance and the parties reach Consensus ad Idem. The parties must have the necessary capacity to _____ and the _____ must not be either trifling, indeterminate, impossible or illegal.

a. 4-4-5 Calendar
c. 529 plan
b. 7-Eleven
d. Contract

29. _____ are a class of computational algorithms that rely on repeated random sampling to compute their results. _____ are often used when simulating physical and mathematical systems. Because of their reliance on repeated computation and random or pseudo-random numbers, _____ are most suited to calculation by a computer.

_____ in finance are often used to calculate the value of companies, to evaluate investments in projects at corporate level or to evaluate financial derivatives. The method is intended for financial analysts who want to construct stochastic or probabilistic financial models as opposed to the traditional static and deterministic models.

a. Semivariance
c. Monte Carlo methods
b. Correlation
d. Sample size

30. _____ is the planning process used to determine whether a firm's long term investments such as new machinery, replacement machinery, new plants, new products, and research development projects are worth pursuing. It is budget for major capital, or investment, expenditures.

Many formal methods are used in _____, including the techniques such as

- Net present value
- Profitability index
- Internal rate of return
- Modified Internal Rate of Return
- Equivalent annuity

These methods use the incremental cash flows from each potential investment, or project. Techniques based on accounting earnings and accounting rules are sometimes used - though economists consider this to be improper - such as the accounting rate of return, and 'return on investment.' Simplified and hybrid methods are used as well, such as payback period and discounted payback period.

a. Preferred stock
c. Shareholder value
b. Capital budgeting
d. Financial distress

31. _____ or net present worth (NPW) is defined as the total present value (PV) of a time series of cash flows. It is a standard method for using the time value of money to appraise long-term projects. Used for capital budgeting, and widely throughout economics, it measures the excess or shortfall of cash flows, in present value terms, once financing charges are met.

a. Negative gearing
c. Tax shield
b. Present value of costs
d. Net present value

32. _____ is the value on a given date of a future payment or series of future payments, discounted to reflect the time value of money and other factors such as investment risk. _____ calculations are widely used in business and economics to provide a means to compare cash flows at different times on a meaningful 'like to like' basis.

The most commonly applied model of the time value of money is compound interest.

a. Negative gearing
c. Net present value
b. Present value of benefits
d. Present value

33. An _____ is any government regulation or law that encourages or discourages foreign investment in the local economy, e.g. currency exchange limits.

As globalization integrates the economies of neighboring and of trading states, they are typically forced to trade off such rules as part of a common tax, tariff and trade regime, e.g. as defined by a free trade pact. _____ favoring local investors over global ones is typically discouraged in such pacts, and the idea of a separate _____ rapidly becomes a fiction or fantasy, as real decisions reflect the real need for nations to compete for investment, even from their own local investors.

a. AAB
c. A Random Walk Down Wall Street
b. ABN Amro
d. Investment policy

34. _____ is a type of bond that allows the issuer of the bond to retain the privilege of redeeming the bond at some point before the bond reaches the date of maturity. In other words, on the call dates, the issuer has the right, but not the obligation, to buy back the bonds from the bond holders at the call price. Technically speaking, the bonds are not really bought and held by the issuer but cancelled immediately.

a. Callable bond
c. Gilts
b. Bond fund
d. Coupon rate

Chapter 23. Options and Corporate Finance: Extensions and Applications

1. An _____ is a contract written by a seller that conveys to the buyer the right -- but not the obligation -- to buy (in the case of a call _____) or to sell (in the case of a put _____) a particular asset, such as a piece of property such as, among others, a futures contract. In return for granting the _____, the seller collects a payment (the premium) from the buyer.

For example, buying a call _____ provides the right to buy a specified quantity of a security at a set strike price at some time on or before expiration, while buying a put _____ provides the right to sell.

a. Option
c. AT'T Mobility LLC
b. Amortization
d. Annuity

2. The term _____ refers to three closely related concepts:

- The _____ model is a mathematical model of the market for an equity, in which the equity's price is a stochastic process.
- The _____ PDE is a partial differential equation which (in the model) must be satisfied by the price of a derivative on the equity.
- The _____ formula is the result obtained by solving the _____ PDE for a European call option.

Fischer Black and Myron Scholes first articulated the _____ formula in their 1973 paper, 'The Pricing of Options and Corporate Liabilities.' The foundation for their research relied on work developed by scholars such as Jack L. Treynor, Paul Samuelson, A. James Boness, Sheen T. Kassouf, and Edward O. Thorp. The fundamental insight of _____ is that the option is implicitly priced if the stock is traded.

Robert C. Merton was the first to publish a paper expanding the mathematical understanding of the options pricing model and coined the term '_____' options pricing model.

a. Perpetuity
c. Modified Internal Rate of Return
b. Black-Scholes
d. Stochastic volatility

3. A _____ is an agreement between a company and an employee (usually upper executive) specifying that the employee will receive certain significant benefits if employment is terminated. Sometimes, certain conditions, typically a change in company ownership, must be met, but often the cause of termination is unspecified. These benefits may include severance pay, cash bonuses, stock options, or other benefits.

a. Market capitalization
c. Trade finance
b. Debtor-in-possession financing
d. Golden parachute

4. In business and accounting, _____s are everything of value that is owned by a person or company. The balance sheet of a firm records the monetary value of the _____s owned by the firm. The two major _____ classes are tangible _____s and intangible _____s.

a. EBITDA
c. Income
b. Accounts payable
d. Asset

Chapter 23. Options and Corporate Finance: Extensions and Applications 153

5. The term _____ is often used to refer to the investment management of collective investments, (not necessarily) whilst the more generic fund management may refer to all forms of institutional investment as well as investment management for private investors. Investment managers who specialize in advisory or discretionary management on behalf of (normally wealthy) private investors may often refer to their services as wealth management or portfolio management often within the context of so-called 'private banking'.

The provision of 'investment management services' includes elements of financial analysis, asset selection, stock selection, plan implementation and ongoing monitoring of investments.

a. Asset management
b. AAB
c. A Random Walk Down Wall Street
d. ABN Amro

6. _____ or financing is to provide capital (funds), which means money for a project, a person, a business or any other private or public institutions.

Those funds can be allocated for either short term or long term purposes. The health fund is a new way of _____ private healthcare centers.

a. Funding
b. Synthetic CDO
c. Proxy fight
d. Product life cycle

7. The phrase _____ refers to the aspect of corporate strategy, corporate finance and management dealing with the buying, selling and combining of different companies that can aid, finance, or help a growing company in a given industry grow rapidly without having to create another business entity.

An acquisition, also known as a takeover, is the buying of one company (the 'target') by another. An acquisition may be friendly or hostile.

a. 529 plan
b. 4-4-5 Calendar
c. 7-Eleven
d. Mergers and acquisitions

8. In finance, the binomial options pricing model (BOPM) provides a generalisable numerical method for the valuation of options. The _____ was first proposed by Cox, Ross and Rubinstein (1979.) Essentially, the model uses a 'discrete-time' model of the varying price over time of the underlying financial instrument.

a. Discount rate
b. Perpetuity
c. Modified Internal Rate of Return
d. Binomial model

9. In finance, _____ is the process of estimating the potential market value of a financial asset or liability. they can be done on assets (for example, investments in marketable securities such as stocks, options, business enterprises, or intangible assets such as patents and trademarks) or on liabilities (e.g., Bonds issued by a company.) _____s are required in many contexts including investment analysis, capital budgeting, merger and acquisition transactions, financial reporting, taxable events to determine the proper tax liability, and in litigation.

a. Procter ' Gamble
b. Margin
c. Share
d. Valuation

10. An _____ is a call option on the common stock of a company, issued as a form of non-cash compensation. Restrictions on the option (such as vesting and limited transferability) attempt to align the holder's interest with those of the business' shareholders. If the company's stock rises, holders of options experience a direct financial benefit.

a. Internal financing
b. Underwriting contract
c. Operating ratio
d. Employee stock option

Chapter 24. Warrants and Convertibles

1. The term _____ refers to three closely related concepts:

   - The _____ model is a mathematical model of the market for an equity, in which the equity's price is a stochastic process.
   - The _____ PDE is a partial differential equation which (in the model) must be satisfied by the price of a derivative on the equity.
   - The _____ formula is the result obtained by solving the _____ PDE for a European call option.

   Fischer Black and Myron Scholes first articulated the _____ formula in their 1973 paper, 'The Pricing of Options and Corporate Liabilities.' The foundation for their research relied on work developed by scholars such as Jack L. Treynor, Paul Samuelson, A. James Boness, Sheen T. Kassouf, and Edward O. Thorp. The fundamental insight of _____ is that the option is implicitly priced if the stock is traded.

   Robert C. Merton was the first to publish a paper expanding the mathematical understanding of the options pricing model and coined the term '_____' options pricing model.

   a. Black-Scholes
   c. Stochastic volatility
   b. Modified Internal Rate of Return
   d. Perpetuity

2. A _____ is a financial contract between two parties, the buyer and the seller of this type of option. Often it is simply labeled a 'call'. The buyer of the option has the right, but not the obligation to buy an agreed quantity of a particular commodity or financial instrument (the underlying instrument) from the seller of the option at a certain time (the expiration date) for a certain price (the strike price.)

   a. Bear spread
   c. Bear call spread
   b. Call option
   d. Bull spread

3. An _____ is a contract written by a seller that conveys to the buyer the right -- but not the obligation -- to buy (in the case of a call _____) or to sell (in the case of a put _____) a particular asset, such as a piece of property such as, among others, a futures contract. In return for granting the _____, the seller collects a payment (the premium) from the buyer.

   For example, buying a call _____ provides the right to buy a specified quantity of a security at a set strike price at some time on or before expiration, while buying a put _____ provides the right to sell.

   a. Annuity
   c. AT'T Mobility LLC
   b. Option
   d. Amortization

4. In finance, a _____ is a security that entitles the holder to buy stock of the company that issued it at a specified price, which is usually higher than the stock price at time of issue.

   _____s are frequently attached to bonds or preferred stock as a sweetener, allowing the issuer to pay lower interest rates or dividends. They can be used to enhance the yield of the bond, and make them more attractive to potential buyers.

   a. Clearing house
   c. Warrant
   b. Clearing
   d. Credit

Chapter 24. Warrants and Convertibles

5. In finance, a _____ is a type of bond that can be converted into shares of stock in the issuing company, usually at some pre-announced ratio. It is a hybrid security with debt- and equity-like features. Although it typically has a low coupon rate, the holder is compensated with the ability to convert the bond to common stock, usually at a substantial discount to the stock's market value.
   a. Bond fund
   b. Gilts
   c. Corporate bond
   d. Convertible bond

6. _____ is typically a higher ranking stock than voting shares, and its terms are negotiated between the corporation and the investor.

   _____ usually carry no voting rights, but may carry superior priority over common stock in the payment of dividends and upon liquidation. _____ may carry a dividend that is paid out prior to any dividends to common stock holders.

   a. Trade-off theory
   b. Second lien loan
   c. Follow-on offering
   d. Preferred stock

7. In finance, a _____ is a debt security, in which the authorized issuer owes the holders a debt and, depending on the terms of the _____, is obliged to pay interest (the coupon) and/or to repay the principal at a later date, termed maturity.

   Thus a _____ is a loan: the issuer is the borrower, the _____ holder is the lender, and the coupon is the interest. _____s provide the borrower with external funds to finance long-term investments, or, in the case of government _____s, to finance current expenditure.

   a. Convertible bond
   b. Catastrophe bonds
   c. Puttable bond
   d. Bond

8. In business and finance, a _____ (also referred to as equity _____) of stock means a _____ of ownership in a corporation (company.) In the plural, stocks is often used as a synonym for _____s especially in the United States, but it is less commonly used that way outside of North America.

   In the United Kingdom, South Africa, and Australia, stock can also refer to completely different financial instruments such as government bonds or, less commonly, to all kinds of marketable securities.

   a. Margin
   b. Bucket shop
   c. Procter ' Gamble
   d. Share

9. In business and accounting, _____s are everything of value that is owned by a person or company. The balance sheet of a firm records the monetary value of the _____s owned by the firm. The two major _____ classes are tangible _____s and intangible _____s.
   a. Accounts payable
   b. Income
   c. Asset
   d. EBITDA

10. The term _____ is often used to refer to the investment management of collective investments, (not necessarily) whilst the more generic fund management may refer to all forms of institutional investment as well as investment management for private investors. Investment managers who specialize in advisory or discretionary management on behalf of (normally wealthy) private investors may often refer to their services as wealth management or portfolio management often within the context of so-called 'private banking'.

The provision of 'investment management services' includes elements of financial analysis, asset selection, stock selection, plan implementation and ongoing monitoring of investments.

a. AAB
b. A Random Walk Down Wall Street
c. ABN Amro
d. Asset management

11. The phrase _____ refers to the aspect of corporate strategy, corporate finance and management dealing with the buying, selling and combining of different companies that can aid, finance, or help a growing company in a given industry grow rapidly without having to create another business entity.

An acquisition, also known as a takeover, is the buying of one company (the 'target') by another. An acquisition may be friendly or hostile.

a. 4-4-5 Calendar
b. 7-Eleven
c. 529 plan
d. Mergers and acquisitions

12. _____ is a form of corporation equity ownership represented in the securities. It is dangerous in comparison to preferred shares and some other investment options, in that in the event of bankruptcy, _____ investors receive their funds after preferred stockholders, bondholders, creditors, etc. On the other hand, common shares on average perform better than preferred shares or bonds over time.

a. Stock market bubble
b. Stop-limit order
c. Stock split
d. Common stock

13. _____ is that which is owed; usually referencing assets owed, but the term can cover other obligations. In the case of assets, _____ is a means of using future purchasing power in the present before a summation has been earned. Some companies and corporations use _____ as a part of their overall corporate finance strategy.

a. Partial Payment
b. Credit cycle
c. Cross-collateralization
d. Debt

14. An _____ is an economic concept that relates to the cost incurred by an entity (such as organizations) associated with problems such as divergent management-shareholder objectives and information asymmetry. The costs consist of two main sources:

1. The costs inherently associated with using an agent (e.g., the risk that agents will use organizational resource for their own benefit) and
2. The costs of techniques used to mitigate the problems associated with using an agent (e.g., the costs of producing financial statements or the use of stock options to align executive interests to shareholder interests.)

Though effects of _____ are present in any agency relationship, the term is most used in business contexts.

The information asymmetry that exists between shareholders and the Chief Executive Officer is generally considered to be a classic example of a principal-agent problem. The agent (the manager) is working on behalf of the principal (the shareholders), who does not observe the actions of the agent.

    a. A Random Walk Down Wall Street
    b. AAB
    c. Agency cost
    d. ABN Amro

15. In economics, business, and accounting, a _____ is the value of money that has been used up to produce something, and hence is not available for use anymore. In business, the _____ may be one of acquisition, in which case the amount of money expended to acquire it is counted as _____. In this case, money is the input that is gone in order to acquire the thing.

    a. Fixed costs
    b. Sliding scale fees
    c. Marginal cost
    d. Cost

Chapter 25. Derivatives and Hedging Risk 159

1. A _____ is a financial contract between two parties, the buyer and the seller of this type of option. Often it is simply labeled a 'call'. The buyer of the option has the right, but not the obligation to buy an agreed quantity of a particular commodity or financial instrument (the underlying instrument) from the seller of the option at a certain time (the expiration date) for a certain price (the strike price.)
   a. Bear call spread
   b. Bear spread
   c. Call option
   d. Bull spread

2. A _____ is a financial contract whose value is derived from the value of something else (known as the underlying.) The underlying on which a _____ is based can be an asset, weather conditions bonds or other forms of credit.
   a. Derivative
   b. 4-4-5 Calendar
   c. 7-Eleven
   d. 529 plan

3. An _____ is a contract written by a seller that conveys to the buyer the right -- but not the obligation -- to buy (in the case of a call _____) or to sell (in the case of a put _____) a particular asset, such as a piece of property such as, among others, a futures contract. In return for granting the _____, the seller collects a payment (the premium) from the buyer.

   For example, buying a call _____ provides the right to buy a specified quantity of a security at a set strike price at some time on or before expiration, while buying a put _____ provides the right to sell.

   a. Amortization
   b. Option
   c. Annuity
   d. AT'T Mobility LLC

4. _____ (in a financial context) is the assumption of the risk of loss, in return for the uncertain possibility of a reward. Only if one may safely say that a particular position involves no risk may one say, strictly speaking, that such a position represents an 'investment.' Financial _____ involves the buying, holding, selling, and short-selling of stocks, bonds, commodities, currencies, collectibles, real estate, derivatives, or any valuable financial instrument to profit from fluctuations in its price as opposed to buying it for use or for income via methods such as dividends or interest. _____ represents one of four market roles in Western financial markets, distinct from hedging, long- or short-term investing, and arbitrage.
   a. Forward market
   b. Central Securities Depository
   c. Market anomaly
   d. Speculation

5. In finance, the _____ of a derivative is an asset, basket of assets, index, or even another derivative, such that the cash flows of the (former) derivative depend on the value of this _____. There must be an independent way to observe this value to avoid conflicts of interest.

   For example, in a stock option to buy 100 shares of Nokia at EUR 50 in September 2006, the _____ is a Nokia share.

   a. A Random Walk Down Wall Street
   b. AAB
   c. ABN Amro
   d. Underlying

6. In business and accounting, _____s are everything of value that is owned by a person or company. The balance sheet of a firm records the monetary value of the _____s owned by the firm. The two major _____ classes are tangible _____s and intangible _____s.

a. Income
b. Accounts payable
c. Asset
d. EBITDA

7. A _____ is an agreement between two parties to buy or sell an asset at a specified point of time in the future. The price of the underlying instrument, in whatever form, is paid before control of the instrument changes. This is one of the many forms of buy/sell orders where the time of trade is not the time where the securities themselves are exchanged.
   a. Constant maturity credit default swap
   b. Derivatives markets
   c. Loan Credit Default Swap Index
   d. Forward contract

8. A _____ is an exchange of promises between two or more parties to do an act which is enforceable in a court of law. It is where an unqualified offer meets a qualified acceptance and the parties reach Consensus ad Idem. The parties must have the necessary capacity to _____ and the _____ must not be either trifling, indeterminate, impossible or illegal.
   a. 4-4-5 Calendar
   b. 529 plan
   c. Contract
   d. 7-Eleven

9. The _____ is an American financial and commodity derivative exchange based in Chicago. The _____ was founded in 1898 as the Chicago Butter and Egg Board. Originally, the exchange was a non-profit organization.
   a. Public Company Accounting Oversight Board
   b. Financial Crimes Enforcement Network
   c. Gamelan Council
   d. Chicago Mercantile Exchange

10. A _____ is a futures contract on a short term interest rate (STIR.) Contracts vary, but are often defined on an interest rate index such as 3-month sterling or US dollar LIBOR.

They are traded across a wide range of currencies, including the G12 country currencies and many others.

   a. Notional amount
   b. Real estate derivatives
   c. Dual currency deposit
   d. Financial Future

11. In finance, a _____ is a standardized contract, to buy or sell a specified commodity of standardized quality at a certain date in the future, at a market determined price (the futures price.)

The price is determined by the instantaneous equilibrium between the forces of supply and demand among competing buy and sell orders on the exchange at the time of the purchase or sale of the contract.

In many cases, the items may be such non-traditional 'commodities' as foreign currencies, commercial or government paper [e.g., bonds], or 'baskets' of corporate equity ['stock indices'] or other financial instruments.

   a. Financial future
   b. Heston model
   c. Repurchase agreement
   d. Futures contract

12. In finance, a _____ is a debt security, in which the authorized issuer owes the holders a debt and, depending on the terms of the _____, is obliged to pay interest (the coupon) and/or to repay the principal at a later date, termed maturity.

Thus a _____ is a loan: the issuer is the borrower, the _____ holder is the lender, and the coupon is the interest. _____s provide the borrower with external funds to finance long-term investments, or, in the case of government _____s, to finance current expenditure.

a. Convertible bond
c. Puttable bond
b. Catastrophe bonds
d. Bond

13. _____ is a fee paid on borrowed assets. It is the price paid for the use of borrowed money, or, money earned by deposited funds. Assets that are sometimes lent with _____ include money, shares, consumer goods through hire purchase, major assets such as aircraft, and even entire factories in finance lease arrangements.

a. A Random Walk Down Wall Street
c. Insolvency
b. AAB
d. Interest

14. An _____ is the price a borrower pays for the use of money they do not own, and the return a lender receives for deferring the use of funds, by lending it to the borrower. _____s are normally expressed as a percentage rate over the period of one year.

_____s targets are also a vital tool of monetary policy and are used to control variables like investment, inflation, and unemployment.

a. ABN Amro
c. A Random Walk Down Wall Street
b. Interest rate
d. AAB

15. An _____ is a futures contract with an interest-bearing instrument as the underlying asset.

Examples include Treasury-bill futures, Treasury-bond futures and Eurodollar futures.

The global market for exchange-traded _____s is notionally valued by the Bank for International Settlements at $5,794,200 million in 2005.

a. Interest rate future
c. Interest rate derivative
b. Open interest
d. Equity swap

16. In financial accounting, _____s are precautions for which the amount or probability of occurrence are not known. Typical examples are _____s for warranty costs and _____ for taxes the term reserve is used instead of term _____; such a use, however, is inconsistent with the terminology suggested by International Accounting Standards Board.

a. Money measurement concept
c. Petty cash
b. Momentum Accounting and Triple-Entry Bookkeeping
d. Provision

17. In finance, a _____ is a position established in one market in an attempt to offset exposure to the price risk of an equal but opposite obligation or position in another market -- usually, but not always, in the context of one's commercial activity. Hedging is a strategy designed to minimize exposure to such business risks as a sharp contraction in demand for one's inventory, while still allowing the business to profit from producing and maintaining that inventory. A typical hedger might be a farmer with 2000 acres of unharvested wheat in the ground, who would rather tend his crop without the distraction of uncertain prices.
   a. 7-Eleven
   b. 529 plan
   c. Hedge
   d. 4-4-5 Calendar

18. _____ is the concept of adding accumulated interest back to the principal, so that interest is earned on interest from that moment on. The act of declaring interest to be principal is called compounding (i.e., interest is compounded.) A loan, for example, may have its interest compounded every month: in this case, a loan with $100 principal and 1% interest per month would have a balance of $101 at the end of the first month.
   a. Penny stock
   b. 4-4-5 Calendar
   c. Compound interest
   d. Risk management

19. _____ are government bonds issued by the United States Department of the Treasury through the Bureau of the Public Debt. They are the debt financing instruments of the U.S. Federal government, and they are often referred to simply as Treasuries or Treasurys. There are four types of marketable _____: Treasury bills, Treasury notes, Treasury bonds, and Treasury Inflation Protected Securities (TIPS.)
   a. Treasury securities
   b. Treasury Inflation Protected Securities
   c. 4-4-5 Calendar
   d. Treasury Inflation-Protected Securities

20. In probability theory and statistics, _____ indicates the strength and direction of a linear relationship between two random variables. That is in contrast with the usage of the term in colloquial speech, which denotes any relationship, not necessarily linear. In general statistical usage, _____ or co-relation refers to the departure of two random variables from independence.
   a. Variance
   b. Geometric mean
   c. Probability distribution
   d. Correlation

21. _____ is a life of security. It may also refer to the final payment date of a loan or other financial instrument, at which point all remaining interest and principal is due to be paid.

1, 3, 6 months _____ band can be calculated by using 30-day per month periods.

   a. Primary market
   b. Replacement cost
   c. False billing
   d. Maturity

22. In finance, the _____ of a financial asset measures the sensitivity of the asset's price to interest rate movements, expressed as a number of years. The reason for expressing this sensitivity in years is that the time that will elapse until a cash flow is received allows more interest to accumulate. Therefore the price of an asset with long term cashflows has more interest rate sensitivity than an asset with cashflows in the near future.
   a. Macaulay duration
   b. Yield to maturity
   c. 4-4-5 Calendar
   d. Duration

Chapter 25. Derivatives and Hedging Risk

23. A _____ is a bond bought at a price lower than its face value, with the face value repaid at the time of maturity. It does not make periodic interest payments, or so-called 'coupons,' hence the term zero-coupon bond. Investors earn return from the compounded interest all paid at maturity plus the difference between the discounted price of the bond and its par value.
    a. Bowie bonds
    b. Callable bond
    c. Municipal bond
    d. Zero coupon bond

24. The coupon or _____ of a bond is the amount of interest paid per year expressed as a percentage of the face value of the bond.

For example if you hold $10,000 nominal of a bond described as a 4.5% loan stock, you will receive $450 in interest each year (probably in two installments of $225 each.)

Not all bonds have coupons.

    a. Zero-coupon bond
    b. Revenue bonds
    c. Puttable bond
    d. Coupon rate

25. A '_____' is a 'Charge' that is paid to obtain the right to delay a payment. Essentially, the payer purchases the right to make a given payment in the future instead of in the Present. The '_____', or 'Charge' that must be paid to delay the payment, is simply the difference between what the payment amount would be if it were paid in the present and what the payment amount would be paid if it were paid in the future.
    a. Discount
    b. Value at risk
    c. Risk modeling
    d. Risk aversion

26. _____ most frequently refers to the standard deviation of the continuously compounded returns of a financial instrument with a specific time horizon. It is often used to quantify the risk of the instrument over that time period. _____ is typically expressed in annualized terms, and it may either be an absolute number ($5) or a fraction of the mean (5%).
    a. Seasoned equity offering
    b. Portfolio insurance
    c. Currency swap
    d. Volatility

27. The phrase _____ refers to the aspect of corporate strategy, corporate finance and management dealing with the buying, selling and combining of different companies that can aid, finance, or help a growing company in a given industry grow rapidly without having to create another business entity.

An acquisition, also known as a takeover, is the buying of one company (the 'target') by another. An acquisition may be friendly or hostile.

    a. 7-Eleven
    b. Mergers and acquisitions
    c. 4-4-5 Calendar
    d. 529 plan

28. An _____ is a derivative in which one party exchanges a stream of interest payments for another party's stream of cash flows. _____s can be used by hedgers to manage their fixed or floating assets and liabilities. They can also be used by speculators to replicate unfunded bond exposures to profit from changes in interest rates.

a. Implied volatility
b. Equity swap
c. International Swaps and Derivatives Association
d. Interest rate swap

29. In finance, a _____ is a derivative in which two counterparties agree to exchange one stream of cash flows against another stream. These streams are called the legs of the _____.

The cash flows are calculated over a notional principal amount, which is usually not exchanged between counterparties.

a. Volatility swap
b. Local volatility
c. Swap
d. Volatility arbitrage

30. A _____ is a foreign exchange agreement between two parties to exchange principal and fixed rate interest payments on a loan in one currency for principal and fixed rate interest payments on an equal (regarding net present value) loan in another currency. They are motivated by comparative advantage.

a. Forex swap
b. Foreign exchange market
c. Currency pair
d. Currency swap

Chapter 26. Short-Term Finance and Planning

1. In financial accounting, a _____ or statement of financial position is a summary of a person's or organization's balances. Assets, liabilities and ownership equity are listed as of a specific date, such as the end of its financial year. A _____ is often described as a snapshot of a company's financial condition.

   a. Statement of retained earnings
   b. Financial statements
   c. Statement on Auditing Standards No. 70: Service Organizations
   d. Balance sheet

2. In accounting, a _____ is an asset on the balance sheet which is expected to be sold or otherwise used up in the near future, usually within one year, or one business cycle - whichever is longer. Typical _____s include cash, cash equivalents, accounts receivable, inventory, the portion of prepaid accounts which will be used within a year, and short-term investments.

   On the balance sheet, assets will typically be classified into _____s and long-term assets.

   a. Write-off
   b. Long-term liabilities
   c. Historical cost
   d. Current asset

3. In accounting, _____ are considered liabilities of the business that are to be settled in cash within the fiscal year or the operating cycle, whichever period is longer.

   For example accounts payable for goods, services or supplies that were purchased for use in the operation of the business and payable within a normal period of time would be _____.

   Bonds, mortgages and loans that are payable over a term exceeding one year would be fixed liabilities.

   a. Current liabilities
   b. Gross sales
   c. Net income
   d. Closing entries

4. _____ is the standard framework of guidelines for financial accounting used in the United States of America. It includes the standards, conventions, and rules accountants follow in recording and summarizing transactions, and in the preparation of financial statements. _____ are now issued by the Financial Accounting Standards Board (FASB).

   a. Generally Accepted Accounting Principles
   b. Revenue
   c. Depreciation
   d. Net income

5. _____ is a measure of the ability of a debtor to pay their debts as and when they fall due. It is usually expressed as a ratio or a percentage of current liabilities.

   For a corporation with a published balance sheet there are various ratios used to calculate a measure of liquidity.

   a. Operating leverage
   b. Operating profit margin
   c. Invested capital
   d. Accounting liquidity

6. In economics, the concept of the _____ refers to the decision-making time frame of a firm in which at least one factor of production is fixed. Costs which are fixed in the _____ have no impact on a firms decisions. For example a firm can raise output by increasing the amount of labour through overtime.

a. Long-run
c. 4-4-5 Calendar
b. 529 plan
d. Short-run

7. In business and accounting, _____s are everything of value that is owned by a person or company. The balance sheet of a firm records the monetary value of the _____s owned by the firm. The two major _____ classes are tangible _____s and intangible _____s.
 a. Accounts payable
 c. Income
 b. Asset
 d. EBITDA

8. The phrase _____ refers to the aspect of corporate strategy, corporate finance and management dealing with the buying, selling and combining of different companies that can aid, finance, or help a growing company in a given industry grow rapidly without having to create another business entity.

An acquisition, also known as a takeover, is the buying of one company (the 'target') by another. An acquisition may be friendly or hostile.

 a. 4-4-5 Calendar
 c. 7-Eleven
 b. Mergers and acquisitions
 d. 529 plan

9. _____ is a financial metric which represents operating liquidity available to a business. Along with fixed assets such as plant and equipment, _____ is considered a part of operating capital. It is calculated as current assets minus current liabilities.
 a. 529 plan
 c. Working capital
 b. 4-4-5 Calendar
 d. Working capital management

10. In marketing, _____ refers to the total cost of holding inventory. This includes warehousing costs such as rent, utilities and salaries, financial costs such as opportunity cost, and inventory costs related to perishibility, shrinkage and insurance.
 a. 4-4-5 Calendar
 c. 7-Eleven
 b. 529 plan
 d. Carrying cost

11. In economics, business, and accounting, a _____ is the value of money that has been used up to produce something, and hence is not available for use anymore. In business, the _____ may be one of acquisition, in which case the amount of money expended to acquire it is counted as _____. In this case, money is the input that is gone in order to acquire the thing.
 a. Sliding scale fees
 c. Cost
 b. Marginal cost
 d. Fixed costs

12. _____ refinancing (in the case of real property) occurs when a loan is taken out on property already owned, and the loan amount is above and beyond the cost of transaction, payoff of existing liens, and related expenses.

Strictly speaking all refinancing of debt is '_____', when funds retrieved are utilized for anything other than repaying an existing lien.

Chapter 26. Short-Term Finance and Planning

In the case of common usage of the term, _____ refinancing refers to when equity is liquidated from a property above and beyond sum of the payoff of existing loans held in lien on the property, loan fees, costs associated with the loan, taxes, insurance, tax reserves, insurance reserves, and in the past any other non-lien debt held in the name of the owner being paid by loan proceeds.

a. Home equity line of credit
b. Fixed rate mortgage
c. Conforming loan
d. Cash-out

13. In financial accounting, the term _____ is most commonly used to describe any part of shareholders' equity, except for basic share capital. Sometimes, the term is used instead of the term provision; such a use, however, is inconsistent with the terminology suggested by International Accounting Standards Board. For more information about provisions, see provision (accounting.)

a. Treasury stock
b. Closing entries
c. FIFO and LIFO accounting
d. Reserve

14. _____ is a life of security. It may also refer to the final payment date of a loan or other financial instrument, at which point all remaining interest and principal is due to be paid.

1, 3, 6 months _____ band can be calculated by using 30-day per month periods.

a. False billing
b. Replacement cost
c. Maturity
d. Primary market

15. _____, in bookkeeping, refers to assets, liabilities, income, and expenses recorded on individual pages of the so called book of final entry or ledger. Changes in _____ value are made by chronologically posting debit (DR) and credit (CR) entries to its page. Examples of _____s are cash, _____s receivable, mortgages, loans, land and buildings, common stock, sales, services provided, wages, and payroll overhead.

a. Alpha
b. Option
c. Account
d. Accretion

16. _____ is a file or account that contains money that a person or company owes to suppliers, but hasn't paid yet (a form of debt.) When you receive an invoice you add it to the file, and then you remove it when you pay. Thus, the A/P is a form of credit that suppliers offer to their purchasers by allowing them to pay for a product or service after it has already been received.

a. Earnings before interest, taxes, depreciation and amortization
b. Outstanding balance
c. Accrual
d. Accounts payable

17. A _____ is an expenditure creating future benefits. A _____ is incurred when a business spends money either to buy fixed assets or to add to the value of an existing fixed asset with a useful life that extends beyond the taxable year. Capex are used by a company to acquire or upgrade physical assets such as equipment, property, or industrial buildings.

a. Cost of capital
b. Weighted average cost of capital
c. 4-4-5 Calendar
d. Capital expenditure

18. In economic models, the _____ time frame assumes no fixed factors of production. Firms can enter or leave the marketplace, and the cost (and availability) of land, labor, raw materials, and capital goods can be assumed to vary. In contrast, in the short-run time frame, certain factors are assumed to be fixed, because there is not sufficient time for them to change.

   a. Short-run
   b. 4-4-5 Calendar
   c. 529 plan
   d. Long-run

19. _____ is one of a series of accounting transactions dealing with the billing of customers who owe money to a person, company or organization for goods and services that have been provided to the customer. In most business entities this is typically done by generating an invoice and mailing or electronically delivering it to the customer, who in turn must pay it within an established timeframe called credit or payment terms.

An example of a common payment term is Net 30, meaning payment is due in the amount of the invoice 30 days from the date of invoice.

   a. Accounting methods
   b. Income
   c. Impaired asset
   d. Accounts receivable

20. _____ is the provision of resources (such as granting a loan) by one party to another party where that second party does not reimburse the first party immediately, thereby generating a debt, and instead arranges either to repay or return those resources (or material(s) of equal value) at a later date. The first party is called a creditor, also known as a lender, while the second party is called a debtor, also known as a borrower.

Movements of financial capital are normally dependent on either _____ or equity transfers.

   a. Warrant
   b. Credit
   c. Comparable
   d. Clearing house

21. _____ is that which is owed; usually referencing assets owed, but the term can cover other obligations. In the case of assets, _____ is a means of using future purchasing power in the present before a summation has been earned. Some companies and corporations use _____ as a part of their overall corporate finance strategy.

   a. Cross-collateralization
   b. Partial Payment
   c. Credit cycle
   d. Debt

22. A _____ is any credit facility extended to a business by a bank or financial institution. A _____ may take several forms such as cash credit, overdraft, demand loan, export packing credit, term loan, discounting or purchase of commercial bills etc. It is like an account that can readily be tapped into if the need arises or not touched at all and saved for emergencies.

   a. Default Notice
   b. Cash credit
   c. Debt-snowball method
   d. Line of credit

23. An _____ is a loan that is not backed by collateral. Also known as a signature loan or personal loan.

_____s are based solely upon the borrower's credit rating.

Chapter 26. Short-Term Finance and Planning

a. Unsecured loan
c. Annualcreditreport.com
b. Intelliscore
d. Event of default

24. A _____, in its most general sense, is a solemn promise to engage in or refrain from a specified action.

More specifically, a _____, in contrast to a contract, is a one-way agreement whereby the _____er is the only party bound by the promise. A _____ may have conditions and prerequisites that qualify the undertaking, including the actions of second or third parties, but there is no inherent agreement by such other parties to fulfill those requirements.

a. Clayton Antitrust Act
c. Partnership
b. Covenant
d. Federal Trade Commission Act

25. In the global money market, _____ is an unsecured promissory note with a fixed maturity of one to 270 days. _____ is a money-market security issued (sold) by large banks and corporations to get money to meet short term debt obligations (for example, payroll), and is only backed by an issuing bank or corporation's promise to pay the face amount on the maturity date specified on the note. Since it is not backed by collateral, only firms with excellent credit ratings from a recognized rating agency will be able to sell their _____ at a reasonable price.

a. Financial distress
c. Trade-off theory
b. Book building
d. Commercial paper

26. _____ is a list for goods and materials held available in stock by a business. It is also used for a list of the contents of a household and for a list for testamentary purposes of the possessions of someone who has died. In accounting _____ is considered an asset.

a. ABN Amro
c. Inventory
b. A Random Walk Down Wall Street
d. AAB

27. In law, a _____ is a form of security interest granted over an item of property to secure the payment of a debt or performance of some other obligation. The owner of the property, who grants the _____, is referred to as the lienor and the person who has the benefit of the _____ is referred to as the _____ee.

The etymological root is: Anglo-French _____, loyen bond, restraint, from Latin ligamen, from ligare to bind.

a. Family and Medical Leave Act
c. Sarbanes-Oxley Act
b. Lien
d. Joint venture

28. Decisions relating to working capital and short term financing are referred to as _____. These involve managing the relationship between a firm's short-term assets and its short-term liabilities. The goal of _____ is to ensure that the firm is able to continue its operations and that it has sufficient cash flow to satisfy both maturing short-term debt and upcoming operational expenses.

a. Working capital management
c. 529 plan
b. Working capital
d. 4-4-5 Calendar

Chapter 27. Cash Management

1. Cash and _____ are the most liquid assets found within the asset portion of a company's balance sheet. _____ are assets that are readily convertible into cash, such as money market holdings, short-term government bonds or Treasury bills, marketable securities and commercial paper. _____ are distinguished from other investments through their short-term existence; they mature within 3 months whereas short-term investments are 12 months or less, and long-term investments are any investments that mature in excess of 12 months.

   a. Tick size
   b. Secured debt
   c. Cash equivalents
   d. Par value

2. In United States banking, _____ is a marketing term for certain services offered primarily to larger business customers. It may be used to describe all bank accounts (such as checking accounts) provided to businesses of a certain size, but it is more often used to describe specific services such as cash concentration, zero balance accounting, and automated clearing house facilities. Sometimes, private banking customers are given _____ services.

   a. Profitability index
   b. Global tactical asset allocation
   c. Capitalization rate
   d. Cash management

3. In accounting, a _____ is an asset on the balance sheet which is expected to be sold or otherwise used up in the near future, usually within one year, or one business cycle - whichever is longer. Typical _____s include cash, cash equivalents, accounts receivable, inventory, the portion of prepaid accounts which will be used within a year, and short-term investments.

   On the balance sheet, assets will typically be classified into _____s and long-term assets.

   a. Write-off
   b. Long-term liabilities
   c. Historical cost
   d. Current asset

4. _____ is a financial metric which represents operating liquidity available to a business. Along with fixed assets such as plant and equipment, _____ is considered a part of operating capital. It is calculated as current assets minus current liabilities.

   a. 4-4-5 Calendar
   b. 529 plan
   c. Working capital management
   d. Working capital

5. In economics, the concept of the _____ refers to the decision-making time frame of a firm in which at least one factor of production is fixed. Costs which are fixed in the _____ have no impact on a firms decisions. For example a firm can raise output by increasing the amount of labour through overtime.

   a. 4-4-5 Calendar
   b. Short-run
   c. Long-run
   d. 529 plan

6. In business and accounting, _____s are everything of value that is owned by a person or company. The balance sheet of a firm records the monetary value of the _____s owned by the firm. The two major _____ classes are tangible _____s and intangible _____s.

   a. Accounts payable
   b. EBITDA
   c. Income
   d. Asset

7. In economics, business, and accounting, a _____ is the value of money that has been used up to produce something, and hence is not available for use anymore. In business, the _____ may be one of acquisition, in which case the amount of money expended to acquire it is counted as _____. In this case, money is the input that is gone in order to acquire the thing.

Chapter 27. Cash Management

a. Marginal cost
b. Fixed costs
c. Sliding scale fees
d. Cost

8. _____ are securities that can be easily converted into cash. Such securities will generally have highly liquid markets allowing the security to be sold at a reasonable price very quickly. This is a usual feature in real estate.
a. Securities lending
b. Book entry
c. Tracking stock
d. Marketable

9. A _____ is a fungible, negotiable instrument representing financial value. They are broadly categorized into debt securities (such as banknotes, bonds and debentures), and equity securities; e.g., common stocks. The company or other entity issuing the _____ is called the issuer.
a. Securities lending
b. Tracking stock
c. Book entry
d. Security

10. A _____ is a situation that involves losing one quality or aspect of something in return for gaining another quality or aspect. It implies a decision to be made with full comprehension of both the upside and downside of a particular choice.

In economics the term is expressed as opportunity cost, referring the most preferred alternative given up.

a. Capital outflow
b. Total revenue
c. Break-even point
d. Trade-off

11. _____ or economic opportunity loss is the value of the next best alternative foregone as the result of making a decision. _____ analysis is an important part of a company's decision-making processes but is not treated as an actual cost in any financial statement. The next best thing that a person can engage in is referred to as the _____ of doing the best thing and ignoring the next best thing to be done.
a. Opportunity cost
b. AAB
c. A Random Walk Down Wall Street
d. ABN Amro

12. In economics, and cost accounting, _____ describes the total economic cost of production and is made up of variable costs, which vary according to the quantity of a good produced and include inputs such as labor and raw materials, plus fixed costs, which are independent of the quantity of a good produced and include inputs (capital) that cannot be varied in the short term, such as buildings and machinery. _____ in economics includes the total opportunity cost of each factor of production in addition to fixed and variable costs.

The rate at which _____ changes as the amount produced changes is called marginal cost.

a. 7-Eleven
b. 529 plan
c. 4-4-5 Calendar
d. Total cost

13. The free _____ of a public company is an estimate of the proportion of shares that are not held by large owners and that are not stock with sales restrictions (restricted stock that cannot be sold until they become unrestricted stock.)

Chapter 27. Cash Management

The free _____ or a public _____ is usually defined as being all shares held by investors other than:

- shares held by owners owning more than 5% of all shares (those could be institutional investors, 'strategic shareholders,' founders, executives, and other insiders' holdings)
- restricted stocks (granted to executives that can be, but don't have to be, registered insiders)
- insider holdings (it is assumed that insiders hold stock for the very long term)

The free _____ is an important criterion in quoting a share on the stock market.

To _____ a company means to list its shares on a public stock exchange through an initial public offering (or 'flotation'.)

- Open market
- Outstanding shares
- Market capitalization
- Public _____ *loat*
- Reverse takeover

a. Golden parachute
c. Synthetic CDO
b. Float
d. Trade finance

14. In banking and finance, _____ denotes all activities from the time a commitment is made for a transaction until it is settled. _____ is necessary because the speed of trades is much faster than the cycle time for completing the underlying transaction.

In its widest sense _____ involves the management of post-trading, pre-settlement credit exposures, to ensure that trades are settled in accordance with market rules, even if a buyer or seller should become insolvent prior to settlement.

a. Clearing house
c. Share
b. Clearing
d. Procter ' Gamble

15. A _____ is a financial services company that provides clearing and settlement services for financial transactions, usually on a futures exchange, and often acts as central counterparty (the payor actually pays the _____, which then pays the payee). A _____ may also offer novation, the substitution of a new contract or debt for an old, or other credit enhancement services to its members.

The term is also used for banks like Suffolk Bank that acted as a restraint on the over-issuance of private bank notes.

a. Valuation
c. Warrant
b. Clearing House
d. Bucket shop

Chapter 27. Cash Management

16. The _____ is the main privately held clearing house for large-value transactions in the United States, settling well over US$1 trillion a day in around 250,000 interbank payments. Together with the Fedwire Funds Service (which is operated by the Federal Reserve Banks), _____ forms the primary U.S. network for large-value domestic and international USD payments (where it has a market share of around 96%).
    a. 7-Eleven
    b. 4-4-5 Calendar
    c. 529 plan
    d. Clearing House Interbank Payments System

17. A _____ can require immediate payment by the second party to the third upon presentation of the _____. This is called a sight _____. A Cheques is a sight _____. An importer might write a _____ promising payment to an exporter for delivery of goods with payment to occur 60 days after the goods are delivered. Such a _____ is called a time _____.
    a. Second lien loan
    b. Cashflow matching
    c. Gross profit margin
    d. Draft

18. _____, in bookkeeping, refers to assets, liabilities, income, and expenses recorded on individual pages of the so called book of final entry or ledger. Changes in _____ value are made by chronologically posting debit (DR) and credit (CR) entries to its page. Examples of _____s are cash, _____s receivable, mortgages, loans, land and buildings, common stock, sales, services provided, wages, and payroll overhead.
    a. Account
    b. Accretion
    c. Alpha
    d. Option

19. The institution most often referenced by the word '_____' is a public or publicly traded _____, the shares of which are traded on a public stock exchange (e.g., the New York Stock Exchange or Nasdaq in the United States) where shares of stock of _____s are bought and sold by and to the general public. Most of the largest businesses in the world are publicly traded _____s. However, the majority of _____s are said to be closely held, privately held or close _____s, meaning that no ready market exists for the trading of shares.
    a. Protect
    b. Federal Home Loan Mortgage Corporation
    c. Depository Trust Company
    d. Corporation

20. In finance, the _____ is the global financial market for short-term borrowing and lending. It provides short-term liquidity funding for the global financial system. The _____ is where short-term obligations such as Treasury bills, commercial paper and bankers' acceptances are bought and sold.
    a. Cramdown
    b. Debt-for-equity swap
    c. Consumer debt
    d. Money market

21. In finance, _____ occurs when a debtor has not met its legal obligations according to the debt contract, e.g. it has not made a scheduled payment, or has violated a loan covenant (condition) of the debt contract. _____ may occur if the debtor is either unwilling or unable to pay their debt. This can occur with all debt obligations including bonds, mortgages, loans, and promissory notes.
    a. Default
    b. Vendor finance
    c. Credit crunch
    d. Debt validation

22. _____ is the risk of loss due to a debtor's non-payment of a loan or other line of credit (either the principal or interest (coupon) or both)

Chapter 27. Cash Management

Most lenders employ their own models (credit scorecards) to rank potential and existing customers according to risk, and then apply appropriate strategies. With products such as unsecured personal loans or mortgages, lenders charge a higher price for higher risk customers and vice versa. With revolving products such as credit cards and overdrafts, risk is controlled through careful setting of credit limits.

a. Market risk
c. Transaction risk
b. Liquidity risk
d. Credit risk

23. _____ is a measure of the ability of a debtor to pay their debts as and when they fall due. It is usually expressed as a ratio or a percentage of current liabilities.

For a corporation with a published balance sheet there are various ratios used to calculate a measure of liquidity.

a. Invested capital
c. Accounting liquidity
b. Operating leverage
d. Operating profit margin

24. _____ is a life of security. It may also refer to the final payment date of a loan or other financial instrument, at which point all remaining interest and principal is due to be paid.

1, 3, 6 months _____ band can be calculated by using 30-day per month periods.

a. Replacement cost
c. Maturity
b. Primary market
d. False billing

25. In finance, a _____ is a debt security, in which the authorized issuer owes the holders a debt and, depending on the terms of the _____, is obliged to pay interest (the coupon) and/or to repay the principal at a later date, termed maturity.

Thus a _____ is a loan: the issuer is the borrower, the _____ holder is the lender, and the coupon is the interest. _____s provide the borrower with external funds to finance long-term investments, or, in the case of government _____s, to finance current expenditure.

a. Puttable bond
c. Convertible bond
b. Catastrophe bonds
d. Bond

26. _____ is a type of bond that allows the issuer of the bond to retain the privilege of redeeming the bond at some point before the bond reaches the date of maturity. In other words, on the call dates, the issuer has the right, but not the obligation, to buy back the bonds from the bond holders at the call price. Technically speaking, the bonds are not really bought and held by the issuer but cancelled immediately.

a. Gilts
c. Coupon rate
b. Callable bond
d. Bond fund

Chapter 27. Cash Management

27. In the global money market, _____ is an unsecured promissory note with a fixed maturity of one to 270 days. _____ is a money-market security issued (sold) by large banks and corporations to get money to meet short term debt obligations (for example, payroll), and is only backed by an issuing bank or corporation's promise to pay the face amount on the maturity date specified on the note. Since it is not backed by collateral, only firms with excellent credit ratings from a recognized rating agency will be able to sell their _____ at a reasonable price.
   a. Financial distress
   b. Book building
   c. Commercial paper
   d. Trade-off theory

28. _____s are deposits denominated in United States dollars at banks outside the United States, and thus are not under the jurisdiction of the Federal Reserve. Consequently, such deposits are subject to much less regulation than similar deposits within the United States, allowing for higher margins. There is nothing 'European' about _____ deposits; a US dollar-denominated deposit in Tokyo or Caracas would likewise be deemed _____ deposits.
   a. ABN Amro
   b. A Random Walk Down Wall Street
   c. AAB
   d. Eurodollar

29. A _____ allows a borrower to use a financial security as collateral for a cash loan at a fixed rate of interest. In a repo, the borrower agrees to immediately sell a security to a lender and also agrees to buy the same security from the lender at a fixed price at some later date. A repo is equivalent to a cash transaction combined with a forward contract.
   a. Total return swap
   b. Contango
   c. Repurchase agreement
   d. Volatility arbitrage

30. _____ mature in one year or less. Like zero-coupon bonds, they do not pay interest prior to maturity; instead they are sold at a discount of the par value to create a positive yield to maturity. Many regard _____ as the least risky investment available to U.S. investors.
   a. 4-4-5 Calendar
   b. Treasury Inflation Protected Securities
   c. Treasury bills
   d. Treasury securities

31. _____ are government bonds issued by the United States Department of the Treasury through the Bureau of the Public Debt. They are the debt financing instruments of the U.S. Federal government, and they are often referred to simply as Treasuries or Treasurys. There are four types of marketable _____: Treasury bills, Treasury notes, Treasury bonds, and Treasury Inflation Protected Securities (TIPS.)
   a. 4-4-5 Calendar
   b. Treasury Inflation-Protected Securities
   c. Treasury securities
   d. Treasury Inflation Protected Securities

Chapter 28. Credit Management

1. _____ is the provision of resources (such as granting a loan) by one party to another party where that second party does not reimburse the first party immediately, thereby generating a debt, and instead arranges either to repay or return those resources (or material(s) of equal value) at a later date. The first party is called a creditor, also known as a lender, while the second party is called a debtor, also known as a borrower.

Movements of financial capital are normally dependent on either _____ or equity transfers.

  a. Credit
  b. Warrant
  c. Comparable
  d. Clearing house

2. An _____ or bill is a commercial document issued by a seller to the buyer, indicating the products, quantities, and agreed prices for products or services the seller has provided the buyer. An _____ indicates the buyer must pay the seller, according to the payment terms.

In the rental industry, an _____ must include a specific reference to the duration of the time being billed, so rather than quantity, price and discount the invoicing amount is based on quantity, price, discount and duration.

  a. Invoice
  b. ABN Amro
  c. A Random Walk Down Wall Street
  d. AAB

3. A '_____' is a 'Charge' that is paid to obtain the right to delay a payment. Essentially, the payer purchases the right to make a given payment in the future instead of in the Present. The '_____', or 'Charge' that must be paid to delay the payment, is simply the difference between what the payment amount would be if it were paid in the present and what the payment amount would be paid if it were paid in the future.

  a. Risk aversion
  b. Risk modeling
  c. Value at risk
  d. Discount

4. A _____, referred to as a note payable in accounting, is a contract where one party (the maker or issuer) makes an unconditional promise in writing to pay a sum of money to the other (the payee), either at a fixed or determinable future time or on demand of the payee, under specific terms. They differ from IOUs in that they contain a specific promise to pay, rather than simply acknowledging that a debt exists.

The terms of a note typically include the principal amount, the interest rate if any, and the maturity date.

  a. Promissory note
  b. Credit repair software
  c. Financial plan
  d. Title loan

5. A _____ can require immediate payment by the second party to the third upon presentation of the _____. This is called a sight _____. A Cheques is a sight _____. An importer might write a _____ promising payment to an exporter for delivery of goods with payment to occur 60 days after the goods are delivered. Such a _____ is called a time _____.

  a. Draft
  b. Cashflow matching
  c. Gross profit margin
  d. Second lien loan

6. _____, in bookkeeping, refers to assets, liabilities, income, and expenses recorded on individual pages of the so called book of final entry or ledger. Changes in _____ value are made by chronologically posting debit (DR) and credit (CR) entries to its page. Examples of _____s are cash, _____s receivable, mortgages, loans, land and buildings, common stock, sales, services provided, wages, and payroll overhead.
   a. Option
   b. Accretion
   c. Alpha
   d. Account

7. A _____ is an exchange of promises between two or more parties to do an act which is enforceable in a court of law. It is where an unqualified offer meets a qualified acceptance and the parties reach Consensus ad Idem. The parties must have the necessary capacity to _____ and the _____ must not be either trifling, indeterminate, impossible or illegal.
   a. 529 plan
   b. 7-Eleven
   c. 4-4-5 Calendar
   d. Contract

8. In marketing, _____ refers to the total cost of holding inventory. This includes warehousing costs such as rent, utilities and salaries, financial costs such as opportunity cost, and inventory costs related to perishibility, shrinkage and insurance.
   a. 4-4-5 Calendar
   b. Carrying cost
   c. 7-Eleven
   d. 529 plan

9. In economics, business, and accounting, a _____ is the value of money that has been used up to produce something, and hence is not available for use anymore. In business, the _____ may be one of acquisition, in which case the amount of money expended to acquire it is counted as _____. In this case, money is the input that is gone in order to acquire the thing.
   a. Marginal cost
   b. Fixed costs
   c. Sliding scale fees
   d. Cost

10. _____ is the method by which one calculates the creditworthiness of a business or organization. The audited financial statements of a large company might be analyzed when it issues or has issued bonds. Or, a bank may analyze the financial statements of a small business before making or renewing a commercial loan.
    a. Credit analysis
    b. Credit crunch
    c. Credit report monitoring
    d. Capital note

11. _____ is one of a series of accounting transactions dealing with the billing of customers who owe money to a person, company or organization for goods and services that have been provided to the customer. In most business entities this is typically done by generating an invoice and mailing or electronically delivering it to the customer, who in turn must pay it within an established timeframe called credit or payment terms.

An example of a common payment term is Net 30, meaning payment is due in the amount of the invoice 30 days from the date of invoice.

   a. Accounts receivable
   b. Impaired asset
   c. Accounting methods
   d. Income

Chapter 28. Credit Management

12. _____ is a financial transaction whereby a business sells its accounts receivable (i.e., invoices) at a discount. _____ differs from a bank loan in three main ways. First, the emphasis is on the value of the receivables (essentially a financial asset), not the firm's credit worthiness.

   a. Debt-for-equity swap
   b. Financial Literacy Month
   c. Factoring
   d. Credit card balance transfer

13. _____ exists when one firm provides goods or services to a customer with an agreement to bill them later, or receive a shipment or service from a supplier under an agreement to pay them later. It can be viewed as an essential element of capitalization in an operating business because it can reduce the required capital investment to operate the business if it is managed properly. _____ is the largest use of capital for a majority of business to business (B2B) sellers in the United States and is a critical source of capital for a majority of all businesses.

   a. 4-4-5 Calendar
   b. 529 plan
   c. Going concern
   d. Trade credit

Chapter 29. Mergers and Acquisitions

1. The phrase _____ refers to the aspect of corporate strategy, corporate finance and management dealing with the buying, selling and combining of different companies that can aid, finance, or help a growing company in a given industry grow rapidly without having to create another business entity.

An acquisition, also known as a takeover, is the buying of one company (the 'target') by another. An acquisition may be friendly or hostile.

   a. 4-4-5 Calendar   b. 529 plan
   c. 7-Eleven   d. Mergers and acquisitions

2. _____ or amalgamation is the act of merging many things into one. In business, it often refers to the mergers or acquisitions of many smaller companies into much larger ones. The financial accounting term of _____ refers to the aggregated financial statements of a group company as consolidated account.
   a. Cost of goods sold   b. Retained earnings
   c. Write-off   d. Consolidation

3. In business and accounting, _____s are everything of value that is owned by a person or company. The balance sheet of a firm records the monetary value of the _____s owned by the firm. The two major _____ classes are tangible _____s and intangible _____s.
   a. Income   b. Accounts payable
   c. EBITDA   d. Asset

4. _____ is a corporate finance term denoting a type of takeover bid. The _____ is a public, open offer or invitation (usually announced in a newspaper advertisement) by a prospective acquirer to all stockholders of a publicly traded corporation (the target corporation) to tender their stock for sale at a specified price during a specified time, subject to the tendering of a minimum and maximum number of shares. In a _____, the bidder contacts shareholders directly; the directors of the company may or may not have endorsed the _____ proposal.
   a. Tender offer   b. Shareholder value
   c. Follow-on offering   d. Cash is king

5. In business, a _____ is the purchase of one company (the target) by another (the acquirer or bidder). In the UK the term refers to the acquisition of a public company whose shares are listed on a stock exchange, in contrast to the acquisition of a private company.

Before a bidder makes an offer for another company, it usually first informs that company's board of directors.

   a. Stock swap   b. 4-4-5 Calendar
   c. 529 plan   d. Takeover

6. In business, _____ is income that a company receives from its normal business activities, usually from the sale of goods and services to customers. Some companies also receive _____ from interest, dividends or royalties paid to them by other companies. _____ may refer to business income in general, or it may refer to the amount, in a monetary unit, received during a period of time, as in 'Last year, Company X had _____ of $32 million.'

In many countries, including the UK, _____ is referred to as turnover.

a. Matching principle
c. Revenue
b. Bottom line
d. Furniture, Fixtures and Equipment

7. In economics, business, and accounting, a _____ is the value of money that has been used up to produce something, and hence is not available for use anymore. In business, the _____ may be one of acquisition, in which case the amount of money expended to acquire it is counted as _____. In this case, money is the input that is gone in order to acquire the thing.
a. Fixed costs
c. Sliding scale fees
b. Marginal cost
d. Cost

8. In microeconomics and management, the term _____ describes a style of management control. Vertically integrated companies are united through a hierarchy with a common owner. Usually each member of the hierarchy produces a different product or (market-specific) service, and the products combine to satisfy a common need.
a. 4-4-5 Calendar
c. 7-Eleven
b. 529 plan
d. Vertical integration

9. The _____ is the rate that a company is expected to pay to finance its assets. WACC is the minimum return that a company must earn on existing asset base to satisfy its creditors, owners, and other providers of capital.

Companies raise money from a number of sources: common equity, preferred equity, straight debt, convertible debt, exchangeable debt, warrants, options, pension liabilities, executive stock options, governmental subsidies, and so on.

a. 4-4-5 Calendar
c. Weighted average cost of capital
b. Cost of capital
d. Capital intensity

10. _____ are costs incurred on the purchase of land, buildings, construction and equipment to be used in the production of goods or the rendering of services. In other words, the total cost needed to bring a project to a commercially operable status. However, _____ are not limited to the initial construction of a factory or other business.
a. Trade-off
c. Defined contribution plan
b. Capital costs
d. Capital outflow

11. The _____ is an expected return that the provider of capital plans to earn on their investment.

Capital (money) used for funding a business should earn returns for the capital providers who risk their capital. For an investment to be worthwhile, the expected return on capital must be greater than the _____.

a. 4-4-5 Calendar
c. Capital intensity
b. Weighted average cost of capital
d. Cost of capital

12. _____ refers to a tax levied by various jurisdictions on the profits made by companies or associations. It is a tax on the value of the corporation's profits.

The measure of taxable profits varies from country to country.

a. Corporate tax
c. Proxy fight
b. Trade finance
d. First-mover advantage

13. _____ is that which is owed; usually referencing assets owed, but the term can cover other obligations. In the case of assets, _____ is a means of using future purchasing power in the present before a summation has been earned. Some companies and corporations use _____ as a part of their overall corporate finance strategy.
   a. Credit cycle
   c. Partial Payment
   b. Debt
   d. Cross-collateralization

14. In investments, _____ refers to the annual rate of growth of earnings. When the dividend payout ratio is the same, the dividend growth rate is equal to the _____ rate.

_____ rate is a key value that is needed when the DCF model, or the Gordon's model is used for stock valuation.

   a. Alternative display facility
   c. Alternative asset
   b. Annuity
   d. Earnings growth

15. A mutual shareholder or _____ is an individual or company (including a corporation) that legally owns one or more shares of stock in a joint stock company. A company's shareholders collectively own that company. Thus, the typical goal of such companies is to enhance shareholder value.
   a. Trading curb
   c. Limit order
   b. Stock market bubble
   d. Stockholder

16. _____ is an insurance-related term that describes a splitting or spreading of risk among multiple parties.

In the US insurance market, _____ is the joint assumption of risk between the insurer and the insured. In title insurance it also means the sharing of risks between two or more title insurance companies.

   a. 7-Eleven
   c. Coinsurance
   b. 529 plan
   d. 4-4-5 Calendar

17. A _____ is a fungible, negotiable instrument representing financial value. They are broadly categorized into debt securities (such as banknotes, bonds and debentures), and equity securities; e.g., common stocks. The company or other entity issuing the _____ is called the issuer.
   a. Book entry
   c. Security
   b. Securities lending
   d. Tracking stock

18. The U.S. _____ is an independent agency of the United States government which holds primary responsibility for enforcing the federal securities laws and regulating the securities industry, the nation's stock and options exchanges, and other electronic securities markets. The SEC was created by section 4 of the SEC of 1934 (now codified as 15 U.S.C. Â§ 78d and commonly referred to as the 1934 Act.)
   a. Securities and Exchange Commission
   c. 7-Eleven
   b. 4-4-5 Calendar
   d. 529 plan

19. The _____ refers to amendments to the Securities Exchange Act of 1934 enacted in 1968 regarding tender offers. The legislation was proposed by Senator Harrison A. Williams of New Jersey.

The _____ requires that bidders must include all details of their tender offer in their filing to the SEC and the target company. Their file must include the terms, cash source, and their plans for the company after takeover. There are also time constraints that stipulate the minimum period of time the offer may be open and the number of days after the offering in which shareholders have the right to change their minds.

 a. Prudent man rule
 b. Williams Act
 c. Rule 144A
 d. Securities Investor Protection Corporation

20. A _____ is an agreement between a company and an employee (usually upper executive) specifying that the employee will receive certain significant benefits if employment is terminated. Sometimes, certain conditions, typically a change in company ownership, must be met, but often the cause of termination is unspecified. These benefits may include severance pay, cash bonuses, stock options, or other benefits.
 a. Debtor-in-possession financing
 b. Trade finance
 c. Market capitalization
 d. Golden parachute

21. In financial accounting, _____s are precautions for which the amount or probability of occurrence are not known. Typical examples are _____s for warranty costs and _____ for taxes the term reserve is used instead of term _____; such a use, however, is inconsistent with the terminology suggested by International Accounting Standards Board.
 a. Money measurement concept
 b. Momentum Accounting and Triple-Entry Bookkeeping
 c. Provision
 d. Petty cash

22. _____ is money paid by a company (or allied company or individual) to acquire its own shares of stock from a shareholder who is threatening to take control of, or unwanted influence of, the company.

The term is a neologism combining the terms greenback and blackmail, invented by journalists and commentators who saw the practices of corporate raiders as a form of blackmail. The target company is financially held hostage, and is legally forced to pay the _____er to go away.

 a. Stock swap
 b. Greenmail
 c. 529 plan
 d. 4-4-5 Calendar

23. In corporate finance, a _____ is a change of the capital structure of the company--usually to substitute debt for equity.

_____s are used by privately held companies as a means of refinancing, generally to provide returns to the shareholders while not requiring a total sale of the company. These types of recapitalizations can be minor adjustments to the capital structure or may involve a change of control.

 a. Leveraged recapitalization
 b. Bed Bath ' Beyond Inc.
 c. Median
 d. Modern portfolio theory

Chapter 29. Mergers and Acquisitions

24. _____ is the corporate management term for the act of reorganizing the legal, ownership, operational, or other structures of a company for the purpose of making it more profitable or better organized for its present needs. Alternate reasons for restructing include a change of ownership or ownership structure, demerger repositioning debt _____ and financial _____.

   a. Day trading
   b. Concentrated stock
   c. Cross-border leasing
   d. Restructuring

25. In business and finance, a _____ (also referred to as equity _____) of stock means a _____ of ownership in a corporation (company.) In the plural, stocks is often used as a synonym for _____ s especially in the United States, but it is less commonly used that way outside of North America.

   In the United Kingdom, South Africa, and Australia, stock can also refer to completely different financial instruments such as government bonds or, less commonly, to all kinds of marketable securities.

   a. Bucket shop
   b. Share
   c. Procter ' Gamble
   d. Margin

26. In some countries, including the United States and the United Kingdom, corporations can buy back their own stock in a share repurchase, also known as a _____ or share buyback. There has been a meteoric rise in the use of share repurchases in the U.S. in the past twenty years, from $5b in 1980 to $349b in 2005. A share repurchase distributes cash to existing shareholders in exchange for a fraction of the firm's outstanding equity.

   a. Trading curb
   b. Common stock
   c. Stockholder
   d. Stock repurchase

27. In finance, an _____ is the difference between the expected return of a security and the actual return. _____ s are sometimes triggered by 'events.' Events can include mergers, dividend announcements, company earning announcements, interest rate increases, lawsuits, etc. all which can contribute to an _____.

   a. A Random Walk Down Wall Street
   b. AAB
   c. Abnormal return
   d. ABN Amro

28. The term _____ is often used to refer to the investment management of collective investments, (not necessarily) whilst the more generic fund management may refer to all forms of institutional investment as well as investment management for private investors. Investment managers who specialize in advisory or discretionary management on behalf of (normally wealthy) private investors may often refer to their services as wealth management or portfolio management often within the context of so-called 'private banking'.

   The provision of 'investment management services' includes elements of financial analysis, asset selection, stock selection, plan implementation and ongoing monitoring of investments.

   a. A Random Walk Down Wall Street
   b. Asset management
   c. ABN Amro
   d. AAB

Chapter 29. Mergers and Acquisitions

29. An _____ is a statistical method to assess the impact of an event on the value of a firm. For example, the announcement of a merger between two firms can be analyzed to see whether investors believe the merger will create or destroy value. Event studies have been used in a large variety of studies, including [mergers and acquisitions], earnings announcements, debt or equity issues, corporate reorganisations, investment decisions and corporate social responsibility (MacKinlay 1997; McWilliams ' Siegel, 1997.)
   a. Event study
   b. AAB
   c. A Random Walk Down Wall Street
   d. ABN Amro

30. An _____ is an economic concept that relates to the cost incurred by an entity (such as organizations) associated with problems such as divergent management-shareholder objectives and information asymmetry. The costs consist of two main sources:

   1. The costs inherently associated with using an agent (e.g., the risk that agents will use organizational resource for their own benefit) and
   2. The costs of techniques used to mitigate the problems associated with using an agent (e.g., the costs of producing financial statements or the use of stock options to align executive interests to shareholder interests.)

   Though effects of _____ are present in any agency relationship, the term is most used in business contexts.

   The information asymmetry that exists between shareholders and the Chief Executive Officer is generally considered to be a classic example of a principal-agent problem. The agent (the manager) is working on behalf of the principal (the shareholders), who does not observe the actions of the agent.

   a. ABN Amro
   b. AAB
   c. A Random Walk Down Wall Street
   d. Agency cost

31. In political science and economics, the _____ or agency dilemma treats the difficulties that arise under conditions of incomplete and asymmetric information when a principal hires an agent. Various mechanisms may be used to try to align the interests of the agent with those of the principal, such as piece rates/commissions, profit sharing, efficiency wages, performance measurement (including financial statements), the agent posting a bond, or fear of firing. The _____ is found in most employer/employee relationships, for example, when stockholders hire top executives of corporations.
   a. 4-4-5 Calendar
   b. 529 plan
   c. 7-Eleven
   d. Principal-agent problem

32. _____ is a fee paid on borrowed assets. It is the price paid for the use of borrowed money , or, money earned by deposited funds . Assets that are sometimes lent with _____ include money, shares, consumer goods through hire purchase, major assets such as aircraft, and even entire factories in finance lease arrangements.
   a. AAB
   b. A Random Walk Down Wall Street
   c. Insolvency
   d. Interest

33. _____ is an accounting term used to reflect the portion of the book value of a business entity not directly attributable to its assets and liabilities; it normally arises only in case of an acquisition. It reflects the ability of the entity to make a higher profit than would be derived from selling the tangible assets. _____ is also known as an intangible asset.

a. Goodwill
c. Cost of goods sold
b. Consolidation
d. Net profit

34. In finance, _____ (or gearing) is borrowing money to supplement existing funds for investment in such a way that the potential positive or negative outcome is magnified and/or enhanced. It generally refers to using borrowed funds, or debt, so as to attempt to increase the returns to equity. Deleveraging is the action of reducing borrowings.
   a. Limited partnership
   c. Pension fund
   b. Financial endowment
   d. Leverage

35. A _____ occurs when a financial sponsor acquires a controlling interest in a company's equity and where a significant percentage of the purchase price is financed through leverage (borrowing.) The assets of the acquired company are used as collateral for the borrowed capital, sometimes with assets of the acquiring company. The bonds or other paper issued for _____s are commonly considered not to be investment grade because of the significant risks involved.
   a. Leveraged buyout
   c. Leverage
   b. Limited partnership
   d. Pension fund

36. In finance and economics, _____ or divestiture is the reduction of some kind of asset for either financial goals or ethical objectives. A _____ is the opposite of an investment.

Often the term is used as a means to grow financially in which a company sells off a business unit in order to focus their resources on a market it judges to be more profitable, or promising.

   a. Portfolio investment
   c. Divestment
   b. Late trading
   d. Certificate in Investment Performance Measurement

37. In accounting, _____ or *Carrying value* is the value of an asset according to its balance sheet account balance. For assets, the value is based on the original cost of the asset less any depreciation, amortization or impairment costs made against the asset. A company's _____ is its total assets minus intangible assets and liabilities.
   a. Pro forma
   c. Book value
   b. Current liabilities
   d. Retained earnings

38. A _____ is a new organization or entity formed by a split from a larger one, such as a television series based on a pre-existing one, or a new company formed from a university research group or business incubator. In literature, especially in milieu-based popular fictional book series like mysteries, westerns, fantasy, or science fiction, the term sub-series is generally used instead of _____, but with essentially the same meaning.

_____s as a descriptive term can also include a dissenting faction of a membership organization, a sect of a cult, or a denomination of a church.

   a. Spin-off
   c. 4-4-5 Calendar
   b. 7-Eleven
   d. 529 plan

39. A _____ is a security issued by a parent company to track the results of one of its subsidiaries or lines of business. The financial results of the subsidiary or line of business are attributed to the _____. Often, the reason for doing so is to separate a high-growth division from a larger parent company.

a. Tracking stock
b. Securities lending
c. Marketable
d. Book entry

Chapter 30. Financial Distress

1. _____ is a term in Corporate Finance used to indicate a condition when promises to creditors of a company are broken or honored with difficulty. Sometimes _____ can lead to bankruptcy. _____ is usually associated with some costs to the company and these are known as Costs of _____.
   a. Commercial paper
   b. Capital structure
   c. Cashflow matching
   d. Financial distress

2. _____ means the inability to pay one's debts as they fall due. Usually used in Business terms, _____ refers to the inability for a 'limited liability' company to pay off debts.

This is defined in two different ways:

Cash flow _____ -
   Unable to pay debts as they fall due.
Balance sheet _____ -
   Having negative net assets: liabilities exceed assets; or net liabilities.

   a. Insolvency
   b. AAB
   c. Interest
   d. A Random Walk Down Wall Street

3. _____ is typically a higher ranking stock than voting shares, and its terms are negotiated between the corporation and the investor.

_____ usually carry no voting rights, but may carry superior priority over common stock in the payment of dividends and upon liquidation. _____ may carry a dividend that is paid out prior to any dividends to common stock holders.

   a. Preferred stock
   b. Second lien loan
   c. Follow-on offering
   d. Trade-off theory

4. In some countries, including the United States and the United Kingdom, corporations can buy back their own stock in a share repurchase, also known as a _____ or share buyback. There has been a meteoric rise in the use of share repurchases in the U.S. in the past twenty years, from $5b in 1980 to $349b in 2005. A share repurchase distributes cash to existing shareholders in exchange for a fraction of the firm's outstanding equity.
   a. Trading curb
   b. Common stock
   c. Stockholder
   d. Stock repurchase

5. In law, _____ refers to the process by which a company (or part of a company) is brought to an end, and the assets and property of the company redistributed. _____ can also be referred to as winding-up or dissolution, although dissolution technically refers to the last stage of _____. The process of _____ also arises when customs, an authority or agency in a country responsible for collecting and safeguarding customs duties, determines the final computation or ascertainment of the duties or drawback accruing on an entry.
   a. 4-4-5 Calendar
   b. 529 plan
   c. Debt settlement
   d. Liquidation

Chapter 30. Financial Distress

6. _____ is a legally declared inability or impairment of ability of an individual or organization to pay their creditors. Creditors may file a _____ petition against a debtor ('involuntary _____') in an effort to recoup a portion of what they are owed or initiate a restructuring. In the majority of cases, however, _____ is initiated by the debtor (a 'voluntary _____' that is filed by the bankrupt individual or organization.)
   - a. 529 plan
   - b. 4-4-5 Calendar
   - c. Debt settlement
   - d. Bankruptcy

7. The _____, was a law enacting several significant changes to the U.S. Bankruptcy Code. Referred to colloquially as the 'New Bankruptcy Law', the Act of Congress attempts to, among other things, make it more difficult for some consumers to file bankruptcy under Chapter 7; some of these consumers may instead utilize Chapter 13.
   - a. Covenant
   - b. Personal property
   - c. Foreclosure
   - d. Bankruptcy Abuse Prevention and Consumer Protection Act of 2005

8. An _____ is an asset that is typically not found in an investment portfolio. Examples include rare coins and stamps, artwork, sports cards, and hedge funds. Due to the nature of these assets, an accurate valuation is sometimes difficult to accomplish.
   - a. Amortising swap
   - b. Advisory capital
   - c. Alternative asset
   - d. Americans for Fairness in Lending

9. In business and accounting, _____s are everything of value that is owned by a person or company. The balance sheet of a firm records the monetary value of the _____s owned by the firm. The two major _____ classes are tangible _____s and intangible _____s.
   - a. Asset
   - b. Income
   - c. Accounts payable
   - d. EBITDA

10. _____ is the corporate management term for the act of reorganizing the legal, ownership, operational, or other structures of a company for the purpose of making it more profitable or better organized for its present needs. Alternate reasons for restructing include a change of ownership or ownership structure, demerger repositioning debt _____ and financial _____.
    - a. Restructuring
    - b. Day trading
    - c. Cross-border leasing
    - d. Concentrated stock

Chapter 31. International Corporate Finance

1. A _____ is a foreign exchange agreement between two parties to exchange principal and fixed rate interest payments on a loan in one currency for principal and fixed rate interest payments on an equal (regarding net present value) loan in another currency. They are motivated by comparative advantage.
   a. Currency pair
   b. Foreign exchange market
   c. Currency swap
   d. Forex swap

2. A _____ is an international bond that is denominated in a currency not native to the country where it is issued. It can be categorised according to the currency in which it is issued. London is one of the centers of the _____ market, but _____s may be traded throughout the world - for example in Singapore or Tokyo.
   a. Education production function
   b. Interest rate option
   c. Economic entity
   d. Eurobond

3. _____ is the term used to describe deposits residing in banks that are located outside the borders of the country that issues the currency the deposit is denominated in. For example a deposit denominated in US dollars residing in a Japanese bank is a _____ deposit, or more specifically a Eurodollar deposit.

   Key points are the location of the bank and the denomination of the currency, not the nationality of the bank or the owner of the deposit/loan.

   a. AAB
   b. A Random Walk Down Wall Street
   c. Eurocurrency
   d. ABN Amro

4. _____ are bonds issued by the governments of the United Kingdom, South Africa, or Ireland. The term is of British origin, and refers to the debt securities issued by the Bank of England, which had a gilt (or gilded) edge. Hence, they are called gilt-edged securities, or _____ for short.

   These are the simplest form of UK government bond and make up the largest share of UK government debt. A conventional gilt is a bond issued by the UK government which pays the holder a fixed cash payment (or coupon) every six months until maturity, at which point the holder receives their final coupon payment and the return of the principal.

   a. Gilts
   b. Zero coupon bond
   c. Zero-coupon bond
   d. Bond fund

5. _____ is a fee paid on borrowed assets. It is the price paid for the use of borrowed money , or, money earned by deposited funds . Assets that are sometimes lent with _____ include money, shares, consumer goods through hire purchase, major assets such as aircraft, and even entire factories in finance lease arrangements.
   a. Insolvency
   b. Interest
   c. AAB
   d. A Random Walk Down Wall Street

6. An _____ is the price a borrower pays for the use of money they do not own, and the return a lender receives for deferring the use of funds, by lending it to the borrower. _____s are normally expressed as a percentage rate over the period of one year.

   _____s targets are also a vital tool of monetary policy and are used to control variables like investment, inflation, and unemployment.

a. A Random Walk Down Wall Street
b. AAB
c. ABN Amro
d. Interest rate

7. An _____ is a derivative in which one party exchanges a stream of interest payments for another party's stream of cash flows. _____s can be used by hedgers to manage their fixed or floating assets and liabilities. They can also be used by speculators to replicate unfunded bond exposures to profit from changes in interest rates.
   a. Equity swap
   b. International Swaps and Derivatives Association
   c. Implied volatility
   d. Interest rate swap

8. The _____ is a daily reference rate based on the interest rates at which banks borrow unsecured funds from banks in the London wholesale money market (or interbank market.) It is roughly comparable to the U.S. Federal funds rate.

During 1984 it became apparent that an increasing number of banks were trading actively in a variety of relatively new market instruments, notably interest rate swaps, foreign currency options and forward rate agreements.

   a. Fixed interest
   b. Risk-free interest rate
   c. Shanghai Interbank Offered Rate
   d. London Interbank Offered Rate

9. In finance, a _____ is a derivative in which two counterparties agree to exchange one stream of cash flows against another stream. These streams are called the legs of the _____.

The cash flows are calculated over a notional principal amount, which is usually not exchanged between counterparties.

   a. Volatility swap
   b. Local volatility
   c. Swap
   d. Volatility arbitrage

10. In finance, a _____ is a debt security, in which the authorized issuer owes the holders a debt and, depending on the terms of the _____, is obliged to pay interest (the coupon) and/or to repay the principal at a later date, termed maturity.

Thus a _____ is a loan: the issuer is the borrower, the _____ holder is the lender, and the coupon is the interest. _____s provide the borrower with external funds to finance long-term investments, or, in the case of government _____s, to finance current expenditure.

   a. Catastrophe bonds
   b. Convertible bond
   c. Puttable bond
   d. Bond

11. A _____ is an exchange of promises between two or more parties to do an act which is enforceable in a court of law. It is where an unqualified offer meets a qualified acceptance and the parties reach Consensus ad Idem. The parties must have the necessary capacity to _____ and the _____ must not be either trifling, indeterminate, impossible or illegal.
   a. 4-4-5 Calendar
   b. 529 plan
   c. 7-Eleven
   d. Contract

Chapter 31. International Corporate Finance

12. In finance, the _____ between two currencies specifies how much one currency is worth in terms of the other. For example an _____ of 102 Japanese yen to the United States dollar means that JPY 102 is worth the same as USD 1. The foreign exchange market is one of the largest markets in the world.
    a. AAB
    b. ABN Amro
    c. A Random Walk Down Wall Street
    d. Exchange rate

13. The _____ is where currency trading takes place. It is where banks and other official institutions facilitate the buying and selling of foreign currencies. FX transactions typically involve one party purchasing a quantity of one currency in exchange for paying a quantity of another.
    a. Floating exchange rate
    b. Foreign exchange option
    c. Spot market
    d. Foreign exchange market

14. _____ is a form of risk that arises from the change in price of one currency against another. Whenever investors or companies have assets or business operations across national borders, they face _____ if their positions are not hedged.

    - Transaction risk is the risk that exchange rates will change unfavourably over time. It can be hedged against using forward currency contracts;
    - Translation risk is an accounting risk, proportional to the amount of assets held in foreign currencies. Changes in the exchange rate over time will render a report inaccurate, and so assets are usually balanced by borrowings in that currency.

    The exchange risk associated with a foreign denominated instrument is a key element in foreign investment. This risk flows from differential monetary policy and growth in real productivity, which results in differential inflation rates.

    a. Currency risk
    b. Market risk
    c. Tracking error
    d. Credit risk

15. In economics and finance, _____ is the practice of taking advantage of a price differential between two or more markets: striking a combination of matching deals that capitalize upon the imbalance, the profit being the difference between the market prices. When used by academics, an _____ is a transaction that involves no negative cash flow at any probabilistic or temporal state and a positive cash flow in at least one state; in simple terms, a risk-free profit.
    a. Arbitrage
    b. Initial margin
    c. Efficient-market hypothesis
    d. Issuer

16. _____ refers to taking advantage of a state of imbalance between three foreign exchange markets: a combination of matching deals are struck that exploit the imbalance, the profit being the difference between the market prices.

    _____ offers a risk-free profit (in theory), so opportunities for _____ usually disappear quickly, as many people are looking for them, or simply never occur as everybody knows the pricing relation.

Consider the three foreign exchange rates among the Canadian dollar, the U.S. dollar, and the Australian dollar.

a. Currency future
b. Floating exchange rate
c. Triangular arbitrage
d. Currency pair

17. _____ refers to a business or organization attempting to acquire goods or services to accomplish the goals of the enterprise. Though there are several organizations that attempt to set standards in the _____ process, processes can vary greatly between organizations. Typically the word '_____' is not used interchangeably with the word 'procurement', since procurement typically includes Expediting, Supplier Quality, and Traffic and Logistics (T'L) in addition to _____.
   a. 7-Eleven
   b. 529 plan
   c. 4-4-5 Calendar
   d. Purchasing

18. _____ is the value of goods/services compared to the amount paid with a currency. Currency can be either a commodity money, like gold or silver, or fiat currency like US dollars which are the world reserve currency. As Adam Smith noted, having money gives one the ability to 'command' others' labor, so _____ to some extent is power over other people, to the extent that they are willing to trade their labor or goods for money or currency.
   a. 529 plan
   b. 7-Eleven
   c. 4-4-5 Calendar
   d. Purchasing power

19. The _____ theory uses the long-term equilibrium exchange rate of two currencies to equalize their purchasing power. Developed by Gustav Cassel in 1920, it is based on the law of one price: the theory states that, in ideally efficient markets, identical goods should have only one price.

This purchasing power SEM rate equalizes the purchasing power of different currencies in their home countries for a given basket of goods.

   a. 4-4-5 Calendar
   b. Gross national product
   c. TED spread
   d. Purchasing power parity

20. The _____ or spot rate of a commodity, a security or a currency is the price that is quoted for immediate (spot) settlement (payment and delivery.) Spot settlement is normally one or two business days from trade date. This is in contrast with the forward price established in a forward contract or futures contract, where contract terms (price) are set now, but delivery and payment will occur at a future date.
   a. Central Securities Depository
   b. Market price
   c. Spot price
   d. Cost of carry

21. The _____ is published by The Economist as an informal way of measuring the purchasing power parity (PPP) between two currencies and provides a test of the extent to which market exchange rates result in goods costing the same in different countries. It 'seeks to make exchange-rate theory a bit more digestible'.
   a. Divisia index
   b. Big Mac Index
   c. 529 plan
   d. 4-4-5 Calendar

22. _____ is the investment strategy where an investor buys a financial instrument denominated in a foreign currency, and hedges his foreign exchange risk by selling a forward contract in the amount of the proceeds of the investment back into his base currency. The proceeds of the investment are only known exactly if the financial instrument is risk-free and only pays interest once, on the date of the forward sale of foreign currency. Otherwise, some foreign exchange risk remains.

a. Currency future
b. Floating exchange rate
c. Triangular arbitrage
d. Covered interest arbitrage

23. _____ is an economic concept, expressed as a basic algebraic identity that relates interest rates and exchange rates. The identity is theoretical, and usually follows from assumptions imposed in economics models. There is evidence to support as well as to refute the concept.
a. A Random Walk Down Wall Street
b. AAB
c. Interest rate parity
d. Unit price

24. In economic models, the _____ time frame assumes no fixed factors of production. Firms can enter or leave the marketplace, and the cost (and availability) of land, labor, raw materials, and capital goods can be assumed to vary. In contrast, in the short-run time frame, certain factors are assumed to be fixed, because there is not sufficient time for them to change.
a. Long-run
b. 4-4-5 Calendar
c. Short-run
d. 529 plan

25. _____ is that which is owed; usually referencing assets owed, but the term can cover other obligations. In the case of assets, _____ is a means of using future purchasing power in the present before a summation has been earned. Some companies and corporations use _____ as a part of their overall corporate finance strategy.
a. Credit cycle
b. Cross-collateralization
c. Partial Payment
d. Debt

26. The _____ of a commodity, a security or a currency is the price that is quoted for immediate (spot) settlement (payment and delivery.) Spot settlement is normally one or two business days from trade date. This is in contrast with the forward price established in a forward contract or futures contract, where contract terms (price) are set now, but delivery and payment will occur at a future date.
a. Market anomaly
b. Limits to arbitrage
c. Spot rate
d. Long position

27. In economics, the _____ is the proposition by Irving Fisher that the real interest rate is independent of monetary measures, especially the nominal interest rate. The Fisher equation is

$$r_r = r_n >- >\pi^e.$$

This means, the real interest rate (r_r) equals the nominal interest rate (r_n) minus expected rate of inflation ($>\pi^e$.) Here all the rates are continuously compounded.

a. 4-4-5 Calendar
b. 529 plan
c. 7-Eleven
d. Fisher hypothesis

28. The _____ is a hypothesis in international finance that says that the difference in the nominal interest rates between two countries determines the movement of the nominal exchange rate between their currencies, with the value of the currency of the country with the lower nominal interest rate increasing. This is also known as the assumption of Uncovered Interest Parity.

The Fisher hypothesis says that the real interest rate in an economy is independent of monetary variables.

a. A Random Walk Down Wall Street
b. Official bank rate
c. Interest rate risk
d. International Fisher effect

29. _____ is the planning process used to determine whether a firm's long term investments such as new machinery, replacement machinery, new plants, new products, and research development projects are worth pursuing. It is budget for major capital, or investment, expenditures.

Many formal methods are used in _____, including the techniques such as

- Net present value
- Profitability index
- Internal rate of return
- Modified Internal Rate of Return
- Equivalent annuity

These methods use the incremental cash flows from each potential investment, or project. Techniques based on accounting earnings and accounting rules are sometimes used - though economists consider this to be improper - such as the accounting rate of return, and 'return on investment.' Simplified and hybrid methods are used as well, such as payback period and discounted payback period.

a. Shareholder value
b. Financial distress
c. Preferred stock
d. Capital budgeting

30. In economics, the concept of the _____ refers to the decision-making time frame of a firm in which at least one factor of production is fixed. Costs which are fixed in the _____ have no impact on a firms decisions. For example a firm can raise output by increasing the amount of labour through overtime.

a. 4-4-5 Calendar
b. 529 plan
c. Long-run
d. Short-run

31. _____ is the balance of the amounts of cash being received and paid by a business during a defined period of time, sometimes tied to a specific project. Measurement of _____ can be used

- to evaluate the state or performance of a business or project.
- to determine problems with liquidity. Being profitable does not necessarily mean being liquid. A company can fail because of a shortage of cash, even while profitable.
- to generate project rate of returns. The time of _____s into and out of projects are used as inputs to financial models such as internal rate of return, and net present value.
- to examine income or growth of a business when it is believed that accrual accounting concepts do not represent economic realities. Alternately, _____ can be used to 'validate' the net income generated by accrual accounting.

Chapter 31. International Corporate Finance

_____ as a generic term may be used differently depending on context, and certain _____ definitions may be adapted by analysts and users for their own uses. Common terms include operating _____ and free _____.

_____s can be classified into:

1. Operational _____s: Cash received or expended as a result of the company's core business activities.
2. Investment _____s: Cash received or expended through capital expenditure, investments or acquisitions.
3. Financing _____s: Cash received or expended as a result of financial activities, such as interests and dividends.

All three together - the net _____ - are necessary to reconcile the beginning cash balance to the ending cash balance. Loan draw downs or equity injections, that is just shifting of capital but no expenditure as such, are not considered in the net _____.

a. Corporate finance
b. Cash flow
c. Shareholder value
d. Real option

32. The role of the _____ is to issue accounting standards in the United Kingdom. It is recognised for that purpose under the Companies Act 1985. It took over the task of setting accounting standards from the Accounting Standards Committee (ASC) in 1990.

a. AAB
b. ABN Amro
c. A Random Walk Down Wall Street
d. Accounting Standards Board

33. _____ is the field of accountancy concerned with the preparation of financial statements for decision makers, such as stockholders, suppliers, banks, employees, government agencies, owners, and other stakeholders. The fundamental need for _____ is to reduce principal-agent problem by measuring and monitoring agents' performance and reporting the results to interested users.

_____ is used to prepare accounting information for people outside the organization or not involved in the day to day running of the company.

a. 7-Eleven
b. 4-4-5 Calendar
c. 529 plan
d. Financial Accounting

34. The _____ is a private, not-for-profit organization whose primary purpose is to develop generally accepted accounting principles (GAAP) within the United States in the public's interest. The Securities and Exchange Commission (SEC) designated the _____ as the organization responsible for setting accounting standards for public companies in the U.S. It was created in 1973, replacing the Accounting Principles Board and the Committee on Accounting Procedure of the American Institute of Certified Public Accountants. The _____'s mission is 'to establish and improve standards of financial accounting and reporting for the guidance and education of the public, including issuers, auditors, and users of financial information.'

The _____ is not a governmental body.

a. Federal Deposit Insurance Corporation
b. Financial Accounting Standards Board
c. World Congress of Accountants
d. KPMG

35. _____ is a type of risk faced by investors, corporations, and governments. It is a risk that can be understood and managed with proper aforethought and investment.

Broadly, _____ refers to the complications businesses and governments may face as a result of what are commonly referred to as political decisions--or 'any political change that alters the expected outcome and value of a given economic action by changing the probability of achieving business objectives.' .

a. Single-index model
b. Capital asset
c. Mid price
d. Political Risk

36. _____, in bookkeeping, refers to assets, liabilities, income, and expenses recorded on individual pages of the so called book of final entry or ledger. Changes in _____ value are made by chronologically posting debit (DR) and credit (CR) entries to its page. Examples of _____s are cash, _____s receivable, mortgages, loans, land and buildings, common stock, sales, services provided, wages, and payroll overhead.

a. Alpha
b. Option
c. Accretion
d. Account

37. In financial accounting, a _____ or statement of financial position is a summary of a person's or organization's balances. Assets, liabilities and ownership equity are listed as of a specific date, such as the end of its financial year. A _____ is often described as a snapshot of a company's financial condition.

a. Balance sheet
b. Financial statements
c. Statement of retained earnings
d. Statement on Auditing Standards No. 70: Service Organizations

38. _____, refers to consumption opportunity gained by an entity within a specified time frame, which is generally expressed in monetary terms. However, for households and individuals, '_____ is the sum of all the wages, salaries, profits, interests payments, rents and other forms of earnings received... in a given period of time.' For firms, _____ generally refers to net-profit: what remains of revenue after expenses have been subtracted.

a. Annual report
b. OIBDA
c. Accrual
d. Income

39. An _____ is a financial statement for companies that indicates how Revenue is transformed into net income The purpose of the _____ is to show managers and investors whether the company made or lost money during the period being reported.

The important thing to remember about an _____ is that it represents a period of time.

a. ABN Amro
b. AAB
c. A Random Walk Down Wall Street
d. Income statement

Chapter 31. International Corporate Finance

40. _____ are business expenses that are not dependent on the level of production or sales. They tend to be time-related, such as salaries or rents being paid per month. This is in contrast to Variable costs, which are volume-related (and are paid per quantity.)
   a. Transaction cost
   b. Marginal cost
   c. Sliding scale fees
   d. Fixed costs

41. In economics, business, and accounting, a _____ is the value of money that has been used up to produce something, and hence is not available for use anymore. In business, the _____ may be one of acquisition, in which case the amount of money expended to acquire it is counted as _____. In this case, money is the input that is gone in order to acquire the thing.
   a. Sliding scale fees
   b. Cost
   c. Marginal cost
   d. Fixed costs

42. _____ is the provision of resources (such as granting a loan) by one party to another party where that second party does not reimburse the first party immediately, thereby generating a debt, and instead arranges either to repay or return those resources (or material(s) of equal value) at a later date. The first party is called a creditor, also known as a lender, while the second party is called a debtor, also known as a borrower.

Movements of financial capital are normally dependent on either _____ or equity transfers.

   a. Comparable
   b. Credit
   c. Warrant
   d. Clearing house

43. In finance, _____ (or gearing) is borrowing money to supplement existing funds for investment in such a way that the potential positive or negative outcome is magnified and/or enhanced. It generally refers to using borrowed funds, or debt, so as to attempt to increase the returns to equity. Deleveraging is the action of reducing borrowings.
   a. Financial endowment
   b. Limited partnership
   c. Leverage
   d. Pension fund

44. An _____ is a contract written by a seller that conveys to the buyer the right -- but not the obligation -- to buy (in the case of a call _____) or to sell (in the case of a put _____) a particular asset, such as a piece of property such as, among others, a futures contract. In return for granting the _____, the seller collects a payment (the premium) from the buyer.

For example, buying a call _____ provides the right to buy a specified quantity of a security at a set strike price at some time on or before expiration, while buying a put _____ provides the right to sell.

   a. Annuity
   b. AT'T Mobility LLC
   c. Option
   d. Amortization

45. _____ is a derivative financial instrument.

The global market for exchange-traded _____s is notionally valued by the Bank for International Settlements at $3,075,400 million in 2005.

a. Eurobond
b. Economic entity
c. Education production function
d. Interest rate Option

46. In finance, _____ is the process of estimating the potential market value of a financial asset or liability. they can be done on assets (for example, investments in marketable securities such as stocks, options, business enterprises, or intangible assets such as patents and trademarks) or on liabilities (e.g., Bonds issued by a company.) _____s are required in many contexts including investment analysis, capital budgeting, merger and acquisition transactions, financial reporting, taxable events to determine the proper tax liability, and in litigation.

a. Procter ' Gamble
b. Share
c. Valuation
d. Margin

47. Under a secondary market offering or seasoned equity offering of shares to raise money, a company can opt for a _____ to raise capital. The _____ is a special form of shelf offering or shelf registration. With the issued rights, existing shareholders have the privilege to buy a specified number of new shares from the firm at a specified price within a specified time.

a. Market for corporate control
b. Corporate finance
c. Tender offer
d. Rights issue

ANSWER KEY

Chapter 1
1. a	2. d	3. b	4. d	5. d	6. d	7. d	8. d	9. d	10. d
11. d	12. d	13. d	14. a	15. a	16. d	17. d	18. a	19. b	20. a
21. a	22. d	23. d	24. a	25. d	26. d	27. d	28. d	29. d	30. d
31. d	32. a	33. d	34. d	35. d	36. b	37. c	38. b	39. a	40. a
41. b	42. a	43. a	44. d	45. d	46. c	47. d	48. a	49. d	50. a

Chapter 2
1. d	2. d	3. b	4. c	5. b	6. a	7. d	8. d	9. a	10. b
11. d	12. d	13. a	14. d	15. c	16. a	17. d	18. d	19. d	20. b
21. d	22. d	23. a	24. c	25. d	26. d	27. c			

Chapter 3
1. c	2. d	3. b	4. b	5. d	6. d	7. c	8. a	9. c	10. b
11. c	12. b	13. d	14. a	15. a	16. a	17. d	18. b	19. b	20. d
21. c	22. d	23. c	24. c	25. d	26. d	27. a	28. b	29. d	30. d
31. d	32. c	33. d	34. a	35. b	36. c	37. a	38. c	39. a	40. d
41. d	42. c	43. d							

Chapter 4
1. a	2. c	3. c	4. c	5. d	6. d	7. d	8. a	9. c	10. b
11. a	12. d	13. b	14. d	15. d	16. c	17. d	18. b	19. c	

Chapter 5
1. d	2. d	3. d	4. c	5. a	6. a	7. b	8. d	9. a	10. d
11. a	12. c	13. d	14. b	15. a	16. a	17. d	18. b	19. d	20. b
21. b	22. d	23. a	24. b	25. a	26. d	27. c	28. a	29. b	30. d
31. d	32. a	33. b	34. a	35. d	36. d	37. b	38. b	39. a	40. a
41. b	42. d	43. d	44. a	45. d	46. d	47. c	48. d	49. d	50. b
51. d	52. c	53. a	54. d	55. c	56. b				

Chapter 6
1. b	2. c	3. d	4. d	5. a	6. d	7. c	8. d	9. c	10. b
11. d	12. d	13. d	14. c	15. d	16. b	17. d	18. c		

Chapter 7
1. d	2. d	3. d	4. c	5. b	6. d	7. b	8. d	9. a	10. d
11. b	12. b	13. d	14. a	15. d	16. b	17. b	18. b	19. d	20. d
21. a	22. d	23. a	24. a	25. b	26. b	27. a	28. a	29. c	30. c

Chapter 8
1. c	2. c	3. b	4. b	5. d	6. d	7. d	8. d	9. a	10. d
11. d	12. c	13. d	14. b	15. d	16. b				

Chapter 9
1. d	2. b	3. d	4. d	5. d	6. c	7. d	8. b	9. c	10. a
11. d	12. d	13. d	14. d	15. b	16. d	17. c	18. a	19. d	20. d
21. c	22. b	23. a	24. b	25. d	26. c	27. c			

Chapter 10
1. a	2. b	3. a	4. c	5. d	6. b	7. d	8. d	9. d	10. b
11. a	12. b	13. d	14. c	15. d	16. c	17. a	18. c	19. d	

Chapter 11
1. d	2. d	3. d	4. d	5. c	6. d	7. c	8. d	9. d	10. a
11. d									

Chapter 12
1. c	2. d	3. d	4. b	5. d	6. a	7. a	8. d	9. d	10. d
11. d	12. d	13. d	14. b	15. a	16. d	17. d	18. c	19. b	20. d
21. c	22. d	23. d	24. a	25. b	26. c	27. d	28. a	29. a	30. a
31. d	32. c	33. c							

Chapter 13
1. b	2. a	3. b	4. d	5. a	6. c	7. d	8. d	9. d	10. d
11. c	12. a	13. b	14. d	15. c	16. c	17. d	18. c	19. b	20. d
21. d	22. b	23. b	24. b	25. d	26. d	27. d	28. c	29. d	30. b
31. d	32. d	33. b	34. d	35. b	36. a				

Chapter 14
1. d	2. d	3. b	4. c	5. d	6. b	7. b	8. b	9. d	10. d
11. d	12. a	13. d	14. a	15. b	16. b	17. a	18. d	19. d	20. d
21. a	22. c	23. a	24. d	25. c	26. b	27. d	28. a	29. d	30. d
31. d	32. a	33. d	34. d	35. d	36. a	37. d	38. c	39. d	40. d
41. b	42. a								

Chapter 15
1. d	2. d	3. d	4. d	5. a	6. d	7. a	8. a	9. d	10. d
11. d	12. d	13. c	14. d	15. a	16. d	17. d	18. a	19. d	20. d
21. b									

Chapter 16
1. c	2. d	3. d	4. b	5. d	6. d	7. d	8. d	9. d	10. d
11. d	12. b	13. d	14. d	15. d	16. a	17. c	18. d	19. c	20. d
21. b	22. d	23. d	24. d	25. d	26. c	27. d	28. d	29. d	30. d

ANSWER KEY

Chapter 17
1. c   2. a   3. d   4. d   5. d   6. a   7. a   8. b   9. b   10. d
11. d   12. c   13. a   14. d   15. a   16. d

Chapter 18
1. b   2. c   3. a   4. d   5. b   6. d   7. d   8. d   9. c   10. d
11. d   12. b   13. d   14. d   15. d   16. d   17. a   18. d   19. c   20. a
21. d   22. c   23. a   24. b   25. d   26. c   27. b   28. b   29. a   30. a
31. b   32. d

Chapter 19
1. a   2. c   3. c   4. d   5. d   6. d   7. a   8. c   9. d   10. a
11. b   12. a   13. d   14. c   15. c   16. d   17. a   18. d   19. a   20. b
21. b   22. d   23. d   24. d   25. d   26. d   27. d   28. a   29. b   30. d
31. a   32. d   33. d   34. d   35. c   36. d   37. c   38. b   39. b   40. a
41. c   42. d

Chapter 20
1. d   2. d   3. a   4. b   5. d   6. a   7. b   8. b   9. a   10. d
11. d   12. c   13. d   14. d   15. d   16. b   17. d   18. d   19. d   20. b
21. d   22. d   23. a   24. d   25. d   26. d   27. a   28. a   29. c   30. d
31. d   32. b   33. a   34. b   35. d   36. d   37. b   38. c   39. d   40. d
41. c   42. d   43. d   44. d   45. d   46. d   47. c

Chapter 21
1. d   2. d   3. d   4. d   5. b   6. d   7. d   8. a   9. d   10. d
11. d   12. c   13. d   14. d   15. c   16. d   17. b   18. d   19. d   20. c
21. d   22. d   23. d   24. d   25. c   26. c   27. a   28. a   29. d   30. c

Chapter 22
1. b   2. d   3. d   4. a   5. d   6. d   7. d   8. a   9. d   10. a
11. d   12. a   13. d   14. d   15. b   16. a   17. b   18. c   19. a   20. d
21. d   22. d   23. a   24. d   25. d   26. d   27. a   28. d   29. c   30. b
31. d   32. d   33. d   34. a

Chapter 23
1. a   2. b   3. d   4. d   5. a   6. a   7. d   8. d   9. d   10. d

Chapter 24
1. a   2. b   3. b   4. c   5. d   6. d   7. d   8. d   9. c   10. d
11. d   12. d   13. d   14. c   15. d

Chapter 25
1. c 2. a 3. b 4. d 5. d 6. c 7. d 8. c 9. d 10. d
11. d 12. d 13. d 14. b 15. a 16. d 17. c 18. c 19. a 20. d
21. d 22. d 23. d 24. d 25. a 26. d 27. b 28. d 29. c 30. d

Chapter 26
1. d 2. d 3. a 4. a 5. d 6. d 7. b 8. b 9. c 10. d
11. c 12. d 13. d 14. c 15. c 16. d 17. d 18. d 19. d 20. b
21. d 22. d 23. a 24. b 25. d 26. c 27. b 28. a

Chapter 27
1. c 2. d 3. d 4. d 5. b 6. d 7. d 8. d 9. d 10. d
11. a 12. d 13. b 14. b 15. b 16. d 17. d 18. a 19. d 20. d
21. a 22. d 23. c 24. c 25. d 26. b 27. c 28. d 29. c 30. c
31. c

Chapter 28
1. a 2. a 3. d 4. a 5. a 6. d 7. d 8. b 9. d 10. a
11. a 12. c 13. d

Chapter 29
1. d 2. d 3. d 4. a 5. d 6. c 7. d 8. d 9. c 10. b
11. d 12. a 13. b 14. d 15. d 16. c 17. c 18. a 19. b 20. d
21. c 22. b 23. a 24. d 25. b 26. d 27. c 28. b 29. a 30. d
31. d 32. d 33. a 34. d 35. a 36. c 37. c 38. a 39. a

Chapter 30
1. d 2. a 3. a 4. d 5. d 6. d 7. d 8. c 9. a 10. a

Chapter 31
1. c 2. d 3. c 4. a 5. b 6. d 7. d 8. d 9. c 10. d
11. d 12. d 13. d 14. a 15. a 16. c 17. d 18. d 19. d 20. c
21. b 22. d 23. c 24. a 25. d 26. c 27. d 28. d 29. d 30. d
31. b 32. d 33. d 34. b 35. d 36. d 37. a 38. d 39. d 40. d
41. b 42. b 43. c 44. c 45. d 46. c 47. d

www.ingramcontent.com/pod-product-compliance
Lightning Source LLC
Chambersburg PA
CBHW081352230426
43667CB00017B/2808